Index to the
Probate Inventories of
York County
Pennsylvania
1749 - 1850

FRONT OF THE COURTHOUSE IN YORK, PENNSYLVANIA, BUILT IN 1839

David A. and Brenda L. Paup

HERITAGE BOOKS
2007

HERITAGE BOOKS
AN IMPRINT OF HERITAGE BOOKS, INC.

Books, CDs, and more—Worldwide

For our listing of thousands of titles see our website
at
www.HeritageBooks.com

Published 2007 by
HERITAGE BOOKS, INC.
Publishing Division
65 East Main Street
Westminster, Maryland 21157-5026

International Standard Book Number: 978-1-58549-239-8

Introduction to the
Probate Inventories
of York County
Pennsylvania

The probate inventories of York County may well be the most overlooked wealth of information, about the lifestyle and material culture of our forebearers. They display a priceless account of the possessions that early York Countians depended upon to survive and flourish, from approximately 1749 to 1850. Only a few inventories after this time frame have been included in this volume.

Reading an inventory is like rummaging through your grandmother's attic. You are filled with wonder and curiosity as you visualize these objects that nolonger play an important part in our "modern lives," but once were depended upon for their survival.

The inventories are filed in twenty-two, four drawer filing cabinets, located in the storage room to the rear of the Clerk of Orphans Court office, in the York County courthouse. They are filed in "alphabetical disorder," however, and one may have a difficult time finding a particular file. An even more distressing item of mention, is that several file holders are now vacant, and it would appear that some documents are being taken by "unscrupulous" persons. Photocopies may be obtained for a small fee.

When searching for a particular individual in these files, remember to check for any spelling variations of the name. The spelling for a family name may vary from one document to the next, and in many cases may have several variations within the same document.

The inventories are listed in this book by file name; date taken; township or boro; any miscellaneous information such as spelling variations of the surname, occupation, husband or wife, German language, or interesting items of mention. In some instances the estate was sold at public auction. These were called "vendues," and listed each item sold along with the name of the buyer. The date of vendue is also listed.

Prior to the formation of Adams County in 1800, all inventories from its townships were filed in the York County courthouse. They are also indexed in this volume and have been identified by this symbol (*).

Inventory of the Estate
of James Petit Dece'd
filed the 11th Day of Febr'y
1771

An Inventory of the Goods and Chattels of James Pettit
late of Berwick Township in the County of York Deceased
Appraised as follows by Abraham Holl and Nicholas Beckener
the Fourth Day of February 1771

	Pounds/Shillings/Pence		
A Suit of Cloaths	3	"	"
One Mans Sadle	"	8	"
One Black Horse	"	10	"
One Brown Horse	8	"	"
One Sorrel Mare	7	"	"
One Wagon and two pair of Geers	2	"	"
One Plow and Irons, and two Clevises	"	15	"
One Seythe	"	1	"
A Set of Black Smith Tools	1	10	"
Four Sheep and Three Lambs	1	8	"
Sundry Iron Tools and two pair of Iron Hopples	"	8	"
One Black Cow	3	5	"
One Brown Spotted Cow	2	15	"
One Red Cow with a white face	2	5	"
One Red Heifer	2	"	"
One Black Calf with a White face	"	2	6
One Gun, Powder Horn and Shot Bag	"	10	"
One Cupboard	1	5	"
The Pewter, Tea Kettle and Tea Ware	1	5	"
Two Iron Ladles, one Flesh fork, one Brass Skillet	"	4	"
Two Iron Pots	"	8	"
The Pot Racks and fire Tongs	"	3	"
One Riddle, Stilyards, Candle molds and Lantron	"	5	"
Linnen Yarn, Woollen Yarn, and Wool	"	9	"
Lamp and Candle Stick	"	1	"
The Threshed Grain in the Garner	7	14	"
Bread Meal	"	12	"
Salt	"	3	"
	48	6	6

iv

```
                                                            L    S  D
Brought Over_ _ _ _ _ _ _ _ _ _ _ _ _ _ _ _ _ _ _ _ _ _ _48   6  6
Two Bells and one Iron Collar_ _ _ _ _ _ _ _ _ _ _ _ _ "    5  "
One Womans Sadle_ _ _ _ _ _ _ _ _ _ _ _ _ _ _ _ _ _ _ _"    4  "
One Iron Harrow_ _ _ _ _ _ _ _ _ _ _ _ _ _ _ _ _ _ _ _"    4  "
One little and one Big Spining Wheels_ _ _ _ _ _ _ _ _"   12  "
Old Barrels and Hogsheads_ _ _ _ _ _ _ _ _ _ _ _ _ _ _"    5  "
Three Pails and two Tubs_ _ _ _ _ _ _ _ _ _ _ _ _ _ _ "    4  "
Cutting Box_ _ _ _ _ _ _ _ _ _ _ _ _ _ _ _ _ _ _ _ _ _"   15  "
Flax_ _ _ _ _ _ _ _ _ _ _ _ _ _ _ _ _ _ _ _ _ _ _ _ _ "    2  "
Two Stacks of Hay_ _ _ _ _ _ _ _ _ _ _ _ _ _ _ _ _ _ _1   "  "
The Hay in the Barn_ _ _ _ _ _ _ _ _ _ _ _ _ _ _ _ _ _2   "  "
Nine Acres of Grain in the Ground_ _ _ _ _ _ _ _ _ _ _4  10  "
Two Sows_ _ _ _ _ _ _ _ _ _ _ _ _ _ _ _ _ _ _ _ _ _ _ "   12  "
One Table and three Chairs_ _ _ _ _ _ _ _ _ _ _ _ _ _ "    5  "
One Bedstead_ _ _ _ _ _ _ _ _ _ _ _ _ _ _ _ _ _ _ _ _ "    5  "
Bedstead, Bed and Bed Cloaths_ _ _ _ _ _ _ _ _ _ _ _ _1   "  "
One Grind Stone_ _ _ _ _ _ _ _ _ _ _ _ _ _ _ _ _ _ _ _"    1  6
One Bay Mare Sadle and Brindle_ _ _ _ _ _ _ _ _ _ _ _ _9  10  "
One Bay Horse Colt_ _ _ _ _ _ _ _ _ _ _ _ _ _ _ _ _ _ _1  15  "
One Brown Heifer with a White face_ _ _ _ _ _ _ _ _ _ _2   "  "
The Pewter_ _ _ _ _ _ _ _ _ _ _ _ _ _ _ _ _ _ _ _ _ _ _2   "  "
Bed and Bed Cloaths_ _ _ _ _ _ _ _ _ _ _ _ _ _ _ _ _ _ 1   "  "
One Spining Wheel_ _ _ _ _ _ _ _ _ _ _ _ _ _ _ _ _ _ _ "   10  "
One Chest_ _ _ _ _ _ _ _ _ _ _ _ _ _ _ _ _ _ _ _ _ _ _ "    5  "
                                                          _____
                                                          77  11  0
```

Leonard Leas Ex'd   Abraham Hol
                                       Nicholas X Bechner

Index to York County Penna.
Probate Inventories

File Name		Date	Twp.	Misc. Info.
Abel,	George	1828	Windsor	-
,	John	1815	"	-
,	John	1835	"	-
,	Peter	1835	"	-
Abbits,	Curtis	1843	Hellam	-
Abbott,	John	1786	Berwick*	-
Acker,	Henry	1843	Monaghan	-
,	Margaret	1845	"	-
Ackerman,	Michael	1782	Reading*	-
Adams,	Alexander	1777	Hamilton Ban*	-
,	George	1823	Chanceford	-
,	Hugh	1793	"	-
,	James	1829	"	-
,	John	1789	Hamilton Ban*	-
,	Martin	1762	Chanceford	-
,	Mathew	1823	Windsor	-
,	Mathew	1812	Chanceford	-
,	Samuel	1777	?	-
,	Thomas	1779	?	-
Addock,	Peter	1768	?	-
Adlum,	John	1772	Yorktowne	-
Africa,	Rosina	1806	Hanover	-
Agnew,	David	1797	Hamilton Ban*	-
,	James	1770	"	-
,	James	1798	"	-
Akins,	William	1817	Fawn	-
Albert,	Andrew	1841	Franklin	-
,	John	1794	Newberry	-
,	Lorince	1797	Huntington*	-
Albright,	Anna May	1840	Hanover Boro	-
,	Appelony	1812	York	-
,	Barnett	1818	Manheim	-
,	Felix	1780	York	-
,	George	1766	Windsor	-
,	Henry	1800	"	-
,	Henry	1842	Hanover Boro	-
,	Henry	1844	York	-
,	Jacob	1840	Manheim	mill items
,	Johannes	1770	"	-
,	John	1760	York	-
,	Michael	1817	"	-
,	Philip	1800	"	-
Alexander,	Elias	1753	?	-
,	James	1837	Hopewell	-

(*) Denotes an area now in Adams county Pa.

File Name		Date	Twp.	Misc. Info.
Alexander,	Jedidiah	1751	?	-
,	John	1769	Hamilton Ban*	-
,	William	1754	Chanceford	-
Alison,	Gavin	1769	Hopewell	-
Alkens,	David	1850	Franklin	-
Allen,	James	1796	Straban*	-
,	John	1796	Fawn	clothing
		1796		
Allison,	Agnes	1789	Hopewell	-
,	Gavin	1782	"	-
,	Jacob	1847	Codorus	-
,	James	1820	Shrewsbury	-
,	John	1763	"	-
,	Joseph	1810	Chanceford	-
,	Margaret	1811	?	German
Alloway,	Stephen	1806	Fawn	-
,	Azariah	1827	"	-
Alt,	Adam	1779	Shrewsbury	-
,	Valentine	1756	?	-
Altland,	Christian	1841	Paradise	-
,	Jacob	1830	Dover	-
,	Jacob	1847	Paradise	-
,	Philip	1804	"	-
,	Philip	1839	Dover	vendue
Ambrose,	Robert	1793	Cumberland*	Doctor
Ament,	Catherine	1782	Yorktowne	-
,	George	1750	?	-
,	George	1770	Hellam	-
,	George L.	1755	York	-
,	Henry	1761	Hellam	-
,	Henry	1774	?	-
Amman,	Conrad	1773	Paradise	-
Ammer,	Daniel	1785	"	-
Ammerman,	Henry	1782	Mt. Pleasant*	-
Amspacker,	Henry	1850	Shrewsbury	-
Anderson,	Abraham	1849	Warrington	-
,	Allen	1774	Fawn filed w/P. Becker	
,	Allen	1844	Peach Bottom	-
,	Andrew	1849	Hopewell	-
,	Agnes	1846	Fawn	-
,	David	1782	Hopewell	-
,	Elisabeth	1847	Carroll	-
,	Esther	1846	Hopewell	-
,	James	1815	York Boro	-
,	James	1839	"	-
,	James	1782	Hopewell	-
		1782		
,	James	1805	Fawn	-
,	James	1832	Hopewell	-

2

File Name		Date	Twp.	Misc. Info.
Anderson,	Jane	1828	Fawn	-
,	Jean	1777	Straban*	-
,	Jennet	1807	Hopewell	books/clothes
,	John	1795	"	-
		1796		
		1796		
,	John	1815	Fawn	-
,	John	1813	Hopewell	-
,	John H.	1842	Lw. Chanceford	-
,	John M.	1844	"	-
,	Mary	1808	Chanceford	-
,	Nathaniel	1825	Fawn	-
,	Ranix	1833	Fairview	-
,	Robert	1819	Hopewell	-
,	Sarah	1838	"	vendue
,	William	1843	Monaghan	-
,	William	1846	Peach Bottom	-
Andrew,	Anna	1841	Wrgvlle. Boro	-
,	Elizabeth	1834	Chanceford	-
,	John	1793	Mt. Pleasant*	-
,	Robert	1803	Chanceford	-
Ansbach,	William	1755	Paradise	-
Anselem,	John	1805	Heidelberg	-
Anspoker,	George	1849	Shrewsbury	-
Anstein,	Catherine	1807	Windsor	-
,	Dorothy	1848	Shrewsbury	-
,	George	1843	Hopewell	-
,	Henry	1819	Chanceford	-
,	Phillip	1799	Windsor	-
,	Simon	1849	"	-
Apfel,	George	1829	Heidelberg	-
Apmeyer,	Melchior	1793	Codorus	-
Appel,	George	1790	Manheim	-
,	Wendell	1781	Manallen*	-
Appelman,	Sarah	1820	Paradise	-
Appleman,	John	1786	"	-
,	Margaret	1817	"	German
Appmeyer,	Michael	1834	Codorus	-
Armold,	Peter	1827	Hellam	-
Armor,	Thomas	1785	Yorktowne	surveyor
Armstrong,	Andrew	1783	Chanceford	-
,	Henry	1806	York Boro	-
,	James	1763	Huntington*	Captain
		1764		negro wench
,	Janet	1827	Chanceford	-
,	Martin	1815	"	-
,	Quinten	1795	Cumberland*	-
,	Thomas	1759	"	-
Arnold,	Abraham	1827	Paradise	-
,	Elizabeth	1814	"	-
,	George	1824	Franklin	-
		1825		items to Peter

3

File Name	Date	Twp.	Misc. Info.
Arnold, George P.	1842	"	-
, Henry	1844	Carroll	-
, John	1845	Chanceford	-
, Peter	1795	Warrington	-
, Samuel	1808	Paradise	-
, Samuel	1846	Washington	-
Arnott, Henry	1806	Hopewell	Doctor
Artey, John	1850	Manheim	-
Arthen, George	1850	Newberry	-
, George	1845	"	-
Arther, Isaiah	1792	"	-
Arthur, Thomas	1787	"	-
Ashenfelter, Peter	1822	Warrington	-
Ashten, George	1823	Fairview	-
Ashton, Mary	1798	Newberry	-
, Thomas	1815	Fairview	-
, William	1794	Newberry	-
, William Jr.	1796	"	-
Asper, Abraham	1831	Washington	-
, Abraham Jr.	1835	"	-
, Frederick	1801	Reading*	-
, Frederick	1841	Washington	-
, George	1832	"	-
, George	1834	Paradise	-
, George	1804	Washington	-
, Jacob	1844	"	-
, Jesse	1846	"	-
, John	1765	Reading*	-
, John	1835	Washington	-
	1836		widow
	1835		vendue
	1835		sale
, Phillip	1850	Washington	-
Atherton, Thomas	1782	Warrington	-
Atkinson, William	1819	Fairview	-
Attick, Henry	1844	Fairview	-
Atticks, John	1782	Newberry	-
Attig, Adam	1821	Windsor	-
, Elizabeth	1840	"	-
, Elizabeth	1827	"	-
, George	1790	"	-
, Rebecca	1834	"	-
	1834		vendue
Au, George	1814	Codorus	-
Aubel, George	1785	Windsor	(Abel)
Aughenbaugh, George	1845	Conewago	-
, Henry	1837	Newberry	-
, John	1835	Dover	-
	1835		vendue
Aulenbeuch, Nicholas	1804	Manheim	-
Ault, Adam	1849	Hanover Boro	-
	1848		

4

File Name	Date	Twp.	Misc. Info.
Ault, Henry	1816	Shrewsbury	-
Aurman, Jacob	1780	Manheim	-
Aymes, John	1796	Manchester	-
Ayres, David	1792	Monaghan	-
, David	1830	"	-
, Susan	1842	Newberry	-
, Rachel	1804	Monaghan	-
, William	1829	"	-

-B-

File Name	Date	Twp.	Misc. Info.
Bachman, Daniel	1844	Manheim	-
, David	1796	Germany*	-
, Francis	1827	Manheim	-
, Frederick	1823	"	-
	1835		
, Frederick	1789	Germany*	-
, John C.	1778	Manheim	-
, John	1783	Warrington	-
Bacon, Samuel Rev.	1820	York Boro	books
Badders, George	1821	Fawn	-
, John	1822	"	-
Baer, Michael	1846	Heidelberg	(Ban)
Bagenhoff, William	1820	Fairview	-
Bahn, Anna Elizabeth	1812	?	German
, Catherine	1840	Hellam	-
, Henry	1815	"	-
, John	1836	"	-
	1837		vendue
, Joseph	1829	"	-
, Nicholas	1804	Manchester	-
Bailetto, George	1820	Fairview	-
, John	1823	"	-
, William	1823	"	-
Bailey, Andrew	1794	Monaghan	-
, Daniel	1785	"	-
, Hannah	1807	York Boro	-
, John	1832	Monaghan	-
, John	1841	Codorus	-
, Joseph	1760	?	-
, Rosanna	1815	Shrewsbury	-
Bair, Barbara	1805	Heidelberg	-
, Christian	1795	"	German
, Daniel	1837	Codorus	-
, Daniel Jr.	1834	Heidelberg	(Baer)
, Daniel Sr.	1836	"	vendue
, David	1832	W. Manchester	-
, Henry	1771	Heidelberg	-
, Henry	1810	W. Manchester	(Baer)
, Henry	1781	Manchester	-

5

File Name	Date	Twp.	Misc. Info.
Bair, Henry	1827	Hanover Boro	(Bear)
, Jacob	1815	Newberry	German
, Jacob	1782	Codorus	-
, Jacob	1778	Germany*	-
, Jacob N.	1822	Manheim	-
, Jeremiah	1807	Dover	(Bear)
, John	1798	Newberry	-
, John	1824	Washington	-
, John	1828	Windsor	(Bear)
, Margarey	1818	(Hempfield)	Lancaster
, Michael	1815	Manheim	(Baer)
, William	1823	Dover	(Baer)
, Samuel	1834	?	(Barr)
Baird, Francis	1839	York Boro	-
, Peter	1847	Newberry	-
, Samuel	1840	"	-
Baish, Elizabeth	1821	Franklin	-
, Joseph	1807	Monaghan	-
Baker, Adolph	1769	Codorus	(Becker)
, Henry	1849	Wrgvlle. Boro	-
, John	1841	Paradise	-
, Nicholas	1794	Berwick*	-
, Philip	1785	Manallen*	-
, Stophel	1777	Shrewsbury	-
Bales, Elizabeth	1802	Huntington*	-
Ballintine, William	1803	Chanceford	-
Baltzly, Jacob	1773	Paradise	-
Bane, James	1814	Newberry	-
Bange, George Wm.	1816	Hanover Boro	-
, John	1829	Heidelberg	-
, John	1837	"	vendue
Banix, Catherine	1839	York Boro	-
Barber, John	1755	?	-
, William	1830	York Boro	-
Bard, Barnet	1786	Germany*	-
, Catharina	1815	Hanover Boro	-
, Dorothy	1795	York Boro	-
, Francis	1788	Germany*	-
, John	1807	Newberry	-
, John	1788	Germany*	(Beard)
, Martin	1756	"	-
, Michael	1778	York	-
, Sivilla	1750	?	-
, Stephen	1782	Germany*	German
, Sussanna	1796	Manheim	clothing
Barger, John	1807	Codorus	German
Barling, Fredrick	1759	?	-
Barnes, Daniel	1821	Conewago	-
, John	1793	Windsor	German
, Johnathan	1835	Hellam	-
, Miller	1833	W. Manchester	vendue
	1835		

File Name	Date	Twp.	Misc. Info.
Barnhart, Catherine	1845	York	-
Barnitz, Charles Jr.	1799	York Boro	-
, Charles A.	1850	"	-
, George Esq.	1844	"	-
, Jacob	1828	"	-
, John	1848	?	-
Barns, William	1845	Conewago	illegible
Baroons, John	1757	?	-
Bar, William	1755	?	(Bair)
Barr, John	1834	Hellam	-
Barshinger, Elizabeth	1842	Windsor	-
, Henry Sr.	1849	"	-
Bart, Jeremiah	1840	Hanover Boro	-
Bartan, John	1850	Fairview	-
Basch, Henry	1798	Manallen*	-
Basserman, Christina	1794	Reading*	-
, Michael	1793	"	-
Bateman, Andrew	1793	Newberry	-
, James	1807	Manchester	-
, John	1832	"	-
Bather, Philip	1784	Berwick*	(Boder)
Baublitz, Michael	1838	Manheim	-
Bauchman, Christian	1845	York Boro	-
Bauger, George Rev.	1791	Berwick*	German
, William	1798	"	-
Baugher, Conrad	1775	Germany*	German
, John	1793	Berwick*	-
Baughman, Henry W.	1849	Manheim	-
Baully, Andrew	1768	Warrington	-
Baum, Jacob	1822	Paradise	-
, Peter	1799	Manheim	-
, Peter	1834	"	-
, Simon	1782	"	-
Bauman, Daniel	1843	Hopewell	-
Baumgardner, Isaac	1837	York Boro	died in Md.
Baumgartner, John	1782	Newberry	-
, Leonard	1839	York Boro	-
Baurgelt, Jacob	1839	Hanover	-
, Michael	1823	"	-
Bauser, Benjamin	1844	Shrewsbury	-
Baxter, George	1805	Hopewell	-
	1805		
Baxtor, William	1815	Manchester	(Backstor)
Bay, Hugh	1758	Yorktowne	attorney
Bayer, George A.	1815	Newberry	-
	1825		widow
, Martin	1791	Heidelberg	-
, Margaret	1793	Manheim	German
Baymiller, Mary	1822	Windsor	-
, Michael	1821	"	-
Beachler, John	1829	Fairview	-
, Margaret	1830	"	-

7

File Name		Date	Twp.	Misc. Info.
Bear,	Catharina	1851	N. Codorus	–
,	George	1838	Manheim	–
,	John	1842	Lw. Windsor	–
,	John	1840	Newberry	–
,	John B.	1848	Shrewsbury	–
,	John	1846	Codorus	–
		1850		widow
,	John E.	1845	W. Manchester	–
,	Mary	1850	Conewago	–
,	Susanna	1840	W. Manchester	–
Beard,	Daniel	1851	York Boro	–
,	Elizabeth	1850	"	–
,	George	1819	"	–
,	George	1812	"	–
,	John	1815	Hopewell	–
		1818		
,	Michael	1843	Heidelberg	–
,	Peter	1848	Newberry	–
,	Samuel	1849	Hopewell	–
,	William	1766	?	–
Beasly,	Samuel	1755	?	–
Beattie,	William	1849	Peach Bottom	–
Beatty,	John	1829	York Boro	–
,	Margaretta	1838	Hellam	–
		1838		vendue
,	Mary	1819	Peach Bottom	–
,	Samuel	1795	Reading*	–
,	Walter	1782	"	–
		1755	(same file/probably wrong)	
Beaver,	Anthony	1835	Paradise	–
Beaverson,	Conrad Jr.	1830	?	–
Beavin,	Mary	1822	Peach Bottom	–
Bechtel,	David	1797	Newberry	German
,	George	1761	?	–
,	George	1796	Germany*	German
,	Samuel Sr.	1848	Heidelberg	–
,	Samuel	1750	?	–
,	Valentine	1762	?	–
Beck,	Burghar	1779	Yorktowne	–
,	George	1768	?	–
		1769		widow
,	George	1849	Manchester	–
,	George	1821	Paradise	–
,	George	1831	"	–
,	Jacob	1797	Shrewsbury	–
,	John	1809	Paradise	–
,	Margaret	1828	"	–
Becker,	Arnold	1765	Windsor	(Backer)
,	Catherine	1804	"	–
,	Christina	1796	York Boro	–
,	Conrad	1795	Manchester	–
,	Esther	1818	Paradise	(Baker)

File Name		Date	Twp.	Misc. Info.
Becker,	Frederick	1782	Manchester	-
,	George	1768	Berwick*	(Backer)
,	Gabriel	1813	Chanceford	-
,	Henery	1805	"	(Baker)
,	Henry	1759	?	(Backer)
,	Henry	1783	Codorus	-
,	Jacob	1808	Shrewsbury	German
,	John	1795	Reading*	-
,	John	1822	York	-
,	John	1806	Paradise	-
,	John	1824	Conewago	(Baker)
,	Mathias	1833	Windsor	-
,	Mathias	1808	Newberry	German
,	Mathias	1789	Heidelberg	-
,	Peter	1819	Shrewsbury	-
,	Peter	1799	Newberry	-
		1774	**This is A. Anderson**	
,	Philip	1818	Shrewsbury	-
,	Philip	1817	Newberry	German
,	Philip	1812	W. Manchester	-
,	Salome	1821	Shrewsbury	-
,	Simon	1784	Reading*	-
,	William	1785	York	-
Beech,	John	1766	Shrewsbury	-
,	John	1770	Cumberland*	-
Beery,	Nicholas	1762	?	-
Behler,	Catherine	1806	Codorus	-
,	Daniel	1795	Manchester	German
,	David	1821	Paradise	-
,	John Sr.	1844	Codorus	-
,	Michael	1789	"	-
Beidler,	Barbara	1789	Hellam	-
,	Daniel	1777	"	German
,	Daniel	1816	"	-
,	Jacob	1770	"	-
,	Ulrich	1757	?	-
Beiglar,	Joseph	1832	Dover	-
Beisel,	Abraham	1826	Monaghan	-
Beitzel,	Benjamin	1832	York	-
,	Catherine	1823	Dover	-
,	Catherena	1836	"	-
,	George	1836	"	-
		1839		vendue
,	Henry	1822	"	-
,	John	1794	"	-
,	John	1814	"	-
,	John	1826	"	son of Lorentz
,	Johnathan	1814	"	the younger
,	Johnathan	1814	"	articles for widow
		1814		
,	Lorentz	1818	"	-
,	Magdalena	1816	"	(Bertzel)

File Name	Date	Twp.	Misc. Info.
Beitzel, Sarah	1847	Dover	-
Bell, David	1823	Warrington	-
, Ebenezer	1834	"	vendue
	1835		"
, James L.	1842	Windsor	-
, John	1765	Manallen*	-
, John	1838	Windsor	-
	1838		vendue
, Peter	1844	Warrington	-
Bellew, Leonard	1782	?	-
Beltz, Jacob	1825	Hanover Boro	-
, John	1804	"	-
, Philip	1819	"	-
Beltze, Herman	1751	Yorktowne	-
Beltzhuber, Anna M.	1786	"	-
, Conrad	1815	Dover	German
Bemer, Henry	1754	Manheim	-
Bender, Jacob	1786	Manallen*	-
Benecoaf, Philip	1758	?	-
Benedick, George	1826	Manchester	-
, George Sr.	1816	Dover	-
, Melchior	1784	"	-
, Michael	1849	Conewago	-
, Philip	1842	Manchester	-
, Susan	1848	Conewago	-
Bener, John	1774	Newberry	-
Bengel, Barbara	1787	Windsor	-
Bennett, Joseph	1816	Newberry	-
, Joshua	1823	"	-
Bennington, Moses	1790	?	-
Bennitsch, Lawrence	1802	Newberry	-
Bentz, Andrew	1825	Codorus	-
, Anna Maria	1796	Yorktowne	w/o George
, Frederick Jr.	1822	Hanover	-
, George	1807	Yorktowne	-
, Henry	1815	Warrington	-
, Jacob	1844	Carroll	-
, Jacob	1835	Warrington	-
	1835		vendue
, John Philip	1781	Yorktowne	-
, John	1814	"	-
, Margaret	1834	W. Manchester	-
	1834		vendue
, Michael	1818	"	-
, Peter	1823	Conewago	-
, Weirich Jr.	1783	Yorktowne	-
	1821		W. Manchester	?
Bentzel, Barbara	1807	Dover	German
, Casper	1809	Paradise	-
, Felix	1798	Warrington	-
, Henry	1785	Dover	-
, Johannes	1770	"	-

File Name		Date	Twp.	Misc. Info.
Bentzel,	John	1828	Paradise	-
,	Mary	1843	Washington	-
,	Sophia	1789	Dover	-
Berdesen,	Jacob	1788	Berwick*	-
Bereridge,	George M.	1848	Wrgvlle. Boro	
Berger,	Andrew	1789	Manheim	German
,	Christian	1829	Newberry	(Burgher)
,	Esther	1830	"	-
,	Jacob Jr.	1830	"	-
,	Jacob Sr.	1828	"	-
,	Margaretta	1778	Hanover Boro	(Burgher)
,	Mathias	1775	"	-
Berkheimer,	Andrew	1831	Codorus	-
,	Henry	1849	Paradise	-
,	Henry	1815	Paradise	h/o Magdalene
,	Magdalene	1847	Berwick*	filed w/Henry
,	Valentine	1814	Paradise	German
,	Valentine	1808	Codorus	(Bergheimer)
Berlin,	Jacob	1790	Berwick*	-
,	Michael	1815	Manheim	-
Berot,	Francis	1778	Yorktowne	-
Berry,	John	1835	Codorus	(Barry)
,	John	1836	"	-
,	Nancy	1822	Monaghan	-
Bersinger,	George	1839	Chanceford	-
,	John	1840	Windsor	-
Berthoff,	Frederick	1805	W. Manchester	Baron
Beshore,	Eliza	1833	York Boro	-
,	John	1821	Yorktowne	(Basehore)
,	John	1837	Manchester	-
Bessor,	Christopher	1754	?	German
Bettinger,	Adam	1770	Berwick*	-
,	Peter	1752	?	-
Beyer,	John	1783	Codorus	-
Bicking,	Casper	1770	Reading*	-
,	Jacob	1796	"	-
Bierer,	Conrad	1772	Yorktowne	-
Bievenower,	Anthony	1821	Paradise	-
,	Elizabeth	1836	"	-
		1836		vendue
,	John	1850	"	-
Bigham,	Hugh	1793	Hamilton Ban*	-
,	John	1796	"	-
,	Martha	1795	"	-
,	Patrick	1796	Mt. Joy*	-
,	Robert	1774	?	-
,	Robert	1798	Hamilton Ban*	-
Bigler,	Jacob	1791	Dover	-
,	John	1806	Fairview	(Beachler)
,	Simon	1849	"	(Bieghler)
Billet,	Baltzer	1846	Hellam	-
,	Catherine	1832	Spr. Garden	-

11

File Name		Date	Twp.	Misc. Info.
Billet,	(Catherine)	1832	Spr. Garden	vendue
,	Jacob	1841	"	-
,	John	1807	?	German
,	Kraft	1807	Hellam	-
,	Michael	1818	Manchester	-
Billmeyer,	Daniel	1828	York Boro	-
,	Elizabeth	1824	"	-
,	Helena	1805	"	-
,	Jacob Jr.	1782	Yorktowne	-
Binder,	Josiah M.	1841	Franklin	-
,	Martin	1797	Washington	-
,	Peter	1837	Franklin	-
		1838		
Bingel,	Leonard	1781	?	German
Bisch,	Adam	1790	Germany*	(Birch)
Bishop,	Henry	1791	"	-
,	William	1834	(Talbot)	MD.
Bitner,	Barbara	1842	Windsor	-
Bittle,	George	1779	Germany*	-
,	John	1777	(Northumberland Co.)	
Bitzberger,	Ulrich	1756	Dover	-
Bivenauer,	Barbara	1840	Paradise	-
,	Jacob	1845	"	-
Bixler,	Conrad	1815	Manchester	-
,	Christian	1795	"	-
,	Christian	1777	"	-
,	John Sr.	1765	Manheim	"Praise King"
,	John Jr.	1803	"	-
,	Magdalena	1806	Manchester	-
Black,	David	1821	Peach Bottom	-
,	Henry	1795	Cumberland*	-
,	Jane	1777	Manallen*	-
,	John	1749	?	-
,	Robert	1760	?	-
,	Robert	1799	Mt. Joy*	h/o Sarah
,	Samuel	1823	Fawn	-
,	Sarah	1787	Mt. Joy*	w/o Robert
,	Thomas Esq.	1821	Monaghan	bed only
,	William T.	1850	Dillsburg	-
Blackburn,	John	1788	Tyrone*	faded
,	John	1767	Manallen*	-
,	John	1752	"	-
,	Thomas	1794	"	-
Blackford,	Mary	1848	Carroll	-
Blacklock,	Nelly	1836	?	-
Blain,	Robert	1823	Chanceford	-
Blair,	Brice	1836	Warrington	h/o Jenny
,	Bryse	1785	"	-
,	Jenny	1801	"	filed James
,	John	1756	?	-
,	John	1813	Warrington	-
Blasser,	Herman	1821	Washington	(Blaesser)

File Name	Date	Twp.	Misc. Info.
Blasser, Mathias	1814	York	(Blafer)
, Nicholas	1799	"	(Blasfer)
Blatchford, Richard	1814	Warrington	-
Blaven, Nathaniel	1782	Hanover	-
	1783		chest of sundries
Blessing, Michael	1820	Hellam	-
, Philip	1849	"	-
Blintzinger, Geo. M.	1849	Hanover	-
, George	1823	"	-
Blocker, Jacob	1842	Manheim	-
, John	1838	"	-
, Mathias	1803	"	-
Bloomenshin, Cathrina	1788	Dover	-
Blouse, George	1825	Windsor	-
, George	1847	Chanceford	(Blaus)
	1848		172 acres
, John	1781	Windsor	-
Blymire, Christian	1805	Hopewell	-
, George M.	1793	York	-
, Mary Eliza.	1837	Hopewell	-
	1837		vendue
Boak, Lewis	1849	Fairview	-
Bodenheimer, William	1789	Reading*(Boudenheimer)	
Bodine, John	1786	York	-
Boeckel, Jacob	1833	Manchester	-
Bogle, Malcom	1799	Straban*	-
Bohly, Daniel	1811	Shrewsbury	German
Bole, Thomas	1776	Cumberland*	-
Bollinger, Abraham	1839	Monaghan	vendue
, Abraham	1839	"	same as above
, Anna Maria	1781	Manheim	w/o Jacob
, Anna Mary	1847	Heidelberg	interest
, George	1831	Shrewsbury	-
, George	1838	Codorus	-
, Isaac	1770	"	-
, Jacob	1777	Manheim	h/o Anna M.
, Jacob	1821	Heidelberg	-
, John	1847	Monaghan	-
Bolton, Elizabeth	1819	Hanover	-
, James	1798	"	-
, Robert Jr.	1787	Hamilton Ban*	-
Bond, Benjamin	1826	Fawn	-
, John	1749	(York Co.)	-
Bone, Valentine	1780	Manchester	-
Bonge, Frederick	1813	York Boro	-
Bonine, James	1783	Newberry	-
, Thomas	1786	" starts w/clothes	
Bonner, Francis	1750	York	-
Boose, Emereth B.	1848	Paradise	-
, Jacob	1837	Dover	-
, Jacob	1849	Chanceford	-
, Jacob	1836	Paradise	-

13

File Name	Date	Twp.	Misc. Info.
Boose, Peter	1835	Paradise	-
Bort, George	1768	Berwick*	-
Bortner, Elizabeth	1843	Codorus	-
, George	1843	"	-
, Ludwick	1816	"	-
Bosler, Frederick	1769	Yorktowne	-
, Veronica	1780	"	(Wagner)
Bosley, Joseph	1815	Paradise	-
Bossert, Catharina	1835	Codorus	-
Bosset, Jacob	1820	"	-
Bosworth, Nathaniel	1846	(New York)	-
Bott, Barbara	1794	Manchester	-
, Henrich Sr.	1783	"	-
, Hermanus	1774	"	-
, Jacob	1808	Manheim	-
, Jonas	1793	Manchester	-
, Mary Elizabeth	1805	"	-
, Peter	1846	W. Manchester	-
, Reinhart	1790	Manchester	-
, Tegenhart	1787	Warrington	-
Bottenfeld, Philip	1805	Manheim	German
Boude, Elizabeth	1839	Hellam	-
Boussel, Frederick	1833	Paradise	-
Bowen, John	1817	Newberry	-
, Thomas	1800	Manallen*	-
Bower, Abraham	1795	Huntington*	-
, Abraham	1825	Washington	-
, Ann	1845	Newberry	-
, Frederick	1782	Huntington*	-
, George	1790	"	-
, George	1847	Manchester	-
, George Sr.	1842	Newberry	-
, George Adam	1807	"	-
, Henry	1814	"	-
, Henry	1833	Manchester	-
, John	1809	Newberry	-
, John	1803	Washington	-
, John	1817	(Lancaster Co.)	-
, Joseph	1841	Washington	-
, Martin	1783	Manchester	-
, Michael	1836	Washington	-
	1837		vendue
, Rosina	1784	Manchester	-
Bowers, Elizabeth	1837	Newberry	-
	1837		
, Jacob	1837	"	-
, John Jacob	1818	Manheim	-
Bowman, Abraham	1785	Dover	-
, Christian H.	1818	Fairview	York property
	1818		Lanc. property
, Henry	1808	Manheim	-
, Henry Sr.	1804	Hanover Boro	-

File Name		Date	Twp.	Misc. Info.
Bowman,	Jacob	1844	Chanceford	-
,	Jacob	1800	Manheim	-
,	John	1787	Heidelberg	-
,	John	1799	Codorus	-
,	John H.	1829	Fairview	-
,	Philip	1838	Chanceford	-
		1838		vendue
,	Samuel	1824	Monaghan	-
,	Sarah	1872	Codorus	-
Bowser,	Daniel	1807	Manheim	(Bauser)
,	Esther	1821	"	-
,	Maria	1834	"	-
,	Mathias	1773	(York Co.)	-
,	Soloman	1844	Manheim	-
Boyd,	George	1796	Warrington	-
,	Jane	1850	Fawn	-
,	John	1771	Warrington	-
,	Moses	1778	Cumberland*	-
,	Robert	1844	Wrgvlle. Boro	-
,	Thomas	1763	? leather sales
,	William	1785	Cumberland*	-
,	William	1767	" blacksmith
Boyer,	Adam	1755	?	-
,	Barbara	1848	Heidelberg	-
,	Christian	1823	"	-
,	Daniel	1823	"	-
,	Daniel	1847	Paradise	-
,	Elizabeth	1816	Heidelberg filed Jn. Sr
,	George	1828	Codorus	-
,	Henry	1812	Manheim	-
,	Jacob	1837	Codorus	-
,	Jacob	1849	Newberry	-
,	Jacob	1847	N. Codorus	-
,	John	?	"	German
,	John	1822	Shrewsbury	-
,	John	1849	Spr. Garden	-
,	John Sr.	1809	Manheim	-
,	Joseph	1749	Hellam	-
,	Magdalena	1834	Heidelberg	-
		1834		vendue
,	Mathias	1772	Newberry	-
Boyers,	Frederick	1846	"	-
Boyle,	Daniel	1771	Mt. Joy*	-
Bracken,	James	1778	Manheim	-
,	John	1782	Huntington*	-
,	Thomas	1785	Monaghan	-
Bradford,	Ebenezer G.	1836	York Boro	Esq.
Bradley,	Allin H.	1815	? formerly Conn.
,	Charles	1822	Chanceford	-
,	Henry	1791	Hopewell	-
,	Henry	1778	Fawn	-
,	Joseph	1797	Monaghan	-

File Name	Date	Twp.	Misc. Info.
Bradley, William	1831	York Boro	-
Bradshaw, Sarah	1831	Chanceford	-
Brandon, George	1793	Huntington*	-
, James	1799	"	-
, James	1758	"	-
	1759		found more property
, John	1794	"	-
, John	1774	"	-
Brandt, Frederick	1822	Paradise	-
, Magdalena	1840	"	-
Brandwood, Andrew	1798	Franklin*	-
Braucher, George	1798	Tyrone*	(Brougher)
Brehm, Jacob	1794	Warrington	German
Breidenbach, Magdalena	1850	Manchester	-
, Susanna	1828	"	German
	1828		vendue/German
Breighner, John	1828	Paradise	-
, Peter	1805	"	-
Breitchbaugh, Paul	1814	Manchester	-
	1814		both in German
Brenam, John	1850	Conewago	-
Breneman, Christian	1840	Codorus	-
Brenemen, Joseph	1845	Washington	-
Brenholte, John	1831	Franklin	-
Brenise, John	1846	York Boro	-
Brenneman, Anthony	1827	Codorus	-
, Benjaman	1805	W. Manchester	-
, David	1845	Hopewell	-
	1846		
, Elizabeth	1839	Codorus	-
, Jacob	1828	"	-
, John	1818	York Boro	-
, Joshua	1798	"	-
, Samuel	1808	Codorus	-
, William	1787	"	-
Brenner, Adam	1783	Paradise	-
, Frederick	1840	N. Codorus	-
, Jacob Jr.	1840	Conewago	-
, Jacob	1839	"	-
	1839		vendue
, Mary	1848	N. Codorus	-
, Michael	1845	Dover	-
, Simon	1791	Mt. Pleasant*	-
Brewbaker, John	1844	Dover	-
Bricker, Anna Maria	1813	Manheim	-
, Christopher	1824	Monaghan	-
, Christopher	1785	Manheim	-
, Jacob	1813	Monaghan	-
, Jacob	1819	Shrewsbury	-
, Jacob	1820	Manheim	-
, Nicholas	1803	"	-
Brickle, George	1849	York Boro	-

File Name		Date	Twp.	Misc. Info.
Brieghner,	Gotlieb	1781	Paradise	-
Brierly,	Rebecca	1785	Manchester	-
Briggle,	Martha	1849	York Boro	-
Brillhart,	Abraham	1830	Shrewsbury	-
,	Anna	1828	Codorus	w/o Christian
,	Catharine	1831	"	-
,	Christian	1811	"	-
,	Jacob	1811	Shrewsbury	-
,	John	1826	"	-
,	Joseph	1833	Codorus	-
,	Margaret	1818	Shrewbury	-
,	Peter	1782	Codorus	-
,	Peter	1837	Washington	-
		1837		vendue
,	Samuel	1830	Codorus	-
,	Samuel	1815	Manheim	-
,	Susanna	1828	"	filed w/Samuel
Brillinger,	John	1820	Manchester	-
Brindly,	Jacob	1785	Warrington	-
Broadbeck,	George	1847	Codorus	-
Broband,	Jacob	1777	Newberry	(Brovand)
Brocaw,	George	1794	Mt. Pleasant*	(Bercaw)
Brockley,	Cora	1946	Hanover City	-
,	Lester	1947	York City	-
Brodbeck,	Catharine	1840	Manheim	-
,	Henry	1830	"	-
,	John	1801	"	(Brothbeck)
,	John	1843	"	-
Brohal,	John	1848	Chanceford	(Brochel)
Brooks,	Edward	1849	Hopewell	-
,	Samuel Allen	1822	York Boro	Doctor
Brose,	John	1834	Hopewell	-
		1834		vendue
Bross,	Frederick	1806	"	-
Brown,	Agnes	1796	Chanceford	-
,	Anna Mary	1839	Hellam	-
,	Barbara	1846	York Boro	-
,	George	1777	Reading*	-
		1781		plantation
,	George	1782	Yorktowne	-
,	George	1802	Manchester	-
,	Henry	1799	Germany*	-
,	James	1818	Fawn	-
,	John	1775	Newberry	-
,	John	1801	Hopewell	-
,	John	1843	Fawn	-
,	John	1846	York Boro	-
,	John	1826	"	-
,	Joseph	1772	(York Co.)	-
,	Joseph	1783	Straban*	-
,	Joshua	1784	Fawn	-
,	Mary	1796	Manchester	-

17

File Name		Date	Twp.	Misc. Info.
Brown,	Paul	1804	Shrewsbury	German
,	Richard	1797	Straban*	-
,	Robert	1764	Hamilton Ban*	-
,	Sarah	1845	York Boro	-
,	Sebastian	1805	Hellam	-
,	Thomas	1789	Fawn	-
,	Thomas	1759	?	-
,	Thomas	1834	York	-
,	William	1791	Hamilton Ban*	-
Browsler,	John	1774	Cumberland*	-
Brua,	Daniel	1838	Manchester	-
		1838		
,	George	1785	Newberry	(Bruah)
,	Mary	1806	Manchester	-
Brubaker,	Christiana	1840	Lw. Windsor	-
,	Conrad	1810	Windsor	-
,	Conrad	1817	"	-
Bruch,	Herman	1796	Berwick*	-
Bruckhard,	Julius	1793	Manchester	-
,	Margaret	1805	"	-
,	Michael	1775	Hellam	-
Brumgart,	Jacob	1848	Manheim	-
Brunck,	David	1816	Newberry	-
,	John	1782	"	-
,	John	1798	"	-
,	John	1819	"	horse stud book
Brunet,	William	1812	York	-
Brungart,	Adam	1821	Manheim	-
,	Christina	1829	"	w/o Adam
Brunk,	Christiana	1823	Newberry	-
Brunner,	Christina	1803	W. Manchester	-
,	George	1817	Dover	-
,	Henry	1793	Manchester	-
,	Peter	1791	(York Co.)	-
Brunson,	Bearfoot	1788	(York Co.)	-
Brunton,	John	1831	Warrington	-
,	Thomas	1774	"	-
Buchanan,	Andrew	1759	Monaghan	-
		1795		
,	James	1775	Fawn	-
,	John	1810	Chanceford	-
,	John	1773	Cumberland*	-
,	Margaret	1775	?	w/o Andrew
,	Mary	1789	?	-
,	Walter	1789	Franklin*	-
,	William	1764	Shrewsbury	-
Bucher,	Henry	1828	Heidelberg	-
,	John	1835	Fairview	-
		1835		vendue
,	Michael	1832	Heidelberg	-
,	Nicholas	1784	Reading*	-
Buehler,	John	1827	York Boro	-

File Name	Date	Twp.	Misc. Info.
Bulette, James	1835	Peach Bottom	-
	1835		vendue
Bull, Elijah	1827	Conewago	-
, Elizabeth	1850	"	-
, John	1817	Dover	-
, Lydia	1835	Manchester	-
, Richard	1827	Dover	-
Bupp, Adam	1837	Codorus	-
, Barnet	1805	Shrewsbury	German
, Barnet	1814	"	-
, Christina	1834	York	-
	1834		vendue
, Ludwig	1834	York	-
, Mathias	1793	Codorus	German
, Peter	1807	Monaghan	-
Burger, George	1837	Newberry	-
	1837		vendue
, Henry	1847	Sp. Garden	-
, Jacob E.	1834	Newberry	-
, John	1841	York	-
, Nancy	1850	Newberry	-
, Stephen Sr.	1844	York	-
Burgert, John	1835	Washington	-
, Paul	1758	Manchester	-
, Maria	1845	Paradise	-
Burgholthous, Geo. C.	1830	Windsor	-
Burk, Henry	1815	York	-
, Thomas	1834	"	-
Burkhart, Jacob	1815	Manheim	-
, Jacob	1828	Paradise	-
, Margaret	1817	Heidelberg	-
Burkholder, Abraham	1798	Chanceford	h/o Catherine
, Abraham	1846	Franklin	-
, Catharine	1805	Chanceford	-
, Christian	1794	(York Co.)	-
, Christian	1800	Chanceford	-
, Christian	1835	Lw. Chanceford	-
	1835		vendue
, Henry	1792	Huntington*	-
, Maria	1847	Lw. Chanceford	-
, Mary	1813	Franklin	-
Burns, Joseph	1808	Fawn	-
, Thomas	1830	Monaghan	-
Busch, John	1781	York	-
Buse, John	1828	Dover	not in a file
Busell, Thomas	1810	Dover	-
Bush, Elizabeth	1844	Newberry	-
, Herman	1801	"	German/to wife
	1801		
, John	1836	York	-
	1837		vendue
, John	1827	York	-

19

File Name	Date	Twp.	Misc. Info.
Bush, Peter	1843	Newberry	-
Bushy, Nicholas	1798	Warrington	-
Buss, Adam	1780	Germany*	(Buhs)
, Elizabeth	1801	Paradise	-
, Peter	1796	"	-
Busser, Henry Sr.	1783	Yorktowne	-
, Henry	1841	York	-
, Jacob	1849	York Boro	-
, Jacob	1814	Codorus	-
, Magdaline	1800	York Boro	-
Butcher, Joseph	1815	Windsor	-
Butler, Abraham	1803	Newberry	-
, Sarah	1783	Heidelberg	-
, Thomas	1769	"	-
	1769		
Buzzel, Daniel	1849	York Boro	-
Byermister, Frederick	1797	Heidelberg	German
Byers, Abraham	1823	Warrington	-
, Charles	1799	Hopewell	-
, David	1762	(York Co.)	-
, Elizabeth	1846	Newberry	-
, Elizabeth	1832	Franklin	-
, John	1777	Windsor	-
, Samuel	1798	Hamilton Ban*	-

-C-

Cable, Philip	1780	Warrington	-
Cadwallader, James	1801	"	-
Cadwallater, John	1787	?	(Cadwallader)
Cain, John	1843	Lw. Windsor	-
, John	1849	Wrgvlle. Boro	-
Caldwell, Charles	1749	?	-
, Hugh	1785	Berwick*	-
, Patrick	1780	(York Co.)	(Colwell)
, William	1778	Fawn	-
, William	1851	Dover	Esq.
Call, William	1828	Chanceford	-
, John	1825	"	-
	1826		vendue
Cameron, Daniel	1804	"	-
, John	1818	"	-
, Robert	1821	Lw. Chanceford	-
Campbell, Ann	1812	Chanceford	-
, Archibald	1784	Monaghan	-
, Elizabeth	1818	Chanceford	-
, Francis	1752	(York Co.)	-
, George	1777	Chanceford	-
, Hugh	1798	Straban*	-
, Isabelle	1836	Carroll	-

20

File Name		Date	Twp.	Misc. Info.
Cambell,	John	1775	Chanceford	–
,	John	1809	"	–
,	John	1791	Franklin*	–
,	Thomas	1762	(York Co.)	–
,	Thomas Col.	1815	Monaghan	–
,	William	1758	Hellam	–
,	William	1835	Lw. Chanceford	–
Candler,	David	1801	York Boro	–
Cannon,	John	1770	Newberry	–
Capell,	George	1832	"	–
Carathers,	James Sr.	1800	Monaghan	–
Cares,	John	1843	(York Co.)	–
Carl,	George	1824	Franklin	–
,	George	1821	Hanover Boro	(Karle)
,	Sarah	1850	Heidelberg	–
Carle,	George	1807	Manheim	–
,	Jacob	1778	Yorktowne	–
,	Michael	1780	Berwick*	–
Carmany,	David	1849	Fairview	–
Carney,	Roger	1826	York Boro	–
Carothers,	Jenkins	1845	Codorus	–
,	John	1795	Monaghan	–
		1801		
Carpenter,	Emanuel	1812	Hanover Boro	–
,	John	1824	Fairview	–
,	Samuel	1816	"	–
,	Thomas	1760	?	–
Carrol,	Thomas	1830	Monaghan	–
Carson,	John	1777	Fawn	–
,	Patrick	1754	?	–
,	Samuel	1760	Mt. Pleasant*	–
,	William	1750	Manallen*	–
,	William	1789	"	–
Cartledge,	Joseph	1757	?	–
Carver,	Casper	1802	Codorus	(Kerver)
,	John	1839	Hopewell	–
Caskey,	Joseph	1837	Peach Bottom	–
Cassat,	David	1824	York Boro	Esq.
,	Henry H.	1827	"	library
Cassel,	Jacob	1840	Newberry	–
Cavin,	James	1776	Cumberland*	(Caven)
Celler,	Henry	1754	York	–
Cesna,	John	1751	Newberry	–
Chalfant,	James	1842	York Boro	–
Chamberlain,	Jeremiah	1776	Reading*	–
,	Sarah	1838	Fairview	–
Chambers,	John	1815	Heidelberg	–
,	John	1800	Mt. Pleasant*	–
,	Robert	1783	(York Co.)	Esq.
,	Robert	1784	Manallen*	–
,	William	1829	Monaghan	–
Chapman,	Matthew	1805	?	–

21

File Name	Date	Twp.	Misc. Info.
Chesney, William	1783	Newberry	-
Chester, Richard	1816	Hanover Boro	-
, Robert J.	1790	Berlin twn.*	-
Christ, Adam	1806	Paradise	-
, Jacob	1843	Washington	-
, Leonard	1772	Yorktowne	-
, Philip	1787	Paradise	-
, Philippina	1813	"	-
Christine, Simon	1832	York Boro	-
Christman, Daniel	1839	Heidelberg	-
, Joseph	1848	"	-
Chronister, Henry	1848	Carroll	-
, John	1782	Huntington*	-
Clagston, Joseph	1798	Hamilton Ban*	-
Clapsaddle, Catherine	1795	Mt. Pleasant*	-
, Michael	1787	"	-
, Rosina	1773	(York Co.)	-
Clark, Edward	1789	Manallen*	-
, Edward	1817	Manchester	-
, George	1760	(Frederick)	MD.
, James	1777	?	-
, John	1783	Hamilton Ban*	-
, John	1820	York Boro	Esq.
, Margaret	1833	?	bedroom items
, Matthew	1847	Peach Bottom	-
, Philip	1841	Wrgvlle. Boro	-
, Thomas	1799	Monaghan	-
, Timothy	1760	Reading*	-
, William	1759	?	-
Clarkson, James	1811	Chanceford	Rev.
Claver, John	1815	Fairview	-
Clay, Nicholas	1776	Heidelberg	-
Cleaver, Peter	1823	Washington	-
, Peter	1795	Warrington	-
Climmer, Valentine	1785	Germany*	Petersburg
Cline, David	1848	Fairview	-
, William	1825	Newberry	-
Clingenmeyer, Conrad	1766	Codorus	-
Clingman, Christopher	1789	(York Co.)	-
, George	1778	Hamilton Ban*	-
Close, Abraham	1803	(Balt.)	MD.
, Christian	1795	Reading*	-
Clover, Philip	1757	?	-
Coble, Christopher	1789	Newberry	-
, David	1775	?	-
, George	1833	Newberry	-
, Margaret	1829	"	-
, Peter	1845	Conewago	-
Cochanour, Eve	1847	Dover	-
Cochenour, Jacob	1834	Washington	-
Cochran, Andrew	1781	Hamilton Ban*	-
, John	1784	"	-

File Name		Date	Twp.	Misc. Info.
Cohick,	William	1817	Manchester	-
Cohoon,	John	1752	"	-
Coleby,	Samuel	1766	Yorktowne	-
Coleman,	Conrad	1799	Dover	-
,	George	1834	Manchester	-
		1834		vendue
,	Joseph	1845	Dover	-
Collings,	John	1768	Reading*	poor cond.
Collingswood,	Richard	1815	Windsor	-
Collins,	David	1840	Lw. Chanceford	-
,	Grace	1813	Hopewell	-
,	John	1812	York Boro	-
,	John	1842	Hopewell	-
,	Margaret	1850	"	-
,	Mary	1830	York Boro	-
,	Samuel	1825	Fawn	-
Colmerry,	William	1789	Manallen*	-
Comfort,	Andrew	1789	Berwick*	s/o Leonard
,	Jacob	1836	Warrington	-
		1836		vendue
,	John	1774	Hellam	s/o Leonard
,	Leonard	1762	"	-
,	Veronica	1769	"	w/o Leonard
Conaway,	Martin	1832	York	-
Condry,	John	1794	Newberry	h/o Leah
		1794		vendue
Conrad,	George	1794	Paradise	-
,	George Sr.	1784	"	-
,	Jacob	1810	Heidelberg	-
,	Jacob	1825	Warrington	-
,	John	1836	Fairview	-
,	Philip	1825	Warrington	-
Consor,	Philip	1813	Fairview	-
Cook,	Abraham	1846	Washington	-
,	Ann	1784	Warrington	d/o Peter Sr.
,	Frederick B.	1843	York Boro	silversmith
,	Jacob	1809	Warrington	-
,	Jesse	1818	Franklin	-
,	Joseph	1788	Warrington	s/o Peter Sr.
,	Peter Sr.	1784	"	h/o Sarah
			lists Ann, Peter, Sarah, Robert Vale, Hannah, Joseph, Samuel, Jesse	
,	Samuel Sr.	1801	Warrington	s/o Peter Sr.
,	Thomas	1751	(York Co.)	-
Cookson,	Daniel	1831	Warrington	7 Daughters
,	Sarah	1823	"	-
Cooley,	David	1792	(York Co.)	-
,	John	1757	Shrewsbury	-
,	William	1767	York	-
Cooper,	Alexander	1816	Peach Bottom	-
,	Archibald	1790	Fawn	-

File Name		Date	Twp.	Misc. Info.
Cooper,	Cornelius	1759	Hellam	–
,	Nicholas	1799	Fawn	–
,	Peter	1766	Shrewsbury	–
,	Stephen	1760	Fawn	letter to widow
		1805		possible widow
,	Thomas	1798	Fawn	–
,	William	1790	"	–
Coover,	Adam	1816	Shrewsbury	–
Cope,	Jacob	1774	Hellam	–
,	John	1784	Tyrone*	–
Copel,	Casper	1846	Newberry	–
Copeland,	William	1759	"	–
		1759		vendue
Coppenheffer,	Elizabeth	1795	York Boro	–
,	Elizabeth	1837	Manheim	–
,	Simon	1833	Heidelberg	–
,	Simon	1802	Newberry	–
Copperstein,	Johannes	1823	Shrewsbury	–
Corbet,	Barnabas	1765	?	–
,	William	1849	York Boro	–
Corly,	Barbara	1812	Hellam	–
Cormenay,	Adam	1847	"	–
Cornelius,	Joseph	1799	Franklin*	–
Cornman,	Margaret	1850	York Boro	–
Cosine,	Cornelius	1786	Straban*	Rev.
,	Peter	1779	(York Co.)	(Cousine)
Coulson,	Charles	1790	Monaghan	–
,	David	1789	"	–
,	Francis Esq.	1835	Franklin	–
		1835		vendue
,	Francis	1844	"	–
Countryman,	John	1815	Fairview	–
Cousler,	John	1755	?	vendue
Cowgill,	Henry	1769	Fawn	–
Cowhock,	Samuel	1834	Paradise	–
		1835		vendue
Cox,	John	1777	Newberry	–
,	Nathaniel	1780	Warrington	–
,	Samuel	1796	(N. Carolina)	–
,	William	1798	Warrington	–
Coxen,	Casper	1844	Dover	–
,	John	1823	"	–
Craig,	John	1754	?	–
,	John	1788	Cumberland*	–
Craley,	Christian	1823	Chanceford	–
,	John	1827	"	–
Crall,	Henry	1834	Dover	–
Cramer,	Adam	1800	York Boro	–
,	Anna Margaret	1815	Codorus	–
,	Daniel	1781	(York Co.)	h/o Anna
,	Daniel	1836	W. Manchester	–
,	David	1817	York Boro	–

24

File Name		Date	Twp.	Misc. Info.
Cramer,	David	1823	York Boro	shoemaker
,	George	1832	W. Manchester	-
,	Helfrich	1797	Manheim	-
,	Henry	1811	Warrington	-
,	Jacob	1836	York Boro	-
,	John	1829	Shrewsbury	-
,	John	1792	Warrington	h/o Marg.
,	Lawrence	1840	Codorus	-
,	Margaret	1793	"	filed w/John
,	Philip	1836	York Boro	-
		1836		vendue
Cranston,	Robert	1821	Peach Bottom	-
Crawford,	Catherine	1801	Fawn	-
,	Elizabeth	1824	Monaghan	-
,	Hugh	1779	Berwick*	-
,	John	1772	Hamilton Ban*	-
,	John	1771	Straban*	-
Creglo,	John	1763	Mt. Joy*	(Kregelo)
Creighton,	Esther	1801	Hopewell	-
,	Robert	1805	Fawn	-
,	Thomas	1781	Cumberland*	-
Cremer,	Charles	1850	Heidelberg	-
,	Margaret	1846	York Boro	-
Cressman,	Baltzer	1783	Yorktowne	-
Crone,	Daniel	1811	Paradise	German
,	Elisabeth	1825	Hellam	-
,	Elizabeth	1811	Dover	filed w/John P.
,	Henry	1832	Fairview	-
,	Henry	1760	Yorktowne	-
,	John	1805	Dover	-
,	John	1785	Windsor	-
,	John Philip	1804	Dover	h/o Elizabeth
,	Lawrence	1823	Hellam	-
,	Michael	1844	Dover	-
,	Simon	1821	"	-
Cronebaugh,	George	1779	"	-
,	Henry	1777	"	-
,	Jacob	1797	"	-
,	Peter	1774	"	-
Cronemiller,	Martin	1771	Manchester	-
Crosby,	James	1803	Windsor	-
,	John	1841	Lw. Windsor	-
,	Sarah	1825	Windsor	-
,	William	1822	"	-
Cross,	James	1845	"	-
,	Randall	1819	"	-
,	Thomas	1776	"	-
		1776		2nd inv.
Crouse,	Christian	1785	Newberry	-
,	Michael	1824	Spr. Garden	-
,	William	1774	Manheim	-
,	William	1774	Newberry	-

File Name	Date	Twp.	Misc. Info.
Crowl, Christian	1758	(York Co.)	wealthy
, Henry	1835	Dover	vendue
, Jacob	1779	Chanceford	-
, Jacob	1811	Newberry	-
, John	1783	Manchester	-
, John	1817	Codorus	German
, Michael	1778	Straban*	-
, Samuel	1793	Fawn	-
Crum, Peter	1785	Manheim	-
Crumrine, Thomas	1772	Yorktowne	-
Culbertson, William	1824	Fairview	Esq.
, William	1783	Cumberland*	-
Culley, Thomas	1772	(Martick)	-
, William	1804	Chanceford	-
Cumings, Nicholas	1842	Fairview	-
, John	1805	Fawn	list of goods
	1805		praisement
Cunkle, John	1848	Franklin	vendue
Cunningham, Benjamin	1803	Fawn	-
, Charles	1777	Windsor	-
, Hugh	1817	York Boro	-
, Jane	1826	Peach Bottom	-
, John	1804	Fawn	-
, Robert	1840	Peach Bottom	-
Cupid, Eli	1838	York Boro	cash only
Curran, James M.	1846	Lw. Windsor	-
Currance, John	1819	(York Co.)	-
Curry, Ann	1782	Manallen*	-
, Barnabas	1767	Berwick*	Will contested
, John	1774	?	-
, Thomas	1777	Cumberland*	-

-D-

Dadisman, John	1838	?	Senator
Dagen, John	1792	Shrewsbury	German
Dahl, George	1825	Newberry	-
Dahlman, Anna Mary	1804	York Boro	filed w/John
, John	1775	Yorktowne	-
, John Sr.	1803	York Boro	h/o Anna M.
Daily, Solomon	1807	Hopewell	-
Danapfel, Charles	1791	Shrewsbury	-
Danner, Abraham Sr.	1833	York Boro	-
, Abraham Jr.	1825	"	-
, Casper	1804	Dover	-
, David Sr.	1842	Heidelberg	-
, Deeter	1759	?	-
, Elizabeth	1828	Heidelberg	filed w/next
, Henry	1814	Manheim	h/o Elizabeth
, Henry	1817	Heidelberg	-

26

File Name	Date	Twp.	Misc. Info.
Danner, John	1820	Hanover Tn.	-
, Michael Sr.	1782	"	-
, Michael Jr.	1781	Manheim	-
, Peter	1812	Dover	-
, Philip	1829	Newberry	-
Darby, John	1758	(York Co.)	-
	1769		plantation
Daron, John	1818	Fairview	(Darron)
Darone, Samuel	1848	Hellam	-
Darvon, Adam	1811	"	-
, Barbara	1815	"	w/o Adam
, Catherine	1824	?	-
Dauber, Christian	1789	Mt. Joy*	-
Daugherty, Adam	1813	Hopewell	-
, George	1783	Monaghan	-
Davidson, Jane	1850	York Boro	-
Davis, Daniel P.	1827	Manchester	-
, David	1785	Huntington*	-
, Elizabeth	1823	Paradise	-
, Henry	1784	Hellam	-
, Issac	1762	Hamilton Ban*	-
, Jacob	1824	Paradise	h/o Rebecca
, Jesse	1833	Shrewsbury	-
, John	1808	Warrington	-
, Jonas	1837	Dover	-
, Phineas	1835	York Boro	-
	1835		vendue
, Rebecca	1838	Paradise	filed w/Jacob
, Thomas	1763	Yorktowne	-
, Treasey	1826	Dover	-
, Walter	1757	Hamilton Ban*	-
Davison, James	1802	Fawn	-
, John	1772	?	-
, Thomas	1756	?	-
Davisson, James	1771	Reading*	-
Davy, John	1773	Huntington*	-
Dawechter, John	1849	Manheim	-
Day, Benjamin	1804	York Boro	-
, Catherine	1824	W. Manchester	-
, Daniel	1824	"	-
, Frederick	1825	Manchester	-
, George	1815	"	-
, Isabelle	1805	"	-
, John	1826	Newberry	-
, John	1760	"	-
, Matthew	1839	Shrewsbury	-
, Nicholas	1789	Manchester	-
Dean, Hance	1773	?	-
Deahl, Jesse	1842	N. Codorus	(Diehl)
Deardorff, Andrew Sr.	1846	Dover	-
, Anna	1803	"	no file
, Anthony	1800	"	no file h/o Anna

27

File Name	Date	Twp.	Misc. Info.
Deardorff, Anthony	1824	Manheim	-
, Anthony	1806	Washington	-
, Daniel	1848	Carroll	-
, Eve	1831	Washington	-
, Henry	1812	Franklin	-
, Jacob	1798	Huntington*	-
, John	1776	Reading*	-
, John	1825	Washington	-
, John	1792	Paradise	-
, John	1806	Monaghan	-
, Peter	1787	Paradise	-
Decker, John	1793	Codorus	-
, George	1794	"	-
Degoma, Adam	1772	Berwick*	-
, Eve	1772	"	w/o Adam
Degroff, Michael	1793	Mt. Pleasant*	-
Degrosch, John	1759	Manheim	-
Dehoff, Christian	1822	Codorus	f/o Elizabeth
, Elizabeth	1830	"	-
, George	1810	"	-
, Henry	1785	Manchester	-
, John	1825	Springfield	-
, Mary	1849	York Boro	-
Deigleman, Adam	1846	Washington	-
Deisman, Henry	1826	Warrington	-
Deisinger, Anna Mary	1832	Paradise	w/o John
, John	1805	Dover	-
Deiss, Andrew	1827	Windsor	-
Deitch, Hartman	1812	York Boro	-
Deitz, Anna Maria	1843	Hellam	(Mary)
, Daniel	1847	"	-
, Galen	1847	"	-
, Henry	1842	Spr. Garden	-
, Magdalena	1846	"	-
Dellinger, Christiana	1830	?	-
, Daniel	1826	Spr. Garden	-
, Daniel	1829	Windsor	-
, Henry	1819	"	-
	1819		2nd sundries
, Henry	1847	Dover	-
, Jacob	1824	Windsor	-
	1840		widow
, John	1817	Manchester	German
, Joseph	1826	Hellam	-
, Joseph	1836	Windsor	-
, Mary Cath.	1820	"	-
, Michael	1849	Lw. Windsor	-
Dello, Catherine	1825	York Boro	-
, Nicholas	1800	Paradise	German
, Peter	1793	"	"
Dellone, Margaret	1841	"	-
Delp, Catherine	1826	Conewago	German

File Name	Date	Twp.	Misc. Info.
Delp, Frederick	1809	Manchester	-
Denniston, James	1812	Warrington	-
Denny, Joseph	1798	Shrewsbury	-
Densel, Christina	1849	York Boro	-
Dentzler, Frederick	1773	Yorktowne	-
Depew, Catherine	1848	Fairview	-
Derr, Elizabeth	1820	"	-
, Gabriel	1807	W. Manchester	-
, Henry	1804	Fairview	-
, George	1808	"	-
, Peter	1831	"	-
Derstine, Michael	1783	Hellam	-
Deshner, John	1786	Windsor	-
Dessenberg, Anthony	1804	Manchester	-
, Margaret	1826	"	-
Detter, Lorentz	1812	Washington	-
, Magdalena	1817	Manchester	filed w/next
, Mathias	1802	Manchester	h/o Magdal.
, Mathias	1848	Washington	-
Detterman, John	1835	York Boro	-
, John	1841	E. Manchester	-
Detwiler, John	1815	Hellam	-
Deveny, Dennis	1846	Springfield	-
, John	1825	Washington	-
Devon, Peter	1836	Peach Bottom	-
Dewald, Henry	1817	Manheim	-
Dewes, Benjamin	1802	Dover	-
, Henry	1790	"	(Dewis)
, John	1808	"	(Devis)
, John	1798	"	(Daves)
	1796		real estate
	1785		(Davis)
Dewinger, Killian	1810	Yorktowne	(Divinger)
, Susanna	1817	York Boro	w/o Killian
Dibble, Eve	1818	Hopewell	(Dipple)
Dick, Adam	1838	Dover	-
, Jacob	1833	W. Manchester	-
Dicks, Peter	1794	Paradise	-
Dickson, James	1794	Straban*	slaves
, Samuel	1777	?	-
, Samuel	1767	Straban*	-
, William	1753	Chanceford	-
Diehl, Adam	1755	York	(Deell)
, Adam	1820	Windsor	-
	1821		
, Adam	1849	Shrewsbury	-
, Alexander	1849	N. Codorus	-
, Charles	1817	Shrewsbury	-
, Charles	1839	Windsor	-
, Daniel	1842	Codorus	-
, Elizabeth	1831	Chanceford	-
, Felix	1797	Huntington*	-

File Name	Date	Twp.	Misc. Info.
Diehl, George	1822	Spr. Garden	-
, George	1804	Codorus	-
, John	1820	"	-
, Nicholas	1790	York	-
, Nicholas	1847	Spr. Garden	-
, Rosina	1847	N. Codorus	-
	1847		filed w/Daniel
, Samuel	1822	Heidelberg	-
Dietrich, Joseph	1788	Mt. Pleasant*	-
Dietz, Barbara	1770	Berwick*	-
, Conrad	1750	?	-
, Conrad	1829	Hellam	-
, Elizabeth	1843	"	-
, George Jr.	1822	"	-
, George Sr.	1823	"	-
, George	1836	Windsor	-
	1836		vendue
, Henry Jr.	1842	Hellam	-
, Jacob	1840	Spr. Garden	-
, John	1843	Hellam	-
, Michael	1843	"	-
Dift, Daniel	1821	Dover	-
Dill, Armstrong	1789	?	Doctor
, Caleb	1805	Manheim	h/o Lydia
, Ellen	1827	Franklin	-
, James	1796	Manheim	-
, James	1850	Chanceford	-
, John	1766	Monaghan	-
, Mary (Rosebrough)	?	?	filed w/Mathew
, Mathew	1750	?	h/o Mary
	1754		
, Priscilla	1825	Monaghan	-
, Thomas	1750	?	-
, Thomas	1798	Manheim	-
Diller, Solomon	1814	Monaghan	-
Dinkel, Elizabeth	1830	York Boro	-
, Peter	1828	"	-
, Peter	1840	Warrington	-
Dinnin, William	1785	?	-
Dinsmore, William G.	1826	Peach Bottom	-
	1829		vendue
Dise, Andrew	1831	York	-
, George	1824	Windsor	poor cond.
, Henry	1833	Shrewsbury	(Deis)
, Michael	1802	York	-
Dittenhafer, Paul	1748	?	stone house
Dixon, James	1768	Chanceford	(Dickson)
Dobbin, James	1785	Yorktowne	-
, John	1821	York Boro	room x room
Dobson, Nicholas	1821	Fairview	-
Dods, Joseph	1798	Huntington*	-
, William	1765	?	-

File Name	Date	Twp.	Misc. Info.
Dods, William	1755	Warrington	–
Doergis, Henry	1793	Manchester	–
Doering, John Henry	1822	Manheim	–
Dohm, Christian	1837	York	–
Doll, Barbara	1811	Codorus	–
, Conrad Sr.	1816	Paradise	–
, Conrad Jr.	1828	"	–
, Elizabeth	1834	"	w/o Conrad
, Elizabeth	1842	Chanceford	–
, Henry	1835	Codorus	–
	1836		vendue
, Henry	1835	Paradise	–
	1835		vendue
, Jacob	1835	E. Manchester	–
, Jacob	1847	W. Manchester	–
, Jacob	1845	Paradise	–
, John	1818	"	–
, John	1815	Windsor	–
, John	1808	Codorus	–
, Joseph	1821	Paradise	–
, Margaret	1818	"	–
, Martin	1831	Chanceford	–
, Susanna	1836	York Boro	–
	1836		vendue
Dombar, John	1771	?	(Dumbar)
Dome, Henry	1846	Windsor	–
, Jacob	1844	Chanceford	–
Donaldson, James	1777	?	–
Donnald, Henry	1767	?	(Donely)
Donoughon, Patrick	1788	?	
Dool, Joseph	1794	Chanceford	(Doole)
Dores, James	1841	Fawn	–
Dorman, John	1776	Hellam	–
Dorrough, John	1755	Reading*	(Darach)
Dosch, Christopher	1825	Windsor	–
, Magdalena	1838	"	–
, Mary	1809	"	(Dosh)
, Michael	1799	"	–
	1803		rent debts
Dotterer, Michael	1776	Germany*	–
, Peter	1803	Warrington	–
Dotterman, John	1843	Shrewsbury	–
Doudel, Jacob	1777	Yorktowne	–
, Michael	1754	"	–
, Michael	1803	York Boro	–
Douglas, Archibald	1792	Cumberland*	–
, John A.	1801	York Boro	–
, Thomas	1792	Cumberland*	–
, William	1797	Chanceford	–
, William	1795	Straban*	–
Dougless, Harriet	1845	Chanceford	–
Downes, Samuel	1845	Newberry	–

File Name	Date	Twp.	Misc. Info.
Downey, Patrick	1829	Peach Bottom	-
Downing, Alexander	1809	Chanceford	-
Downs, Samuel	1849	Hopewell	-
Drawbaugh, Adam	1770	Shrewsbury	-
, Adam	1836	Fairview	-
, Michael	1771	York	-
, Peter	1835	Fairview	-
	1835		vendue
Dreher, William	1805	York	-
Drennan, David	1801	Windsor	-
Dressler, George	1812	Paradise	German
Drever, John	1816	Dover	-
Dritt, Elisabeth	1826	Windsor	-
, Henry	1819	"	-
, Jacob	1834	York Boro	-
, Jacob	1817	Windsor	-
, John	1823	"	-
, Peter	1768	"	-
Druck, George	1840	Hellam	-
Drumgold, Michael	1767	Straban*	-
Dryewers, Lewis	1781	?	-
Dubbs, Oswald	1843	Manheim	-
, Oswald	1766	"	(Tup)
Dubs, Daniel Sr.	1837	"	-
, George	1848	Codorus	-
, Salome	1804	Manheim	-
Duffield, George	1794	Tyrone*	-
, John	1758	?	-
, Philip	1828	Hellam	-
Dugan, James	1840	Newberry	-
, Michael	1848	York Boro	-
Dugen, Elizabeth	1840	Newberry	w/o James
Dull, Elisabeth	1834	Chanceford	-
Dunbar, John	1770	?	-
, William	1798	Tyrone*	-
Duncan, Andrew	1828	Hopewell	-
, James	1782	Chanceford	-
, James	1843	Fawn	-
, James	1845	Lw. Chanceford	-
, John	1824	"	-
, Robert	1829	Fawn	-
, Robert	1849	(Ohio)	money only
, Seth	1793	Berwick*	-
, Solomon	1797	Germany*	Doctor
, Thomas	1837	York Boro	-
Dundore, Henry	1817	Dover	-
, John	1774	"	-
Dunkel, Matthias	1835	Paradise	-
	1836		vendue
Dunlap, Jane (Jean)	1798	Hopewell	-
, James	1793	"	-
, William	1892	Chanceford	-

32

File Name	Date	Twp.	Misc. Info.
Dunn, Daniel D.	1832	York Boro	-
, Margaret	1840	"	-
, Robert	1815	"	-
, Thomas	1793	Manchester	-
Dunwoody, Hugh	1777	Hamilton Ban*	-
, John	1780	?	-
Durffil, Lewis	1827	Manheim	(Derfel)
Dwinn, Patrick Jr.	1838	York Boro	Rev.

-E-

Eagle, Barnet	1765	?	-
Early, Edward	1752	Newberry	-
Eaton, George	1848	Hopewell	-
Ebaugh, John	1833	"	-
Eberly, Martin	1846	Washington	-
Ebersold, Henry	1843	Heidelberg	-
Ebersole, Anna Magdalena	1831	"	-
, George	1813	Manheim	slave
Ebert, Adam	1807	York Boro	-
, Elizabeth	1836	Hanover Boro	-
	1836		vendue
, George	1840	Hanover Boro	-
, Martin	1814	W. Manchester	-
, Michael	1785	Manchester	-
, Michael Jr.	1785	"	-
, Michael	1820	York Boro	-
, Philip	1804	W. Manchester	-
, Susanna	1840	York Boro	-
Eby, Esther	1839	Shrewsbury	-
, John	1825	"	-
, John	1783	Windsor	-
Eck, Anthony	1848	York Boro	-
Edgar, Elenor	1831	Peach Bottom	w/o Hugh
, Hugh	1823	"	-
, James	1774	Fawn	-
, James	1779	"	-
, James	1832	Peach Bottom	-
, Libby	1828	Hopewell	-
, Margaret	1779	Fawn	-
, Samuel	1824	Peach Bottom	-
, William	1799	Hopewell	-
, William	1826	Peach Bottom	-
, William	1850	Hopewell	-
Edger, Joseph	1838	"	-
Edie, James	1849	"	-
, John	1751	?	(Eady)
, William	1829	Hopewell	-
Edinger, Adam	1809	Dover	-
Edmundson, John	1783	Warrington	-

File Name		Date	Twp.	Misc. Info.
Edmundson,	Mary	1825	Franklin	–
,	Samuel	1757	?	–
,	Thomas	1811	Warrington	–
,	William	1815	"	–
Edwards,	Edward	1805	Hopewell	–
,	John	1753	?	–
,	John	1841	Spr. Garden	–
Ehresman,	Jacob	1793	Manchester	–
Ehrhart,	Catherine	1807	Shrewsbury	–
,	David	1849	N. Codorus	–
,	David	1775	Reading*	–
,	Jacob	1829	Shrewsbury	–
,	John	1825	"	–
,	Michael	1812	Manheim	–
,	Thomas	1789	Shrewsbury	–
,	William	1826	"	–
,	William	1850	York	–
,	William	1849	Hopewell	farmer
,	William	1781	Shrewsbury	–
Ehrman,	David	1845	"	–
,	George	1828	"	–
,	Jacob	1811	?	h/o Elizabeth
,	Joseph	1798	Heidelberg	(Erman)
Eib,	Matthias	1802	Manchester	–
,	Matthias	1830	"	–
,	Matthias	1808	"	German
Eichelberger,	Adam	1788	Manheim	–
,	Barnet	1781	Yorktowne	Baltimore
,	Barnet	1817	W. Manchester	–
,	Barnitz	1848	York Boro	Distillery
,	Catherine	1843	Heidelberg	–
,	Catherine	1849	York Boro	Bonds
,	Frederick	1776	Hanover	–
,	George	1782	Yorktowne	–
		1752	?	prob. wrong file
,	Jacob	1843	Hanover Boro	–
,	John	1821	York Boro	–
,	Leonard	1811	Monaghan	–
,	Magdalene	1822	Heidelberg	–
,	Magdalene	1790	"	–
,	Martin Sr.	1781	Manchester	–
,	Martin	1829	W. Manchester	–
,	Michael	1801	Manheim	–
,	Michael	1842	York Boro	–
,	Samuel Sr.	1828	Heidelberg	–
,	Susanna	1804	Manheim	–
,	Susanna	1850	York Boro	–
,	William	1825	W. Manchester	–
Eichholtz,	John	1843	Conewago	–
Eicholtz,	Catherine	1811	Dover	–
,	Frederick,	1797	"	German
,	Mathias	1824	Conewago	–

34

File Name	Date	Twp.	Misc. Info.
Eicholtz, Peter	1817	Dover	-
Eirich, Sebastian	1810	York	(Ihrich/Ihrig)
Eisenhart, Conrad	1782	Manchester	-
, Jacob	1812	Dover	German
, John	1844	"	-
Elcock, Mary	1847	Warrington	-
, Richard	1844	?	-
Elder, James	1790	Hamilton Ban*	-
Eley, George	1837	?	-
Elicker, Barbara	1837	?	-
, Casper	1766	?	-
, Casper	1835	Washington	-
	1835		vendue
, George	1837	Franklin	-
	1837		vendue
, Jacob	1832	Warrington	-
Eliofrats, George	1749	?	-
Ellenberger, Peter	1796	Manchester	h/o Eva
, Eva	1802	?	filed w/Peter
, Ulrich	1782	Windsor	-
Elliot, Andrew	1751	?	-
, Andrew	1782	Monaghan	-
, Benjamin	1803	"	-
, John	1776	Reading*	-
, John	1778	Tyrone*	-
, Thomas	1760	Reading*	h/o Margaret
Ellis, James	1785	Hamilton Ban*	-
Elsroth, Valentine	1775	Manheim	-
Emack, Jane	1758	?	-
Emig, Anna M.	1850	N. Codorus	-
, Anna	1819	Codorus	filed w/Philip
, Daniel	1846	N. Codorus	-
, George	1820	Codorus	-
, George	1827	"	-
, George	1844	Dover	-
, John	1787	Manchester	-
, John	1834	W. Manchester	h/o Marg.
, John	1795	Manheim	German
, John Sr.	1848	N. Codorus	blacksmith
, John	1824	Hanover Boro	-
, John	1842	W. Manchester	-
, Margaret	1839	" filed w/Jn. 1834
, Michael	1836	Codorus	-
	1836		vendue
Emlet, Jacob	1821	Heidelberg	-
Emment, George	1841	Hanover Boro	-
Emmit, Josiah	1780	?	-
, Sarah	1790	Hamilton Ban*	-
, William	1757	Fawn	-
Emory, Samuel	1783	Yorktowne	money only
Emrich, Mary	1803	Fairview	-
Emswiler, Henry	1811	W. Manchester	-

35

File Name	Date	Twp.	Misc. Info.
Enders, Nicholas	1810	Paradise	(Anders)
	1833		(Anders)
Endler, Jacob	1804	York Boro	−
Englert, Christophell	1757	?	half German
Enic, Catharina	1839	Dover	−
Ensely, George	1808	Codorus	−
Ensminger, Conrad	1783	Manchester	−
, George	1815	Fairview	−
, Henry	1790	Newberry	−
Entler, Jacob	1824	Hanover Boro	−
Epley, John W.	1849	York Boro	−
Eppley, Anna Maria	1843	"	filed w/Jacob
, Elizabeth	1835	Codorus	filed w/Jacob
	1836		vendue
, Elizabeth	1832	Fairview	−
, Emanuel	1834	"	−
, Frederick	1849	Codorus	−
, George	1835	York Boro	−
, Jacob	1831	"	h/o Anna M.
, Jacob	1845	Newberry	−
, Jacob	1820	Codorus	h/o Elizabeth
, John	1797	Newberry	−
, John	1837	Codorus	−
, John	1826	Fairview	−
, John	1794	Manheim	−
, Rosina	1795	"	−
, Sophia	1800	Newberry	−
Erb, Elizabeth	1848	Spr. Garden	w/o John
, Jacob	1779	(Warwick)	Lanc.
, John	1841	Spr. Garden	−
Erion, Jacob	1804	York Boro	−
Ermold, George	1806	Hellam	−
Erney, Henry	1848	Dover	−
Ernst, Adam	1812	Franklin	−
, Andrew	1829	Manchester	−
, Jacob	1841	Paradise	−
, Jesse	1836	Conewago	−
, John	1809	W. Manchester	−
, Susanna	1840	Franklin	−
Erter, Abraham	1818	Manheim	−
, William	1818	"	−
Erther, Peter	1844	(Carroll Co.)	Md.
Erwin, Julianna	1843	Spr. Garden	−
, Patrick	1822	York	−
Eshelman, Peter	1775	Newberry	−
Etter, Christian	1804	Codorus	−
, Henry	1849	Newberry	−
, Lawrence	1804	Shrewsbury	−
, Mary	1818	"	−
Ettinger, Anna Maria	1842	Dover	−
, Philip	1786	Manchester	−
Etzler, Andrew	1824	Heidelberg	−

File Name		Date	Twp.	Misc. Info.
Etzler,	George	1813	Heidelberg	-
,	Jacob	1830	"	-
,	Mary	1833	"	-
,	Michael	1843	"	-
Evans,	Ann	1850	Wrgvlle. Boro	-
,	David	1776	Dover	-
,	David	1798	Warrington	-
,	Henry	1771	Windsor	-
,	James	1848	Carroll	-
,	James	1825	Windsor	-
,	James	1799	Hopewell	-
,	Margaret	1819	Fairview	-
,	Peter	1833	Franklin	-
,	Samuel	1769	Windsor	-
,	Thomas	1827	Franklin	-
Everhart,	John	1790	Codorus	-
,	Michael	1845	Heidelberg	-
,	Wendel	1780	Codorus	-
Ewing,	Alexander	1832	Fawn	Rev.
,	Henry	1825	"	-
,	James	1786	Franklin*	-
,	James	1806	Hellam	General
,	John	1768	Mt. Pleasant*	-
,	Samuel	1793	"	-
Eyler,	Christian	1820	Hanover Boro	-
,	John	1804	Manheim	(Eiler)
,	Salome	1844	Hanover Boro	-
Eyres,	Henry	1786	Newberry	-
Eyster,	Catherine	1842	Paradise	-
,	Daniel	1819	Heidelberg	h/o Eliz.
,	Elias	1829	Manchester	-
,	Elizabeth	1835	Heidelberg	filed w/Dan
		1836		vendue
,	George	1810	W. Manchester	-
,	George	1831	"	-
,	Peter	1804	Paradise	-
,	William	1824	"	-

-F-

Fackler,	Adam	1771	Yorktowne	-
,	Daniel	1842	W. Manchester	-
,	George	1841	"	-
,	Jacob	1775	Yorktowne	-
Faddis,	Jacob H.	1821	Manchester	-
Fahs,	Christian	1795	Manheim	-
,	Henry	1808	(Graceham)	Md.
,	Jacob	1785	Berwick*	-
,	Jacob	1873	York Boro	-
,	Jacob	1837	"	-

File Name	Date	Twp.	Misc. Info.
Fahs, John	1840	Dover	–
, John	1834	W. Manchester	–
, Mary	1849	"	–
, Susanna	1805	Paradise	–
, William	1845	Spr. Garden	–
Fairfield, Charles	1833	Carroll	–
Fake, Leonard	1848	Windsor	–
Falkner, John Sr.	1807	Hopewell	–
Faller, John	1784	Mt. Pleasant*	–
	1786		2nd inv.
, John	1786	Hanover	–
Falls, Daniel W.	1770	(York Co.)	–
Farmer, John	1782	Fawn	–
Farra, George	1752	(York Co.)	in pcs.
, James	1778	Dover	–
, John	1799	Warrington	–
, William	1795	"	–
Fauble, John	1794	Manheim	–
Faust, Baltzer	1826	Peach Bottom	–
, Baltzer	1827	Shrewsbury	–
Fedrow, Philip	1791	Newberry	–
Feeney, James	1837	Hellam	–
	1837		2nd inv.
Feeser, Anna Maria	1796	Germany*	–
, Jacob	1777	"	–
, John	1781	Dover	–
, Peter Sr.	1806	York Boro	–
, Peter	1826	Shrewsbury	–
Fegely, Paul	1796	Paradise	–
Fehl, Daniel	1762	Codorus	(Fhel)
	1762		vendue
Feigly, Martin	1822	Shrewsbury	–
Feiser, Daniel	1838	Springfield	–
Feister, Catharine	1821	Windsor	–
, Jacob	1806	"	–
Felde, John	1817	Shrewsbury	–
Felger, Dorothea	1804	Manchester	–
, Frederick	1786	"	–
, Henry	1788	Manheim	–
Feltenberger, Jacob	1831	Manchester	–
Felty, Henry	1836	Hanover Boro	–
	1836		vendue
, Ignatius	1841	Lw. Chanceford	–
, John	1825	Heidelberg	–
Fensel, Christian	1847	Newberry	–
Feree, Andrew	1836	Spr. Garden	–
	1836		vendue
Ferguson, John	1778	Manallen*	–
, Robert	1778	?	–
, Samuel	1778	Manallen*	–
Fernster, George	1789	Codorus	–
Ferree, Andrew	1831	Spr. Garden	–

File Name		Date	Twp.	Misc. Info.
Ferree,	Andrew C.	1850	Hellam	-
,	Joseph	1831	Spr. Garden	-
,	Peter	1824	Washington	-
Fetrow,	Abraham	1827	Newberry	-
,	John	1820	Conewago	-
,	Jonas	1849	Newberry	-
,	Joseph	1818	Fairview	-
,	Michael	1826	Newberry	-
		1834		vendue
,	Philip	1834	York Boro	-
Fetter,	Michael	1801	Codorus	-
Fettrow,	Elizabeth	1834	Conewago	-
Ficht,	John	1832	Spr. Garden	-
Fickes,	Jacob	1783	Huntington*	-
,	John	1832	Franklin	-
,	Martin	1821	"	-
,	Valentine	1782	Huntington*	-
Field,	Barbara	1843	Hanover Boro	-
,	Joseph	1831	Newberry	-
Fields,	John	1778	(York Co.)	-
,	John	1836	York Boro	-
		1836		vendue
Fife,	George	1841	Shrewsbury	-
,	Jacob	1847	"	-
,	James	1842	"	-
,	William	1823	?	-
Filey,	George	1790	Monaghan	-
,	Jacob	1832	"	-
		1836		vendue
,	John Sr.	1804	"	-
Finder,	Anna Mary	1784	Manchester	-
Fink,	Adam	1769	?	-
,	Christina	1804	Newberry	-
,	Ferdinand	1874	York Boro	-
,	Henry	1804	Manchester	-
,	Jacob	1838	"	-
,	John	1828	Conewago	-
,	John Sr.	1757	?	-
,	Mary	1837	Spr. Garden	-
,	Michael	1782	Paradise	-
,	William	1843	Newberry	-
Finley,	Aaron	1794	Straban*	-
,	Andrew	1807	Hopewell	-
,	David	1799	Chanceford	-
,	James	1783	Cumberland*	-
,	James	1764	Hamilton Ban*	vendue
,	John	1782	Chanceford	-
,	Martha	1807	"	-
,	Michael	1785	(York Co.)	-
,	William	1825	Lw. Chanceford	-
Firestone,	George	1835	Washington	-
		1835		vendue

File Name		Date	Twp.	Misc. Info.
Firestone,	John	1825	Fairview	-
,	Nicholas	1768	Heidelberg	-
		1769		2nd inv.
,	Samuel	1844	Washington	-
,	William	1835	"	-
		1835		vendue
Fishel,	Anna Maria	1835	Paradise	-
,	Barbara	1824	"	German
,	Conrad	1809	?	German
,	Daniel	1818	Hellam	-
,	Daniel	1834	Codorus	-
,	David	1830	Paradise	-
,	Frederick	1817	"	-
,	Frederick	1777	Shrewsbury	h/o Anna.
,	Henry	1802	Manheim	-
,	Henry Sr.	1812	Paradise	-
,	Henry	1830	"	-
,	John Sr.	1820	Codorus	-
,	John	1794	Huntington*	-
		1794		2nd inv.
,	John Sr.	1786	Yorktowne	-
,	John	1834	Hopewell	-
,	Magdalena	1842	Paradise	-
,	Michael	1816	"	-
,	Michael	1804	York	-
,	Michael	1810	Paradise	-
,	Nicholas	1823	Hanover	-
,	Philip	1778	Paradise	-
,	Philipina	1837	Liverpool twn.	-
		1837		vendue
,	Wendel	1790	Paradise	-
Fisher,	Abraham	1822	Monaghan	-
,	Casper	1819	York	-
,	Catherina	1822	York Boro	-
,	Charles F.	1842	"	-
,	Christian	1815	Codorus	-
,	David	1827	Fairview	-
,	Frederick Sr.	1791	York	-
,	George	1848	Codorus	Esq.
,	George	1837	?	-
,	Goodlieb	1792	Newberry	-
,	Gotlieb	1823	Fairview	-
,	Henry	1837	"	-
		1837		vendue
,	Henry	1844	Hellam	-
,	James	1770	Newberry	-
,	John	1797	Shrewsbury	-
,	John Sr.	1809	York Boro	-
,	John	1834	Manheim	-
,	John Sr.	1832	York Boro	-
,	John Ludwig	1821	"	-
,	Nicholas	1785	Manheim	-

40

File Name		Date	Twp.	Misc. Info.
Fisher,	Thomas	1793	York Boro	Esq.
,	William	1830	"	–
Fissel,	Killian	1790	Codorus	–
,	Philip	1845	Paradise	–
Fitz,	Baltzer	1803	Hellam	–
,	Elizabeth	1823	"	–
,	Elizabeth	1825	Windsor	–
,	Frederick	1817	"	–
,	Jacob	1839	Hellam	–
,	John	1820	Windsor	–
,	John Sr.	1845	N. Codorus	–
Fitzgerald,	William	1754	?	–
Flecks,	Valentine	1796	Huntington*	–
Fleishman,	Martin	1806	Shrewsbury	German
Fleming,	George	1797	Straban*	–
,	Robert	1784	Hamilton Ban*	–
Flemming,	John	1783	Cumberland*	–
Fletcher,	Jacob	1758	?	–
,	Robert	1786	Cumberland*	–
Flickinger,	Andrew	1789	Manheim	–
,	Andrew	1844	Hanover	–
,	Christina	1831	Heidelberg	–
,	Eve	1823	"	filed w/Sam
,	Peter	1821	"	–
,	Rachel	1846	"	–
,	Samuel	1843	"	–
,	Samuel	1816	"	h/o Eve
Flinchbaugh,	Adam	1820	Hopewell	–
,	Adam	1842	York	–
,	Frederick	1837	Windsor	–
,	John	1819	Hopewell	–
,	Ludwick	1776	York	–
,	Martin	1802	Hopewell	–
,	Melchoir	1772	York	–
Flohr,	Valentine	1804	Dover	–
Flory,	Abraham	1777	Hellam	–
,	Abraham	1850	(Harrison)	Indiana
,	Barbara	1827	Wrgvlle. Boro	–
,	Francis	1782	Hellam	–
,	Isaac	1809	"	–
,	Jacob	1813	"	–
,	John Jr.	1823	"	–
,	Magdelina	1787	"	–
Flowers,	Benjamin	1826	Hopewell	–
,	John	1772	Shrewsbury	–
,	John	1775	York	–
,	John	1817	Hopewell	–
Flury,	Abraham	1832	Hellam	–
,	Catherine	1849	Lw. Windsor	–
,	Daniel	1841	Wrgvlle. Boro	–
Focht,	Daniel	1835	Windsor	–
		1835		vendue

File Name	Date	Twp.	Misc. Info.
Fockenroth, George	1830	Codorus	–
Foerster, Henry Sr.	1796	Warrington	–
Fogel, Christian	1778	Manchester	–
, Nicholas	1766	Codorus	–
Fogelsang, Philip	1797	Warrington	–
, Philip	1804	Washington	–
Fogelsong, Barbara	1807	Warrington	–
Foght, Jacob	1824	York Boro	–
Folcommer, Anna Maria	1833	Shrewsbury	–
Folk, George	1821	Manheim	–
Folkenruth, Valentine	1811	Codorus	–
Folkomer, Jane	1850	Shrewsbury	–
Folkommer, Jacob	1829	"	–
Follmer, John	1826	Manheim	–
Forbes, Lucretia	1832	York Boro	–
, Robert	1816	Fairview	–
Fordenbaugh, Andrew	1823	Newberry	–
, Henry	1824	"	–
, Henry	1835	"	–
, Peter	1805	"	–
, William	1812	"	–
Foreman, Elizabeth	1783	Berwick*	–
Forney, Adam	1752	?	–
, Adam	1822	Heidelberg	–
, Adam	1845	"	–
, Christian	1824	"	–
, Marx (Marks)	1804	"	–
, Philip	1783	"	–
, Rachel	1845	Hanover Boro	–
, Rachel	1846	Heidelberg	–
, Samuel	1836	"	–
	1844		2nd inv.
Forry, Christian	1783	Newberry	–
	1785		2nd inv.
, Henry Sr.	1836	Hellam	–
	1837		vendue
, Henry	1766	"	–
, Jacob	1807	Manchester	–
, John	1782	Newberry	–
, John Sr.	1841	Heidelberg	–
, Randolph	1841	York Boro	–
, Ulrick	1825	Hellam	–
Forsh, Barbara	1817	Dover	–
, Martin	1844	Washington	–
Forsht, Adam	1804	Dover	–
Forsyth, John	1820	York Boro	–
, Robert	1782	Chanceford	–
Fortenbaugh, Anna	1844	Newberry	–
, Peter	1830	"	–
Fortney, Christopher	1809	Monaghan	–
, Jacob	1831	"	–
Foster, Hugh	1827	Newberry	–

File Name		Date	Twp.	Misc. Info.
Fotsh,	Mary	1794	Chanceford	German
Foust,	Henry	1843	E. Manchester	-
Fowler,	Thomas	1796	Fawn	-
Fox,	Christian	1795	Franklin*	-
,	George	1808	Windsor	-
,	George	1789	Paradise	(Fuchs)
,	Henry	1772	Reading*	-
,	Peter	1796	"	(Fuchs)
Fraelig,	Jacob	1809	Newberry	-
Frank,	David	1785	Manheim	-
,	Ernest	1849	York Boro	-
,	George Philip J.	1772	Manchester	-
,	John	1836	Wrgvlle. Boro	-
,	Ludwig	1799	Hanover twn.	Doctor
Frankelberger,	Jacob	1847	Lewisbury Boro	-
,	John	1788	Paradise	-
,	John	1777	"	-
Franklin,	Walter S.	1838	York Boro	Esq.
Frantz,	Abraham	1838	Manchester	-
,	Jonas	1848	Dover	-
Frazer,	Alexander	1816	Newberry	-
,	Joshua	1820	Monaghan	-
Frederick,	Andrew Sr.	1778	Paradise	h/o Anna
,	Anna Eliz.	1781	"	-
,	Philip	1834	York	-
Free,	Conrad	1814	Shrewsbury	German
,	Conrad	1834	"	-
		1834		vendue
,	John	1821	New Holland twn.	-
Freed,	Henry	1817	Hellam	-
,	Paul	1814	"	-
,	Peter	1778	York	-
Freeland,	James	1766	Shrewsbury	-
,	Stephen	1771	"	-
Freeman,	Nathaniel	1804	Fairview	-
Freet,	Paul	1842	Wrgvlle. Boro	-
Freetz,	George	1770	Chanceford	-
,	Michael	1793	Windsor	-
,	Philip	1756	Hellam	-
French,	Philip	1761	?	-
Frend,	Charles	1847	York Boro	(Freund)
Frey,	Adam	1846	Windsor	-
,	Anna Maria	1822	Shrewsbury	-
,	Benjamin	1850	York Boro	-
,	Christopher	1833	Manchester	-
,	Conrad	1812	Newberry	-
,	Conrad	1811	Manchester	German
,	Frederick	1814	Windsor	"
,	George	1804	Manchester	-
,	George	1830	Windsor	-
		1830		vendue
,	Goteried	1782	York	-

File Name	Date	Twp.	Misc. Info.
Frey, John	1822	Windsor	-
, John	1850	Fawn	-
, John	1846	Chanceford	-
, Martin	1780	Yorktowne	-
, Peter	1789	Monaghan	German
, Peter	1825	Windsor	-
, Philip	1789	(York Co.)	-
, Samuel	1827	Windsor	-
Friedly, Christopher	1794	Chanceford	-
, Frederick	1794	Manheim	-
Fries, George	1833	Hellam	-
, Simon	1826	"	-
Friesinger, Jacob	1845	Conewago	-
Fringer, Nicholas	1773	Manheim	-
Fritsel, George	1800	Germany*	-
Fritz, Philip Sr.	1807	Hellam	-
Froesher, Catharine	1815	Codorus	filed w/Fred German
, Frederick	1811	"	h/o Cath.
Frohn, Peter T.	1837	Spr. Garden	-
Fry, Diedrick	1839	Wrgvlle. Boro	-
, Elizabeth	1842	"	-
, Philip	1841	Spr. Garden	-
Frymiller, Joseph	1752	?	-
Frysinger, Elizabeth	1818	Conewago	-
, Jacob	1831	Monaghan	-
	1832		grain planted
, Lewis	1850	Monaghan	-
, Ludwig	1792	Dover	German
Fuhrman, Henry	1848	Manheim	-
, Jacob	1830	"	-
, Peter	1835	"	-
, Stephen	1781	"	-
, Susanna	1822	Heidelberg	German
, Valentine	1838	Manheim	-
Fullerton, John	1788	Chanceford	-
, William	1812	Lw. Chanceford	-
Fulton, David	1826	Hopewell	-
, James Sr.	1808	Chanceford	-
, James	1800	"	"of the ferry"
, James	1772	Hopewell	-
, Margaret	1805	Chanceford	-
, Samuel	1807	Lw. Chanceford	-
, Samuel B. (G)	1832	"	-
, William	1781	?	-
Fulwiler, Jacob	1757	?	German
, Michael	1819	Washington	-
Funk, Benedict	1801	York Boro	-
, Jacob	1816	"	(Funck)
, Jacob	1843	Spr. Garden	-
, John	1844	York Boro	-
, John	1804	Dover	-

File Name	Date	Twp.	Misc. Info.
Funk, John	1830	Fairview	-
, Martin	1840	Windsor	-
, Michael	1798	Manheim	s/o Adam
Furman, Michael	1817	"	-
Furst, Adam	1827	Dover	(Forst)

-G-

Gable, Conrad	1839	Spr. Garden	-
, Henry	1844	N. Codorus	-
, John	1791	Shrewsbury	German
, Peter	1790	Manallen*	-
, Valentine	1825	Chanceford	-
Gabriel, Philip	1834	York Boro	-
	1834		vendue
Galbraith, Alexander	1819	Peach Bottom	-
, Henry	1782	Hamilton Ban*	-
, James	1772	Straban*	-
, John	1770	Mt. Pleasant*	-
, Mathew	1822	Peach Bottom	-
, Thomas	1778	Mt. Pleasant*	-
Gallagher, Abraham	1810	Windsor	-
, Jennet	1811	"	-
, John	1841	Lw. Chanceford	-
Galloway, Samuel	1778	Manallen*	-
Galt, Rosanna	1793	Mt. Pleasant*	-
Gantz, Catharine	1841	Shrewsbury	-
, Esther	1828	Manheim	-
, George	1816	Codorus	-
, Henry	1850	Springfield	-
, John	1792	Codorus	German
, John Sr.	1835	"	-
	1835		vendue
, John	1846	Springfield	-
Gantzer, Andrew	1776	Dover	-
, Mathias	1772	"	-
Gantzert, Catherina	1776	"	d/o Mathias
Gap, George	1757	?	German
Gardner, Adam	1780	Yorktowne	-
, Eleanor	1836	York Boro	-
, Jacob	1807	"	-
, Louisa	1822	Warrington	-
, Margaret	1824	York Boro	-
, Peter Sr.	1793	Hellam	-
, Philip Sr.	1804	"	-
, Philip	1834	"	-
	1835		vendue
Garlitz, Christopher	1834	Manheim	-
Garner, George	1799	Germany*	-
, Mark	1799	Windsor	-

File Name	Date	Twp.	Misc. Info.
Garner, Michael	1825	Windsor	-
Garretson, Cornelus	1829	W. Manchester	-
, Elizabeth	1849	Newberry	-
, Hannah	1836	York Boro	-
	1836		vendue
, Jacob	1830	Newberry	-
, James	1810	"	-
, Joel	1837	"	-
, John	1797	"	-
, John	1815	York Boro	-
, John	1829	Newberry	-
, Joseph	1814	"	-
, Rachel	1832	"	-
, Rebecca	1815	"	w/o Joseph
, Samuel	1822	"	-
, William	1797	Warrington	-
Gartman, Catharine	1806	York Boro	-
, Isaac Sr.	1789	Yorktowne	-
, Isaac	1808	"	-
, Isaac	1800	York Boro	-
Garver, Christian	1849	Fairview	-
Gashaw, Peter	1777	Yorktowne	(Cashaw)
Gass, Catherine	1812	Chanceford	filed w/Geo.
, George	1804	"	h/o Cath.
	1804		to widow
Gates, John	1830	New Holland twn.	-
Gauf, George	1792	Dover	-
, Jacob	1783	"	-
, Philip Sr.	1776	"	-
, Philip Jr.	1777	"	-
Geary, James Sr.	1779	Mt. Pleasant*	-
Gebby, William	1826	Lw. Chanceford	-
Geber, Catharine	1815	Manheim	-
Geesey, Conrad	1831	York	-
, Elizabeth	1839	Shrewsbury	-
, Julian	1834	Manchester	-
, Samuel	1847	Shrewsbury	-
Gehly, John	1846	Windsor	-
Gehr, Andrew	1804	Fairview	-
, Elizabeth	1832	"	-
Geib, Henry	1841	Hellam	-
Geigel, Gotlieb	1816	York Boro	-
Geis, Adam	1793	Manallen*	-
, Peter	1804	Paradise	(Gise)
Geise, Elizabeth	1823	"	-
Geiselman, George	1834	Shrewsbury	-
, Michael	1784	"	-
Geisly, Anna Mary	1846	N. Codorus	-
Geistweit, George	1837	York Boro	Rev.
	1837		vendue
, Magdalena	1837	"	-
	1837		vendue

46

File Name		Date	Twp.	Misc. Info.
Gelby,	John	1823	Lw. Chanceford	-
Gelhaus,	John	1803	Dover	-
Gellesph,	John	1793	Mt. Pleasant*	-
Gelwicks,	Frederick	1783	Hanover	-
,	Frederick	1812	Manheim	-
Gelwicks,	Nicholas	1817	Hanover	h/o Mary
Gelwix,	Mary	1838	"	-
Gemling,	Barnhard	1766	?	-
Gemmill,	James	1816	Lw. Chanceford	-
,	James	1799	Hopewell	-
,	Jane	1839	Chanceford	-
,	John Jr.	1837	Hopewell	-
		1837		vendue
,	John	1832	Hopewell	-
,	John	1798	"	-
,	John	1807	"	-
,	Margaret	1844	Chanceford	-
,	Mary	1805	?	-
,	Robert	1843	Manchester	-
,	Robert	1813	Hopewell	-
,	Sarah	1830	"	-
,	Thomas	1849	"	-
,	William	1849	"	-
,	William	1789	"	-
		1789		land
,	William	1820	?	-
Gennings,	Mary	1845	Newberry	-
Gentzler,	Conrad	1778	Paradise	-
		1778		2nd inv.
,	George P.	1816	Codorus	-
,	Peter Sr.	1839	N. Codorus	-
Gerber,	Abraham	1850	Heidelberg	-
,	Andrew	1829	Hellam	poor cond.
,	Christopher	1815	Dover	-
,	George	1791	York Boro	-
,	Jacob	1840	Dover	-
,	Jacob	1822	Heidelberg	-
,	John	1759	Manchester	German
,	John	1805	Manheim	-
,	Joseph	1850	Codorus	-
,	Nicholas	1804	Manheim	-
,	Philip	1759	Yorktowne	-
Gerberich,	George	1838	Codorus	-
,	Jacob	1814	York Boro	-
,	John	1846	Shrewsbury	-
Gerberick,	Margaret	1802	Codorus	-
,	Michael	1835	Shrewsbury	-
		1835		vendue
,	Peter	1805	Codorus	German
Gerbrick,	Frederick	1827	"	-
Gering,	Elizabeth	1831	York Boro	-
,	Elizabeth	1833	"	filed w/John

File Name	Date	Twp.	Misc. Info.
Gering, Jacob	1780	Chanceford	-
, John	1833	York Boro	-
Gets, Martin	1807	Monaghan	(Gates)
Geyer, Adam	1779	Windsor	(Gyger)
	1794		German
, Paul	1771	Yorktowne	-
Gibbs, Burroughs H.	1816	Hanover Boro	-
Gibhs, Isaac	1837	Springfield	vendue
	1836&37		vendue
Gibons, Henry	1850	Lw. Windsor	-
Gibony, James	1807	Lw. Chanceford	-
, Thomas	1826	"	-
Gibson, Jacob Esq.	1809	Fawn	-
, Jacob	1849	Peach Bottom	-
, Jane	1850	"	-
, James	1763	?	-
, John	1750	(York Co.)	-
, John	1763	"	-
, John	1783	Hopewell	-
, Robert	1787	"	-
, Thomas	1840	Fawn	-
, William	1769	Mt. Joy*	-
	1769		2nd inv.
Giep, Daniel	1843	York Boro	poor cond.
Giesey, Conrad	1833	York	-
Giesy, Christian	1831	Shrewsbury	-
, Conrad	1802	York	-
, Henry	1825	"	-
, John	1831	Manchester	-
Gilbert, Andrew	1816	Windsor	-
, Eleazor	1839	Shrewsbury	-
, John	1846	Lw. Windsor	-
, John	1765	?	-
Gilberthorp, William	1835	York Boro	-
	1835		vendue
Gilkey, John	1751	Tyrone*	-
	?		vendue
Gillespie, John R.	1848	Hellam	-
, Simon	1836	?	Rev.
Gilliland, Archibald	1777	Hopewell	-
, John	1789	Manallen*	-
Gillis, William	1817	Fawn	-
Gillman, Daniel	1848	Hellam	-
Ginder, Christina	1788	Dover	-
, Conrad	1828	Conewago	-
	1835		Bonds
, Dewalt	1774	Dover	-
Ginder, Jacob	1801	Manchester	-
, John	1808	Newberry	German
, Michael	1800	Manchester	"
, Susanna	1829	"	-
Gingerich, Benjamin	1796	Codorus	-

File Name		Date	Twp.	Misc. Info.
Gingerich,	Maria	1811	Manchester	-
Gingrich,	Jacob	1822	Spr. Garden	-
,	Michael	1803	Manchester	-
Ginter,	George	1828	"	-
,	Jacob	1842	Conewago	-
Gipe,	Jacob	1844	Chanceford	-
,	Jacob	1831	"	-
Girvin,	Mary	1790	Cumberland*	-
Gise,	Peter	1849	Paradise	-
Gist,	Reuben	1815	Windsor	-
Gitchell,	Justus	1821	Fairview	-
Given,	John	1845	Newberry	-
Gladdy,	Martin	1790	Reading*	-
Gladfelter,	Elizabeth	1827	Codorus	-
,	Jacob	1841	"	-
Glancy,	Joseph	1807	York Boro	-
Glasgow,	Hugh	1818	Peach Bottom	-
,	Marie (Maria)	1820	"	w/o Hugh
Glasick,	John	1776	Codorus	-
Glass,	Daniel	1821	Warrington	-
Glassbrenner,	Frederick	1784	Windsor	-
Glasser,	John	1783	Manheim	-
Glassick,	Catherine	1822	Codorus	-
Glassmyer,	Jacob	1832	W. Manchester	-
Glatfelder,	Philip	1825	Codorus	-
Glatfelter,	Anna Eliz.	1840	Newberry	-
,	Casper Jr.	1823	Shrewsbury	-
,	Casper Sr.	1775	Codorus	poor cond.
,	Catharine	1826	York Boro	-
,	Felix	1815	Shrewsbury	-
,	Frederick	1845	N. Codorus	-
,	Henry Sr.	1833	Codorus	-
,	Jacob Sr.	1827	"	-
		1827		2nd inv.
,	Jacob	1849	N. Codorus	-
,	John	1821	Shrewsbury	-
,	John	1811	"	-
,	Jonathan	1827	Codorus	-
,	Margaret	1847	N. Codorus	-
,	Michael	1836	"	-
Glenn,	Joseph	1841	Lw. Chanceford	-
,	Thomas	1820	"	-
,	William	1846	"	-
Gobrecht,	Christopher	1815	Hanover Boro	Rev.
Godfrey,	Jonathan	1842	Fawn	-
,	Sallome/Sarah	1840	Springfield	-
,	Thomas	1831	Franklin	-
,	William	1812	"	-
Godwalt,	George	1842	E. Manchester	-
Goforth,	Thomas	1832	Fairview	Doctor
Gohn,	Adam	1773	Windsor	h/o Cath.
,	Andrew J.	1791	Chanceford	-

49

File Name	Date	Twp.	Misc. Info.
Gohn, Andrew Jr.	1804	Chanceford	(Kuhn)
, Catharine	1793	Windsor	filed w/Adam
, Daniel	1846	Lw. Windsor	-
, Elizabeth	1817	Windsor	w/o Phil.
, George	1841	"	-
, Henry	1822	"	-
, Margaret	1797	"	spinstress
, Philip	1811	"	h/o Eliz.
	1817		Eliz. inv.
, Philip	1751	Hellam	-
Golden, Charles	1817	Manheim	-
Good, Abraham	1843	(New York)	-
, Barbara	1843	Manchester	-
, Dewalt	1787	Windsor	-
, Elizabeth	1841	Manchester	-
, John	1831	Conewago	-
, Mary	1791	Windsor	-
Goodbread, Ludwig	1776	Yorktowne	-
, Turless	1778	"	w/o Ludwig
			(Goodbroth)
Gooding, Stephen	1761	?	-
Goodling, Jacob	1843	Springfield	-
, Peter	1815	Shrewsbury	-
, Peter	1775	Cumberland*	-
Goodwin, Seth	1832	Dover	-
Goodyear, George	1837	York Boro	-
Gordon, Alexander	1842	Lw. Chanceford	-
, John	1815	"	-
, John	1810	Hopewell	-
, Robert	1813	Lw. Chanceford	-
, Robert	1843	Peach Bottom	-
Gossler, George Adam	1791	York	-
Gossuch, John	1816	"	-
Gottwald, Andrew	1806	Manchester	h/o Mary
			German
, Felix	1819	York	-
, George	1806	York Boro	-
, Jacob	1790	Manchester	-
, Mary Magdal.	1847	"	filed w/Andrew
Gotwalt, Catharina	1823	"	-
, Margaret	1823	?	-
Gouchenour, Daniel	1834	Dover	-
	1834		vendue
, John	1810	Monaghan	-
, Joseph	1811	Dover	(Gouchenouer)
, Martin	1812	Manchester	-
Goudy, George	1792	Manheim	-
, William	1769	Cumberland*	-
Gould, Thomas	1804	Newberry	-
Gowan, Alexander	1803	Chanceford	-
, Thomas	1784	"	-
, William Alex.	1782	Fawn	-

50

File Name		Date	Twp.	Misc. Info.
Grabill,	Samuel	1849	Dillsburg twn.	-
Graff,	Christian	1822	Paradise	-
,	Christley	1775	Newberry	(Christian)
,	Elizabeth	1802	Paradise	-
,	Francis	1809	Manheim	-
,	Gerhart (Garret)	1777	Dover	-
,	Gertrude	1823	Paradise	w/o Mathias
,	Gotlieb Ernst	1831	Windsor	-
,	Henry	1778	Paradise	-
		?		vendue
,	Jacob	1760	Manchester	-
,	Mathias	1793	Paradise	-
,	Michael	1804	"	-
Graham,	James	1781	Manallen*	-
,	Thomas Jr.	1828	Chanceford	-
,	Thomas Sr.	1832	"	-
,	William	1795	Manallen*	-
Gram,	Conrad Sr.	1807	Fairview	-
Grant,	Henry	1833	Shrewsbury	-
Grass,	Andreas	1752	?	-
,	Andrew	1804	Manchester	-
,	Andrew	1818	"	German
,	Catharine	1846	"	-
,	Catherine	1820	"	-
,	John	1802	"	-
Grasser,	Adam	1798	Berwick*	-
Graver,	Barbara	1816	Manheim	-
Gray,	Joel	1821	York Boro	-
,	Thomas	1787	?	-
,	Thomas	1811	Warrington	-
Graybill,	Barbara	1830	W. Manchester	-
,	Hannah	1801	York Boro	-
,	John	1774	Manchester	-
		1775	(Donegal)	-
,	John	1801	Manchester	-
,	Michael	1800	York Boro	-
,	Michael	1823	W. Manchester	-
Graydon,	Nancy	1808	Hopewell	(Greton)
Greely,	John	1764	?	-
Green,	George W.	1843	Spr. Garden	-
,	John	1759	?	-
		1759		vendue
,	Joshua	1848	Shrewsbury	Doctor
Greenawalt,	Anna Maria	1848	Hellam	-
Greenblatt,	Philip	1806	Codorus	-
Greenewalt,	Christopher	1805	Manchester	(Greenawalt)
,	Jacob	1831	"	(Greenawalt)
,	John	1847	Hellam	(Greenawalt)
,	Mary	1833	York Boro	(Greenawalt)
Greenwald,	Abraham	1825	"	-
Greenway,	William	1765	Manallen*	-
Greesinger,	David	1840	Lewisbury Boro	-

51

File Name	Date	Twp.	Misc. Info.
Greitinger, Sabina	1790	Cumberland*	(Kryling)
Grele, Christian	1841	Chanceford	-
Grenewalt, Alexander	1845	York Boro	(Greenawalt)
Gresemer, Henry	1786	Heidelberg	-
Grett, John	1797	Hanover Boro	-
Grever, Anthony	1771	Manheim	(Grabers)
Gribble, Jane	1790	Huntington*	-
, John	1787	"	-
Grieb, John C.	1843	Newberry	-
Grier, Ann	1849	York Boro	-
	1849		real estate
, James	1823	Chanceford	-
, Jane	1849	York Boro	-
, Jennet	1813	?	w/o David
, John	1813	York Boro	-
Griest, David	1821	Dover	-
, Willing	1833	Warrington	-
Griffey, Stephen	1766	Yorktowne	-
Griffin, James	1800	Monaghan	weaver
	1802	(Dauphin Co.)	2nd inv.
Griffith, Abraham	1841	Warrington	-
, Ann	1816	Washington	filed w/Dave
, David	1800	Paradise	h/o Ann
, David	1781	Hopewell	-
, Deborah	1845	Warrington	-
, Elizabeth	1832	Chanceford	-
, Evan	1790	Hopewell	-
, James	1813	"	-
, James	1818	Chanceford	-
, John	1814	"	-
, John	1786	Cumberland*	-
, John	1795	Hopewell	-
, Thomas	1769	?	-
	1769		vendue
, Thomas	1769	Manallen*	-
, William	1799	Warrington	-
, William	1778	"	-
	1779		2nd inv.
, William	1815	Washington	-
Grim, Daniel	1817	Hopewell	-
, Peter	1845	York Boro	-
, Valentine	1809	Dover	-
Grimes, John	1815	Newberry	-
, Margaret	1793	Chanceford	-
, Nathan	1783	Manallen*	-
Grimm, Charles	1835	Conewago	-
	1835		vendue
, Jacob	1835	Manchester	-
	1835		vendue
, John	1774	Berwick*	-
, Philip Sr.	1794	Yorktowne	-
Grisinger, Adam	1833	Fairview	-

File Name		Date	Twp.	Misc. Info.
Grisinger,	Henry	1839	Fairview	-
,	John	1838	"	-
Grist,	Daniel	1787	Monaghan	-
,	Isaac M.	1842	"	-
,	John	1751	Warrington	-
,	Solomon	1844	"	-
Groff,	David	1831	Washington	-
,	Isaac	1828	Spr. Garden	-
,	John	1826	Washington	-
Grogan,	Bernard	1762	?	-
Groming,	Christian	1825	Windsor	-
Groom,	William	1843	Newberry	-
Gross,	Adam	1756	?	-
,	Andreas	1758	Dover	-
,	Andrew	1817	"	-
,	Andrew Jr.	1798	"	-
,	Charles	1833	"	vendue
,	Christina	1844	"	-
,	Daniel	1822	"	-
,	Jacob	1792	"	-
,	John	1850	Manchester	-
,	John Sr.	1835	Dover	-
		1835		vendue
,	Michael	1822	"	-
,	Philip	1838	"	-
,	Samuel A.	1839	Lw. Chanceford	-
,	Samuel	1831	Manchester	-
,	Samuel M.	1847	W. Manchester	-
,	Wendel	1828	Dover	-
Grove,	Barbara	1845	Codorus	-
,	Daniel	1813	?	-
,	Elizabeth	1815	Paradise	-
,	Fran	1833	Windsor	-
,	Frances	1830	Paradise	-
		1831	Windsor	bonds
,	Francis	1782	"	-
,	Frederick	1849	"	-
,	Henry	1780	Manchester	-
,	Jacob Sr.	1828	Windsor	-
,	Jacob	1836	Chanceford	-
		1836		vendue
,	Jacob Jr.	1812	Windsor	-
,	John	1847	Manheim	-
,	Michael	1815	Codorus	-
,	Philip	1839	W. Manchester	-
,	Samuel	1834	Lewisbury Boro	-
		1834		vendue
,	Samuel	1822	"	-
,	Thomas	1802	Chanceford	-
,	Vinger	1836	Lewisbury Boro	-
Grubb,	Christian	1823	Fairview	-
,	Michael	1816	"	-

53

File Name		Date	Twp.	Misc. Info.
Gruber,	George	1825	W. Manchester	–
,	Henry	1818	Codorus	–
,	Henry	1833	Newberry	–
,	Margaret	1830	Codorus	–
Guicht,	Ludwick	1813	Chanceford	–
,	Margaret	1820		–
Gump,	George	1792	York Boro	–
Gundel,	Adam	1784	Dover	–
,	Casper	1788	"	–
Gundy,	Jacob	1817	Newberry	–
		1817		vendue
Gunnet,	John	1836	Codorus	–
Guth,	Peter	1823	Manchester	German
,	Susanna	1822	Fairview	–

–H–

Haack,	Anna Maria	1828	York Boro	–
Haar,	George	1837	Paradise	–
,	Jacob	1813	"	–
		1837		vendue
,	Susanna	1852	Paradise	filed w/Geo.
Haas,	Adam	1826	Yorktowne	–
,	Casper	1850	Codorus	–
,	George	1826	Hanover Boro	–
,	John	1804	Dover	–
,	Joseph	1844	"	–
Hackin,	Nicholas	1758	Heidelberg	(Hagen)
Hackman,	Abraham	1776	Manchester	–
Hageman,	Jacob	1829	Monaghan	–
Hagen,	Edward	1779	Mt. Pleasant*	–
Hager,	John	1822	?	–
Hagner,	John	1794	(Balt.)	MD./rents
Hahn,	David	1801	Hanover Boro	–
,	Elizabeth	1802	York Boro	w/o Michael
,	Jacob	1785	Manchester	–
,	Jacob	1843	W. Manchester	–
,	John	1758	Manchester	German
,	Michael	1791	York Boro	–
Hail,	Robert	1843	Spr. Garden	–
Haines,	Anthony	1764	?	(Heins)
,	Jacob	1776	Shrewsbury	sundries
		1778		2nd inv.
,	John	1754	?	German
,	John Valentine	1826	Fairview	–
,	Philip	1778	Manchester	–
,	Philip Sr.	1781	"	–
Hake,	Andrew	1832	"	–
,	Anna Marie	1836	"	–
,	Catharine	1843	Chanceford	–

File Name	Date	Twp.	Misc. Info.
Hake, Christian	1848	Manchester	-
, Frederick	1771	?	-
, Frederick	1836	Manchester	-
	1836		vendue
, Frederick	1830	Conewago	-
, Frederick	1816	Manchester	-
, Jacob	1850	"	-
, Jacob	1804	"	German
, John	1811	Chanceford	-
	1811		bonds
, John	1846	Manchester	-
, William	1823	Chanceford	-
Hakov, Christill	1759	(Adillbark)	-
Halbert, John	1811	?	-
Haldeman, Jacob	1819	Manheim	-
Hale, Richard	1768	?	-
, Thomas	1761	Warrington	-
Halferdx, Edward	1850	Monaghan	-
Hall, Anna	1803	York Boro	-
, Edward	1775	Cumberland*	-
, Michael	1790	Codorus	-
Haller, Adam	1817	York Boro	-
, Christopher	1777	Yorktowne	-
, George	1821	York Boro	-
, John	1824	"	-
Ham, Daniel	1795	Codorus	-
	1795		2nd inv.
, Louisa	1809	Dover	(Hamme)
, Valentine	1766	"	-
Hamaker, Joseph	1823	?	-
Hamersly, William	1796	Newberry	-
Hamilton, Hance (Hans)	1772	Manallen*	Col.
, John	1806	York	h/o Marg.
, John	1784	Hamilton Ban*	-
, Margaret	1807	York	w/o John
, Margaret	1820	Manchester	-
, Pricilla	1825	Monaghan	-
Hamm, Catharine	1843	Manheim	-
, Samuel	1824	Codorus	-
Hamme, Adam	1827	Dover	-
, Baltzer	1826	"	-
, Christian	1837	"	-
	1837		vendue
	1843		?
, John	1821	Manchester	-
Hammell, Philip	1786	Paradise	-
Hammer, Apollonia	1790	Manchester	-
	1780		German
, Conrad	1796	Heidelberg	-
, George	1834	Spr. Garden	-
, Henry	1841	Windsor	-
, Margaret	1849	York	-

File Name		Date	Twp.	Misc. Info.
Hammond,	Elisha	1824	Fairview	–
,	James	1793	Tyrone*	–
,	John	1787	Manallen*	–
,	Philip	1828	Hopewell	–
Hamsher,	John	1785	Codorus	–
Hand,	Jacob	1756	?	–
Hanes,	Henry	1850	Windsor	–
Haney,	Ludwick	1839	Hopewell	–
Hantz,	Andrew	1787	Dover	–
,	Andrew	1828	"	–
,	Andrew	1822	"	–
,	John	1826	"	–
Hapbell,	Conrad	1791	Hellam	(Habble)
Harbach,	John	1800	York	–
Harbaugh,	Jacob	1793	"	–
Harbold,	Daniel	1837	Paradise	–
		1837		vendue
,	Doratha	1822	Dover	–
,	George	1790	"	(Herbold)
,	Henry	1843	Washington	–
,	John	1848	"	–
,	Lydia	1823	Paradise	–
,	William	1816	Dover	–
Harding,	Michael	1795	Berwick*	–
Hare,	Michael	1778	Manheim	–
		1781		2nd inv.
Harlacker,	Benjamin	1832	Paradise	–
,	Benjamin	1829	Washington	–
Harman,	Adam	1834	Warrington	–
,	Adam	1783	Huntington*	–
,	Frederick	1838	Warrington	–
,	Hanichle	1764	?	(Nicholas)
,	Henry	1815	Paradise	–
,	Melchor	1763	Windsor	–
,	Samuel	1817	York Boro	–
Harnish,	Christian	1823	Heidelberg	–
,	Elizabeth	1821	"	–
,	John	1790	?	–
,	Samuel	1813	Manheim	–
,	Samuel	1843	Heidelberg	–
Harper,	Samuel	1761	?	–
,	Samuel	1781	Hopewell	–
Harr,	John	1824	Hellam	–
Harrier,	Andrew	1750	Heidelberg	–
Harrington,	Isaac	1777	Chanceford	–
,	Jacob	1755	?	–
,	Jacob	1770	Windsor	–
Harrington,	Nicholas	1800	York Boro	(Herrington)
Harris,	Abraham	1841	Wrgvlle. Boro	–
,	Daniel	1820	York Boro	–
,	George	1806	Newberry	–
,	John	1805	York Boro	–

File Name		Date	Twp.	Misc. Info.
Harris,	John	1843	Hellam	-
,	Thomas	1808	"	-
,	William	1826	"	-
,	William C.	1818	York Boro	-
Harrison,	Anne	1800	Monaghan	-
,	John	1790	"	-
Harry,	Reuben	1823	York Boro	-
,	Stephen	1815	"	-
Hart,	Adam	1825	Newberry	-
,	Andrew	1792	Hamilton Ban*	-
,	Andrew	1775	"	-
,	David	1779	Hopewell	-
,	David	1783	Hamilton Ban*	-
,	Francis	1789	(York Co.)	-
,	Isaac	1839	Fairview	-
,	Jacob	1842	"	-
,	Jacob	1819	"	-
,	Jacob	1843	Lw. Chanceford	-
,	Joseph	1827	Fairview	-
,	Michael	1828	"	Esq.
Hartley,	Thomas	1801	Yorktowne	books
Hartman,	Christian	1836	Manchester	-
		1836		vendue
,	Elizabeth	1833	York Boro	-
,	Francis	1814	Hopewell	-
,	Frederick	1816	York Boro	-
,	Frederick	1838	Springfield	-
,	George	1826	Hanover Boro	-
,	Henry	1835	Hopewell	-
		1835		vendue
,	John Sr.	1815	York Boro	-
,	John	1799	Franklin*	-
,	John	1844	Spr. Garden	-
,	Lorentz	1791	Manchester	-
,	Ludwig	1828	York	-
,	Nicholas	1849	Hopewell	-
,	Susanna	1847	Manchester	-
,	Tobias	1817	Shrewsbury	-
,	Tobias	1844	Spr. Garden	-
Hartzough,	George	1771	Yorktowne	-
Harvey,	Archabald	1824	Peach Bottom	-
Harvin,	John	1795	Cumberland*	-
Haslet,	James	1769	Yorktowne	-
,	Joseph	1767	Cumberland*	-
Hassler,	Abraham	1803	Codorus	-
,	Christian	1813	Monaghan	-
,	Joseph	1833	Carroll	(Hossler)
,	Michael	1775	Codorus	-
,	Peter	1816	Warrington	-
Hatton,	Edward	1779	Huntington*	-
,	Robert	1777	"	-
Haubburd,	Philip	1823	Lw. Chanceford	-

File Name		Date	Twp.	Misc. Info.
Hauck,	Anna Maria	1822	Hanover Boro	–
,	Catharine	1786	Heidelberg	–
,	David	1806	Hanover Boro	–
,	Dominicus	1773	Yorktowne	–
,	Jacob	1790	Hanover Boro	–
,	Lorentz	1790	"	–
,	Ludwig	1754	York	–
Haverstock,	Andrew	1821	Paradise	–
,	Andrew	1835	"	–
		1835		vendue
,	Magdalena	1836	Paradise	–
		1836		vendue
Hay, Michael		1850	York Boro	Esq.
Hays,	Edward	1767	Yorktowne	–
,	Thomas	1804	Chanceford	–
,	Thomas	1829	(York Co.)	–
Hebeisen,	Phillip	1792	Reading*	–
Heck,	Martin	1778	Hopewell	–
Heckendorn,	John Sr.	1788	York Boro	–
,	John Sr.	1789	Windsor	–
Heckert,	Charles	1833	Carroll	–
,	Dorothy	1844	York Boro	–
,	Francis	1751	Manchester	–
,	George	1821	York Boro	–
,	Jacob	1772	Manchester	–
,	Joseph	1840	York Boro	–
,	Jullana	1849	"	–
,	Magdalena	1811	"	–
,	Philip	1831	"	–
,	Philip	1845	"	–
,	Philip	1812	"	–
Heckler,	George	1774	Manchester	–
Heckley,	John M.	1829	Windsor	–
Heckman,	William	1828	York Boro	–
Hefener,	Christian	1841	Chanceford	(Hafener)
Heffener,	John	1836	"	–
		1836		vendue
,	Mathias	1785	Manheim	–
Heffer,	John	1793	Warrington	–
Heid,	Adam	1817	W. Manchester	–
Heide,	Catharine	1848	Lewisbury Boro	–
Heidler,	Jacob	1760	?	–
,	John	1806	Paradise	h/o Judith
,	Judith	1814	"	filed w/John
Heiges,	Abraham	1819	Franklin	–
,	Christian	1827	"	–
,	Christian	1801	Huntington*	–
,	Esther	1845	Franklin	–
,	George	1809	Franklin	–
,	George	1800	Huntington*	–
,	George	1801	"	–
,	George	1804	Monaghan	–

File Name		Date	Twp.	Misc. Info.
Heiges,	Lawrence	1806	"	-
,	Leonard	1843	Franklin	-
,	Margaret	1808	Monaghan	-
,	Philip	1827	Franklin	owned nothing
,	Susanna	1804	Washington	-
Heildebaugh,	John	1802	Manchester	-
Heilman,	Daniel	1825	Paradise	-
,	Dolly	1836	Codorus	-
,	John	1787	"	-
,	Peter	1838	Paradise	-
,	Philip	1797	Shrewsbury	German
Heindel,	Adam	1785	Windsor	-
,	Adam	1811	"	-
,	Anna M.	1841	"	-
,	Barbara	1832	"	-
,	Christian	1814	"	-
,	Christian	1830	"	-
,	Christopher	1831	"	-
,	George Sr.	1843	York	-
,	Jacob	1850	Windsor	-
,	Jacob	1847	"	-
,	John	1815	"	-
,	Michael	1838	Windsor	-
,	Peter	1815	York	incomplete
,	Philip	1792	Windsor	-
Heindell,	Adam	1805	York	-
Heindle,	Lorentz	1846	N. Codorus	(Lawrence)
Heiner,	George	1839	Paradise	-
,	Henry	1826	"	-
,	Ludwig	1828	"	-
		1830		2nd inv.
,	Yost	1816	"	-
Heise,	Elizabeth	1818	Shrewsbury	kitchen
,	Wendel	1816	"	h/o Eliz.
Helfrig,	George	1793	Mt. Pleasant*	-
Hellman,	Elizabeth	1844	Codorus	-
,	Jacob Sr.	1789	Hanover	-
,	Jacob	1786	Yorktowne	-
,	Margaret	1834	Hanover	-
,	Michael	1818	"	-
Heltzel,	Anna Mary	1798	Paradise	-
,	Christina	1829	Windsor	-
,	Jacob	1818	"	-
		?		2nd inv.
,	Jacob	1821	Windsor	-
,	Philip	1800	Paradise	-
,	Philip	1763	?	-
,	Stoffel	1772	Windsor	-
,	Tobias	1792	Paradise	-
Hemler,	Christian	1792	Germany*	-
Hemrich,	Sabastian	1785	Newberry	-
Henderson,	Hugh	1816	Windsor	-

File Name		Date	Twp.	Misc. Info.
Henderson,	Margaret	1834	Windsor	-
,	Matthew	?	?	incomplete
Hendricks,	Adam	1788	Shrewsbury	-
,	Isaac	1817	"	-
,	Samuel	1782	Manallen*	jury list
,	William	1768	Hanover twn.	-
Hendrickson,	Caleb	1749	?	-
,	John	1749	?	adm. w/Caleb
Hendrix,	Rachel	1842	Shrewsbury	-
Heneise,	Philip	1841	Dover	-
Heneman,	Philip	1775	Reading*	-
Heney,	Patrick	1787	Hamilton Ban*	-
,	Peter	1826	Hopewell	-
Hengst,	George	1826	Windsor	-
,	John	1826	"	-
,	Michael	1802	York Boro	-
,	Michael	1848	Shrewsbury	-
,	Zachariah	1845	Windsor	-
Henico,	Adam	1782	York	(Heinge)
Henig,	Peter	1821	Codorus	(Henny)
Heniker,	Henry	1822	Spr. Garden	-
Henise,	John	1810	Dover	-
Henley,	John	1788	Cumberland*	-
Hennish,	Elizabeth	1822	Shrewsbury	-
Hennison,	John Jr.	1804	Dover	-
Henry,	Christian	1827	Codorus	-
,	George	1782	Chanceford	-
,	George	1827	Shrewsbury	-
,	John	1793	Warrington	-
,	John	1847	Paradise	-
,	Michael	1802	Windsor	-
,	Nicholas	1794	Shrewsbury	-
,	Nicholas	1847	Paradise	-
,	Peter	1848	Codorus	-
,	Peter	1796	Monaghan	-
,	Valentine	1830	Washington	-
,	William	1807	Chanceford	-
Hentzel,	Casper	1804	Manheim	German
Heny,	Peter	1831	Hopewell	(Haney)
Hep,	John	1773	Warrington	-
Hepburn,	George	1759	York	-
Heps,	Jennet	1850	Peach Bottom	-
Herington,	Issac	1769	Chanceford	-
Herliman,	Sebastian	1794	Codorus	-
Herman,	Andrew	1826	York Boro	-
,	Catherine	1833	W. Manchester	-
,	Christian	1842	Manchester	-
,	Christman	1786	Yorktowne	(Christian)
,	Elisabeth	1828	Windsor	-
,	Emanuel	1797	Manchester	-
,	Eve	1794	"	-
,	Henry	1789	Berwick*	-

File Name		Date	Twp.	Misc. Info.
Herman,	John	1825	Fairview	-
,	John	1819	Washington	-
,	Joseph	1807	Fairview	-
,	Kraft	1825	Windsor	-
,	Randolph	1823	Warrington	-
,	Samuel	1813	Newberry	-
,	Samuel	1838	Fairview	-
Herold,	Peter	1793	Newberry	-
Herr,	John	1800	Hellam	bad cond.
,	Rudolph	1813	"	-
Herran,	Samuel	1792	Franklin*	-
Herring,	George	1807	Manheim	(Hering)
,	Henry	1801	"	-
,	Henry	1779	Paradise	(Hering)
,	Henry	1825	Dover	-
,	John	1823	"	-
,	Julianna	1805	Manheim	-
Herron,	John	1796	Hopewell	-
Herschner,	Andrew	1802	"	-
,	Anna Mary	1812	Windsor	-
,	John	1761	"	-
,	Lorentz	1779	"	old rate
		1779		new rate
Hersey,	Andrew	1800	Paradise	-
Hersh,	Christian	1823	Manchester	-
,	Mary	1808	York Boro	-
Hershey,	Andrew	1750	Manheim	-
,	Christian	1810	Paradise	-
,	Christian	1825	Heidelberg	-
,	Christian	1848	"	-
,	Christian	1782	Manheim	-
,	Jacob	1831	Dover	-
,	Jacob Sr.	1847	Paradise	-
,	John	1829	Heidelberg	-
,	Joseph	1798	Paradise	-
,	Peter	1823	Dover	-
,	Samuel	1824	"	-
Hershy,	Andrew	1846	Paradise	-
Hertzler,	Abraham	1818	Windsor	3 inv.
,	Susanna	1831	"	-
Hess,	Casper	1759	?	-
,	Elizabeth	1844	Springfield	-
,	Henry	1799	Shrewsbury	German
,	Jacob	1823	Manchester	-
,	Jacob	1843	N. Codorus	-
,	John	1816	York Boro	-
,	John	1824	Fawn	-
,	Michael	1823	Fairview	-
,	Peter	1822	"	-
,	Valentine	1793	Huntington*	-
,	Valentine	1785	"	-
Hetrich,	Jacob	1820	Shrewsbury	-

File Name	Date	Twp.	Misc. Info.
Hetrich, Ludwig	1794	York Boro	–
Hetrick, Catharine	1838	Codorus	–
, Christian	1827	"	–
, Jacob	1829	"	–
, John	1810	Manheim	–
Hetterich, Jacob	1789	Codorus	–
Hetzer, Adam	1813	Dover	–
Hevel, John	1820	Conewago	–
Heyd, Leah	1850	Spr. Garden	–
, Nancy	1850	"	–
Heydt, Christian	1773	Manchester	–
Heyer, Charles	1831	Conewago	–
, Frederick	1816	Codorus	–
, Jacob	1801	Newberry	–
, John	1780	Hellam	old rate
	1780		new rate
, Peter	1827	Conewago	–
Hibner, Frederick	1840	York Boro	–
Hickernell, Jacob	1832	Fairview	–
Hiestand, Jacob	1767	York	–
, John	1808	Manchester	German
Higas, Benjamin	1841	Franklin	–
Higes, Jacob	1816	"	–
Higgins, Cornelius	1798	Manallen*	–
, Francis	1806	York Boro	–
Hildebrand, Casper	1841	Springfield	–
, Christian	1842	York Boro	–
, Christian	1829	"	–
, John	1783	Shrewsbury	–
Hill, Alexander	1755	Fawn	–
, Isaac	1817	Fairview	–
, James Sr.	1819	Chanceford	–
, James	1826	Lw. Chanceford	–
, John	1754	?	–
, Rachael	1757	Chanceford	–
, William	1828	Lw. Chanceford	–
Hillard, William	1830	York Boro	–
Hillegas, Lawrence	1773	Paradise	–
Hiller, Martin	1798	Manheim	–
Hilt, Joseph	1839	Hanover Boro	–
Himes, Benjamin	1828	Washington	–
, Christian	1816	Paradise	–
, Peter	1827	Monaghan	–
, William	1818	Hanover Boro	–
Himmen, Gotlieb	1809	Shrewsbury	–
Hindle, Jacob	1842	Lw. Windsor	–
Hines, Anthony	1829	Windsor	Esq.
, James	1807	"	–
, Jeremiah	1811	"	–
, Susanna	1808	"	–
Hinesman, John	1850	"	–
Hinkle, Anthony	1838	Hanover Boro	–

File Name		Date	Twp.	Misc. Info.
Hinkle,	John	1816	Heidelberg	-
		1818		2nd inv.
,	John L.	1846	Hanover Boro	-
,	Josh	1828	Hellam	-
Hipple,	Frederick	1788	Huntington*	(Hibble)
,	Mary	1789	"	w/o Fred
Hirt,	Martin	1799	Shrewsbury	-
Hitchcock,	Henry	1817	Hellam	-
Hively,	Christopher	1798	"	(Heibly) German
,	Christopher	1783	"	-
,	Jacob	1786	Shrewsbury	-
,	Sophia	1810	York Boro	-
Hobach,	Conrad	1826	Warrington	-
Hobaugh,	John	1844	"	-
Hobbach,	Dietrich	1799	"	-
Hobias,	Frederick	1784	Codorus	-
Hobson,	Francis	1779	Manallen*	-
Hodge,	William Sr.	1767	Reading*	-
Hoff,	Adam	1813	Newberry	-
,	Adam	1786	Codorus	-
,	Adam	1834	"	-
,	Andrew	1823	Newberry	-
,	Daniel	1819	Heidelberg	-
,	David	1828	"	-
,	Elizabeth	1835	"	filed w/Mike
,	Francis	1811	Codorus	-
,	Henry Sr.	1838	Paradise	-
,	Henry	1783	Manheim	-
,	Henry	1820	Heidelberg	-
,	Henry	1850	N. Codorus	-
,	Jacob	1804	Manchester	-
,	John	1831	Newberry	-
,	Michael	1832	Heidelberg	h/o Eliz.
		1835		vendue
,	Peter	1816	Newberry	-
,	Philip	1785	Codorus	-
,	Samuel	1839	Manheim	-
,	William	1833	Manchester	-
Hoffhantz,	Adam	1784	Dover	-
,	George	1750	York Boro	(Hofhans)
,	Margaret	1800	"	(Hoffheim)
Hoffman,	Adam	1820	Codorus	-
,	Adam	1838	Franklin	-
,	Barbara	1821	Dover formerly Jacobs
,	Barbara	1835	Codorus only 3 items
,	Catherine	1838	Manheim	-
,	Catherine	1812	Newberry	-
,	Charles	1820	Dover	-
,	Christiana	1801	Manchester filed w/Phil
,	Christopher	1797	Monaghan	-
,	David	1844	Franklin	-
,	Eve	1832	Manchester	-

File Name		Date	Twp.	Misc. Info.
Hoffman,	George	1838	Franklin	-
,	Henry	1773	York	-
,	Henry	1817	Manchester	-
,	Jacob	1775	Dover	-
,	John Jr.	1780	Newberry	-
,	John	1816	"	-
,	John Sr.	1773	Manchester	-
,	John	1805	Newberry	-
,	John	1839	Washington	-
,	John	1846	Conewago	-
,	Mary Elizabeth	1774	Newberry	-
,	Mary	1796	Dover	-
,	Mathias	1790	Manheim	-
,	Michael	1810	Newberry	German
,	Michael	1814	Hanover Boro	-
,	Nicholas	1784	Dover	-
,	Nicholas	1815	"	-
,	Nicholas	1847	"	-
,	Philip	1799	Manchester	weaver h/o Chris
,	Philip	1802	Manchester	-
,	Philip	1817	Newberry	-
,	Philip Jacob	1822	Dover	-
,	Philip	1806	Manchester	(Hufman)
,	Susanna	1822	Conewago	-
,	William	1761	Paradise	-
Hoffstadt,	John	1829	Fairview	-
,	Nancy	1843	Newberry	-
,	Peter Sr.	1820	"	-
,	Urcilla	1835	"	-
		1836		vendue
Hofocker,	Michael	1818	Manheim	-
Hogan,	James	1846	Chanceford	-
Hogg,	James	1814	Lw. Chanceford	-
,	James	1824	Wrgvlle. Boro	-
Hoke,	Anna Margaret	1785	Manchester	-
,	Casper	1821	Paradise	h/o Marg.
,	Casper	1849	"	-
,	Frederick	1771	Manchester	-
,	Frederick	1844	Carroll	-
,	George	1849	W. Manchester	-
,	George Sr.	1844	Paradise	-
,	Jacob	1815	"	-
,	Jacob	1820	W. Manchester	-
,	John	1781	Manchester	-
,	Margaret	1831	Paradise	filed w/Casper
,	Martin	1776	Manchester	-
,	Michael	1780	Newberry	-
,	Peter	1829	W. Manchester	-
,	Samuel	1826	Paradise	-
Holder,	John	1802	Windsor	-
,	Mary	1809	"	-

File Name	Date	Twp.	Misc. Info.
Holder, Michael	1782	Windsor	-
Holdsworth, Samuel	1787	Straban*	-
Holl, Abraham	1788	Berwick*	-
, George	1785	Codorus	(Helly)
, Isaac	1785	Warrington	-
, Jacob	1781	"	-
, John	1801	Hellam	German
Holland, Henry	1787	Warrington	-
, Thomas	1777	"	-
Hollinger, Christopher	1823	York	-
, Jacob	1826	Washington	-
, Jacob	1829	Paradise	-
, Jacob	1835	Franklin	-
	1835		vendue
Hollobush, Daniel	1837	Conewago	-
	1837		vendue
Hollopeter, Barbara	1827	Warrington	d/o Mathias
, Mathias	1799	"	-
Holton, Francis	1779	Chanceford	-
Holtz, John Jr.	1823	Warrington	-
, Ludwig (Lewis)	1826	"	-
, Michael	1835	"	-
	1835		vendue
, William	1836	Monaghan	-
	1836		vendue
Holtzapple, Barnet	1820	W. Manchester	German
, Erasmus	1793	Manchester	-
, Erasmus	1798	Manchester	-
, George	1846	W. Manchester	-
, Jacob	1849	"	-
, Magdalena	1832	"	German
Holtzbaum, Conrad	1775	Yorktowne	-
Holtzinger, Elizabeth	1777	"	-
, Jacob	1785	"	-
, John	1837	Hellam	-
	1837		vendue
, John	1847	Spr. Garden	-
Holtzwart, Adam	1808	York	-
Homan, Michael	1766	Shrewsbury	-
Honey, John	1755	?	-
, John (Nicholas)	1752	Manheim	-
Honheman, Yost Sausman	1753	Manchester	-
Honsicker, Catherine	1770	?	-
, Jacob	1762	Manheim	-
Hood, Elizabeth	1758	?	-
Hooke, Jacob	1766	Manchester	-
Hoope, Augustus	1785	Mt. Joy*	-
Hooper, Robert	1776	Chanceford	-
Hoopes, William	1843	Newberry	-
	1857		prob. new William
	1858		vendue
Hoops, Job	1847	Newberry	-

File Name	Date	Twp.	Misc. Info.
Hoops, William Jr.	1846	Newberry	-
Hoover, Adeline	1850	Conewago	-
, Anna Mary	1808	Dover	-
, Catherine	1848	Conewago	-
, Christian	1771	Heidelberg	-
, Christian	1823	Hellam	-
, Conrad	1806	Dover	-
, Daniel	1848	Conewago	-
, Elizabeth	1837	Dover	-
, George	1775	"	-
, George	1786	Germany*	-
, John	1783	Warrington	-
, John	1800	Germany*	-
, John	1846	Conewago	-
, Jonas	1823	Dover	-
, Maria	1777	Heidelberg	-
, Martin	1788	Hellam	(Huber)
, Peter	1848	Manchester	-
, Samuel	1831	Shrewsbury	-
, Soloman	1824	York	-
Hopkins, Levin Hill	1785	(Hartford Co.)	MD.
Horn, Henry	1789	Heidelberg	(Horne)
, Michael	1801	Windsor	-
Horne, Jacob	1778	Monaghan	-
Horner, Daniel	1842	N. Codorus	-
, John	1816	Chanceford	-
Horney, Benedict	1792	Germany*	-
Horst, Jacob	1774	Newberry	-
, John	1804	Monaghan	-
Hosack, John	1789	Franklin*	-
, Thomas	1793	"	-
Hoschaar, John	1795	Manheim	-
, John	1817	Heidelberg	-
Hose, Philip	1788	York	-
Hoselberger, George	1766	Yorktowne	-
, Maria	1770	"	-
Hosler, Henry	1842	N. Codorus	-
Houck, Bernard	1762	Manheim	-
Houdeshell, Jacob	1844	Dover	-
Hough, Jonathan	1835	New Holland twn.	-
House, Benjamin	1819	Fairview	-
Householder, Henry	1813	Hopewell	-
, Jacob Sr.	1813	York	-
, Jacob	1822	Hopewell	-
, Jacob	1847	York	Esq.
Houser, John	1763	Codorus	-
, John Sr.	1841	Hellam	-
Housihl, Ludwick (Lewis)	1816	York Boro	-
Housman, Christian	1822	Windsor	-
Houston, John Sr.	1847	Hellam	-
, William F.	1838	Wrgvlle. Boro	Doctor
Houts, John	1781	Mt. Pleasant*	-

File Name	Date	Twp.	Misc. Info.
Hovis, Frederick	1825	Shrewsbury	-
, Jacob	1827	"	-
How, Abraham	1766	Manallen*	-
Howard, Anthony	1810	Chanceford	-
, Henry	1840	Springfield	-
, Henry	1824	Chanceford	-
Howe, William	1831	York Boro	-
Hower, Michael	1807	Manheim	-
Hubbard, Adam Sr.	1781	"	-
, Catharine	1793	Mt. Pleasant*	-
, Catharine	1812	Manheim	-
, George	1792	Mt. Pleasant*	-
Huber, George	1824	Dover	-
, John	1833	Shrewsbury	-
, John	1841	Hellam	-
, John	1832	Dover	-
, Magdalena	1841	Hellam	w/o John
, Martin	1817	"	-
, Martin	1826	"	-
Hubley, Frederick	1800	Manchester	-
Huffsmith, Christian	1810	"	-
Huggins, Jacob	1783	"	-
Hughes, Daniel	1801	York Boro	-
, Jonathan	1769	Manallen*	-
, Patrick	1778	Berwick*	-
, Peter	1812	Newberry	-
, Rowland	1779	?	-
Hughy, James	1755	Fawn	-
, Mary	1759	?	-
Hugler, Mary	1842	Hanover Boro	-
Hulick, Peter	1790	Mt. Joy*	-
Hull, Abraham	1834	Fairview	(Hell)
, Abraham	1846	Washington	-
, John	1834	"	-
Hume, Charles	1815	Chanceford	(Humes)
, William	1776	Yorktowne	-
Humer, Joseph	1803	Chanceford	vendue
Hummel, Barbara	1782	?	German
, Gerald	1791	Newberry	-
Hummer, John	1814	Paradise	-
Humrichousan, John	1771	Manchester	-
Humrickhousen, John	1819	Dover	-
Hunt, John	1783	Huntington*	-
, Roger	1786	"	-
, William	1793	Hamilton Ban*	-
, William	1783	Huntington*	-
Hunter, David	1766	Windsor	-
, James	1770	Fawn	-
, James	1778	Mt. Joy*	-
, John	1823	Spr. Garden	-
, Joseph	1782	Mt. Joy*	-
, Joseph	1774	Reading*	-

File Name	Date	Twp.	Misc. Info.
Hunter, Thomas	1777	Newberry	-
Huppert, Adam	1800	Manheim	-
Hurl, Edward	1817	York Boro	-
Hursh, Christian	1823	Monaghan	-
, Henry	1843	Fairview	-
, Joseph	1849	"	-
Huss, John	1818	Chanceford	-
Hussey, Amos	1822	Franklin	-
, Jediah	1823	Warrington	-
, Jediah	1828	"	-
, John	1770	Newberry	-
, Miriam	1808	Warrington	-
, Nathan	1775	Yorktowne	-
, Nathan	1808	Warrington	-
, Ricord	1784	"	-
Hutchison, Daniel	1774	Windsor	-
, James	1794	Mt. Joy*	-
Hutton, Joseph	1774	Newberry	-
, Simeon	1836	Warrington	-
Hyde, Valentine	1829	W. Manchester	-
Hyder, William	1829	Manchester	-
Hymes, Charles	1814	Paradise	-
Hyson, David	1841	Hopewell	-

-I-

File Name	Date	Twp.	Misc. Info.
Idle, John	1832	Chanceford	-
Ilgenfritz, Christian	1818	York Boro	-
, Daniel	1833	"	-
, Elizabeth	1843	Conewago	-
, Frederick	1823	"	-
, George	1810	York Boro	-
, Jacob	1823	Hellam	-
, Martin	1812	Manchester	-
, Samuel	1835	York Boro	-
	1836		widow
Ilges, George	1801	Chanceford	-
, Philip	1794	"	-
Illges, David	1843	"	-
Illias, Paul	1837	Spr. Garden	-
	1837		vendue
Imfeld, Jacob	1817	Windsor	-
, Joseph	1836	York Boro	-
, William	1813	"	-
Immel, Daniel	1810	York	-
, George	1817	Hanover Boro	-
, John	1788	York	-
, Leonard	1778	"	h/o Mary
, Mary	1785	"	-
Immenheiser, Jacob	1829	Windsor	-

File Name		Date	Twp.	Misc. Info.
Imswiller,	Eve	1773	Windsor	filed w/Peter
	, Peter	1822	"	-
	, Peter	1773	"	h/o Eve
Ingram,	Samuel	1755	?	-
Inloze,	Samuel	1849	Newberry	-
		1849		vendue
Inners,	Jacob	1770	York	-
	, Jacob	1839	"	-
Irvine,	Isabella	1837	Fawn	-
Irwin,	Arthur	1806	Fairview	-
	, Christopher	1814	Fawn	-
	, George	1812	York Boro	-
	, Gerrerd	1803	Fairview	-
	, John	1785	Reading*	-
	, John	1811	York Boro	-
	, John	1838	Fawn	-
	, Joseph	1772	Reading*	-
	, Rebecca	1840	Fawn	-
	, William	1774	Cumberland*	-
Isaacs,	Jeremiah	1833	Windsor	-
	, John	1790	Hellam	-
	, John	1832	Windsor	-

-J-

File Name		Date	Twp.	Misc. Info.
Jack,	James	1780	Hamilton Ban*	-
Jackson,	Margaret	1758	Tyrone*	-
Jacobs,	Christopher	1826	York Boro	-
	, George	1848	Manchester	-
	, George	1802	Windsor	-
	, George Sr.	1820	York Boro	-
	, George	1822	Paradise	-
	, George	1806	"	-
	, Henry	1774	?	-
	, Henry	1824	Paradise	-
	, Henry	1788	"	-
	, Jacob	1754	?	-
	, James	1816	Fairview	-
	, John	1842	Manchester	-
	, Mary	1846	"	-
	, Michael	1818	York	-
		1818		vendue
	, Philip	1818	Windsor	-
	, Philip	1792	Paradise	-
	, Samuel	1775	Berwick*	-
Jacoby,	David	1821	Manchester	-
	, John	1846	Conewago	-
	, John	1805	Newberry	-
James,	Absolom	1824	Fairview	-
	, John	1823	Newberry	-

File Name	Date	Twp.	Misc. Info.
James, Thomas	1844	Fairview	-
Jameson, David	1820	Codorus	-
, David Sr.	1800	(Shippensbg.)	Doctor
, Samuel	1774	Reading*	-
, William	1805	Hopewell	-
Jay, Thomas	1838	Fawn	-
Jenkins, Moses	1789	Franklin*	-
, William	1773	?	-
Jenner, Peter	1849	York Boro	-
Jennings, Esther	1801	Newberry	-
, Thomas	1773	"	-
John, Ann	1831	W. Manchester	-
, Jane	1828	Newberry	-
, Joshua	1798	"	-
, Rachel	1798	"	-
, Rachel	1843	York Boro	-
, Samuel	1769	Newberry	-
, William	1822	Fawn	-
Johnson, Jacob	1843	Lw. Chanceford	-
, James	1849	York Boro	-
, James	1839	Peach Bottom	-
, Thomas H.	1843	Lw. Chanceford	-
Johnston, Alexander	1777	Cumberland*	-
, Asa	1842	Newberry	-
, Benjamin	1770	Fawn	-
, Elizabeth	1806	Chanceford	-
, Elizabeth	1773	Warrington	-
, Ephraim	1780	Cumberland*	-
, Ephraim	1782	Manallen*	-
, Henry	1814	W. Manchester	-
, Jacob	1803	Fawn	-
, James	?	?	-
, James	1795	Franklin*	-
, John	1807	Chanceford	-
, John	1754	Yorktowne	-
, Mary	1847	York Boro	-
, William	1793	Chanceford	-
, William	1792	York	-
, William	1811	Lw. Chanceford	-
, William	1828	Franklin	-
, William	1837	Spr. Garden	-
	1837		vendue
Joiner, Mary Elizabeth	1777	Tyrone*	-
Jolly, John	1772	Shrewsbury	-
Jonas, Amos	1848	Fawn	-
, Engel	1761	Manheim	-
Jones, Charles	1770	Yorktowne	-
, Daniel	1814	Monaghan	Rev.
, Edward	1823	Newberry	weaver
, Edward	1823	"	-
, Edward Jr.	1802	"	-

File Name	Date	Twp.	Misc. Info.
Jones, Isaac	1841	Peach Bottom	-
, Jacob	1836	Hopewell	-
, James	1836	York Boro	-
, James	1816	"	-
, John	1831	Warrington	-
, John	1770	Codorus	-
, Morgan	1762	Hellam	-
, Naphthali	1797	Newberry	-
, Peter	1822	"	-
, Richard	1782	Windsor	-
, Robert	1810	York Boro	-
, Robert	1790	Manchester	-
, Samuel	1845	Newberry	-
, Samuel	1839	"	-
, Theophilus	1783	Fawn	-
Jordon, Joseph	1848	Hopewell	-
, Josiah	1791	York Boro	-
, Samuel	1828	Peach Bottom	-
Joseph, George Henry	1766	Paradise	-
, John	1840	"	-
Josey, Martin	1763	?	vendue
, Nicholas	1763	?	-
Jueryens, Sarah	1849	York Boro	-
Julius, John	1844	Dover	-
, Peter	1833	"	-

-K-

File Name	Date	Twp.	Misc. Info.
Kagey, Jacob Sr.	1789	Heidelberg	German
Kain, Christina	1824	Codorus	-
Kaldreider, George	1848	Windsor	-
Kalklaser, Solomon	1811	Hellam	-
Kaltreiter, Henry	1819	Windsor	(Kaltwriter)
Kaltrider, Christiena	1841	"	-
Kane, Edward	1834	Dover	-
Kann, Anna Mary	1823	Conewago	-
, George	1820	Dover	-
, George	1794	Paradise	-
, Henry	1798	Manchester	-
, Jacob	1797	"	-
, Martin	1799	"	-
, Michael	1762	Dover	-
Karch, Susanna	1815	Hopewell	-
Katler, Magdalena	1789	Berwick*	-
Kauffelt, David	1847	Wrgvlle. Boro	-
, Jacob	1817	Windsor	-
, Michael	1830	"	-
Kauffman, Abraham	1834	Dover	(Cafman)
, Andrew	1819	Fairview	-
, Anna	1807	?	-

71

File Name		Date	Twp.	Misc. Info.
Kauffman,	Catharine	1835	York Boro	–
		1835		vendue
,	Charles	1817	York Boro	–
,	Christina	1804	York	German
,	Daniel	1842	Spr. Garden	–
,	Henry	1796	York	–
,	Jacob	1823	Hopewell	–
,	John	1824	York	(Kaufman)
,	John	1827	York Boro	"
,	Joseph	1816	Hellam	–
,	Samuel	1843	York	(Kafman)
,	Solomon	1802	York Boro	(Kaufman)
Kaufman,	John	1828	Fairview	–
Kauter,	Bernard	1797	Manchester	–
Kean,	Daniel	1770	?	–
Keas,	John	1793	Straban*	–
Kedy,	John	1824	Fawn	–
Keech,	Joseph	1821	Lw. Chanceford	–
Keefer,	Abraham	1764	Codorus	–
,	Casper	1769	"	–
,	Dorothy Eliz.	1812	York Boro	–
,	Frederick	1786	Petersbg. twn.	(Keffer)
,	Joseph	1849	Hanover Boro	–
,	Mathias	1795	Berwick*	(Keifer)
Keeffer,	Peter	1771	Yorktowne	–
Keelough,	John	1783	?	–
Keener,	John	1840	Conewago	–
,	John	1831	"	–
Keeney,	Abraham	1912	Warrington	–
Keentz,	George	1775	Yorktowne	h/o Maria
,	Maria E.	1777	"	(Kintz)
Keeny,	Michael	1850	Codorus	farmer
Keeports,	John	1841	Lw. Chanceford	–
		1841		2nd inv.
Kefauver,	Conrad	1798	Manheim	(Kefahber)
Kehlbaugh,	Henry	1839	"	–
Kehler,	Daniel	1826	Windsor	–
,	Henry	1838	Paradise	–
,	Martin	1784	Yorktowne	–
Kehr,	Christian	1829	Heidelberg	room x room
,	Magdalena	1829	"	–
,	Mary	1823	"	w/o John
,	Samuel	1832	"	–
Kehrman,	Mathias	1809	Hellam	h/o Mary/German
Keiser,	Jacob	1847	N. Codorus	–
,	Samuel	1806	York	–
Keller,	Christian	1844	Manchester	–
,	Christian	1826	"	German
,	George	1792	Codorus	–
,	George	1798	Manheim	–
,	Jacob	1786	York	–
,	Jacob	1828	Manheim	–

File Name		Date	Twp.	Misc. Info.
Keller,	Jacob	1791	Shrewsbury	German
,	Johann Jacob	1810	"	-
,	John	1802	Hellam	-
,	John	1806	Manheim	-
,	Mary (Meary)	1804	Hellam	-
,	Michael	1781	Yorktowne	(Kellar)
,	Samuel	1850	Shrewsbury	farmer
Kelly,	Charles	1767	?	-
,	Eleanor(Leonora)	1816	York Boro	-
,	James	1822	Heidelberg	-
,	James	1819	York Boro	-
,	James	1772	?	-
,	James	1848	York Boro	stone cutter
,	John	1835	Chanceford	-
		1835		vendue
,	Mary	1816	Manheim	German
,	Thomas	1813	"	-
,	Thomas	1786	Chanceford	-
,	Thomas	1842	York Boro	-
Kemerly,	George	1825	Windsor	-
,	Jacob	1792	"	(Kemeleys)
Kemmerling,	John	1828	Codorus	-
,	Margaret	1831	"	-
Kennard,	Anthony	1793	Fawn	-
,	Hannah	1794	"	-
,	Joseph	1834	"	-
		1842		widow
Kennedy,	Bailey	1790	Monaghan	-
,	David	1788	Hopewell	-
,	Robert	1805	York Boro	-
Kenworthy,	David	1775	Huntington*	(Kenwary)
Kepler,	Jacob	1805	Newberry	-
Keplinger,	Peter	1795	Manheim	-
Kerbach,	George	1791	Berwick*	-
,	John	1823	Monaghan	-
Kerchner,	Jacob	1827	Codorus	farmer
Kerline,	Valentine	1810	Windsor	-
Kern,	Conrad	1775	York	-
,	Conrad	1821	Newberry	-
,	Frederick	1845	Manchester	-
		1846		grain
,	Jacob	1799	York Boro	-
,	Michael	1803	Newberry	-
Kernan,	James	1819	York Boro	-
Kerr,	Agnes (Nancy)	1822	Lw. Chanceford	-
,	Alexander	1776	Mt. Pleasant*	-
,	James	1771	Mt. Joy*	-
,	James	1837	Fairview	-
,	John	1759	Hamilton Ban*	-
,	John	1773	"	-
,	John	1788	"	-
		1786		?

File Name	Date	Twp.	Misc. Info.
Kerr, John	1839	Lw. Chanceford	-
, John	1794	Manheim	(Kehr)
, Joseph	1806	Chanceford	-
, Josiah	1784	Mt. Pleasant*	-
, Robert	1793	?	-
, William	1791	Hamilton Ban*	-
, William	1794	"	-
Kerwer, Henry	1773	Manheim	-
Kessler, Michael	1804	Codorus	-
Ketterman, Andrew	1800	Newberry	-
, John	1799	"	-
, Michael	1798	Mt. Pleasant*	-
Kettlewell, Isaac	1812	Newberry	-
, John	1807	Warrington	-
Keys, Hugh	1814	?	-
Keyser, Jacob	1816	Shrewsbury	-
Kilgore, John	1846	Peach Bottom	-
, Levi	1840	Lw. Chanceford	-
	1840		to Jennet
, Solomon	1847	Lw. Chanceford	-
, William	1846	"	-
Kilmer, Joseph	1797	?	German
Kilmore, Jacob	1847	Newberry	-
Kimmel, Joel	1843	Carroll	-
Kimmell, Philip	1800	Reading*	-
Kinard, Christian	1798	Monaghan	-
, Emanuel	1811	Franklin	-
, Henry	1811	"	-
, Jacob	1787	Windsor	German
	1787		English
Kincaid, Samuel	1810	Fawn	-
Kind, Christian	1803	Manheim	German
Kinder, Anna Maria	1778	Monaghan	(Kindor)
, Valentine	1766	"	-
, Valentine	1814	Franklin	-
Kindick, Daniel	1842	Fairview	-
Kindig, Anna	1798	Manchester	German
, David	1827	Wrgvlle. Boro	store
, George	1839	Dover	-
, Henry	1824	Hellam	-
, Jacob	1795	Manchester	-
, Mary	1836	Hellam	-
	1836		vendue
Kinerd, Frederick	1840	Lw. Windsor	-
King, Abraham	1766	?	-
, Adam	1835	York Boro	1/2 Gazette
	1836		vendue
, Catharine	1826	York Boro	w/o Phil.
, Charles	1787	Hellam	-
, Daniel	1838	Springfield	-
, David	1764	Warrington	-
, Godfrey	1805	W. Manchester	-

74

File Name	Date	Twp.	Misc. Info.
King, Henry	1777	Yorktowne	-
, Jacob	1829	Warrington	-
, Jacob Sr.	1792	Manchester	-
, Nicholas	1776	Yorktowne	-
, Peter	1847	York	-
, Philip	1821	Warrington	-
, Samuel	1829	"	-
, Victor	1775	Tyrone*	f/o James, Samuel, William Thomas
, William	1795	Tyrone*	-
Kinkead, Samuel	1779	?	-
Kinsler, Michael	1806	Shrewsbury	-
, Rebecca	1808	"	-
Kinsley, Samuel	1790	Dover	-
Kinter, John	1842	Franklin	-
Kintt, Jacob	1784	Germany*	(Kindt)
Kintzlein, Elizabeth	1808	York Boro	(Kinsley)
Kirckhoff, Mary	1811	Fairview	-
Kirk, Caleb	1772	Manchester	-
, Eli	1797	York Boro	-
, Elisha	1790	"	clockmaker
, Isaac	1833	Lewisberry Boro	-
	1833		vendue
, Isaac Jr.	1832	"	6 items
, Jacob	1782	Newberry	-
, Joseph	1806	?	-
, Samuel	1835	Newberry	-
, Slater B.	1848	Peach Bottom	Firm of
Kirkhark, Anthony	1774	York	-
	1774		vendue
, Sophronia	1783	"	w/o Anthony
Kirkpatrick, David	1768	Chanceford	-
, William	1824	Lw. Chanceford	-
Kissinger, Conrad	1784	York	-
, Philip	1822	Spr. Garden	-
Kister, Adam	1821	Newberry	-
, Ann	1844	"	-
, Anna	1843	"	-
, Christian	1828	Fairview	-
, David	1842	Newberry	-
, David L.	1825	"	-
, George	1815	"	-
, George Jr.	1814	"	-
, Henry E.	1835	"	-
	1835		vendue
, Henry	1832	Newberry	-
, John	1833	"	-
, Ludwick	1799	"	-
, Margaret	1843	"	-
, Thomas	1793	York	-
Kitzmiller, Julianna	1790	Manheim	-

File Name	Date	Twp.	Misc. Info.
Kitzmiller, Martin	1788	Manheim	–
Klein, Andrew	1778	Manchester	(Kline)
	1780		2nd inv.
, Conrad	1842	Dover	–
, Elizabeth	1823	Shrewsbury	–
, Henry	1823	Windsor	–
, Jacob	1836	Hanover Boro	–
Kleinfelter, Adam	1816	Hopewell	–
, Barbara	1817	"	–
Kline, Adam	1785	Hellam	–
, Elizabeth	1835	Spr. Garden/Hellam	
, Gerlach	1785	Berwick*	–
, Henry	1814	Newstrasbg. twn.	–
, Henry	1786	Manheim	–
, Henry	1849	Lw. Windsor	–
, Jacob	1756	?	(Klyne)
, Jacob	1828	Wrgvlle. Boro	General
, Johan Handill	1760	Warrington	–
, John	1839	Newberry	–
, John	1840	Wrgvlle. Boro	–
, John	1840	Shrewsbury Boro	–
, John	1756	?	–
, John	1798	Manheim	–
, Peter	1822	Hellam	–
Klinedinst, Christian	1836	Codorus	–
	1836		vendue
, Christian	1848	N. Codorus	–
, David	1798	Hanover	–
, David	1798	Codorus	–
, Eve	1815	"	–
, Eve	1838	N. Codorus	–
, Margaret	1850	" filed	w/Godfrey
Klinefelder, Daniel	1825	Shrewsbury	–
Klinefelter, Elizabeth	1842	"	–
, George	1794	"	–
, Jacob	1830	"	–
, Jacob	1815	"	–
, Joseph	1837	"	–
, Michael	1807	"	–
Klinepeter, Casper	1827	Franklin	–
, Rudolph	1809	Paradise	–
Klinger, Catherine	1796	Huntington*	–
Klipfer, Joseph	1774	Dover	–
Klugh, Frederick	1847	Washington	–
Klunk, John	1811	Hanover	–
, Martin	1795	Berwick*	–
, Peter	1777	"	–
, Peter	1837	Heidelberg	–
Knab, Anna Maria	1801	York Boro	(Knabb)
, Casper	1781	Manchester	–
, Casper	1823	"	–
, Jacob	1811	"	–

File Name	Date	Twp.	Misc. Info.
Knab, John	1804	York Boro	(Knabb)
Knatzer, Adam	1846	"	-
Knaub, Jacob	1849	"	-
, Juliana	1827	"	(knab)
, Leonard	1817	Manchester	(Knob)
, Margaret	1836	York Boro	-
, Peter	1817	"	(Knab)
Knaus, Daniel	1777	?	-
, David	1799	Manallen*	German
Knertzer, Baltzer	1769	Yorktowne	-
Kneyer, Leonard	1783	Codorus	(Kneier)
, Rosina	1799	York Boro	-
Knipple, Anna Maria	1775	Manchester	-
, Christopher	1766	"	(Knepple)
, George	1819	Manheim	-
Kniseley, Eve	1850	Lw. Windsor	(Knisely)
Knisely, Christian	1835	Chanceford	(Knizely)
, John	1842	Windsor	(Knisly)
, Mary	1817	Dover	-
, Mary	1848	Franklin	-
, Michael	1823	"	-
Knisley, Abraham	1764	Reading*	-
, Anthony	1801	Warrington	-
, Anthony	1839	Monaghan	-
Knoll, George	1830	Spr. Garden	-
Knox, John	1778	Hopewell	-
Koch, George	1792	York Boro	-
, Jacob	1790	York	-
, John	1849	York Boro	-
, John Michael	1811	York	-
, Joseph	1821	Conewago	-
, Margaret	1804	York Boro	-
, Mary	1798	Managhan	-
, Mary	1832	York Boro	-
, Mary	1832	"	-
, Michael	1800	Newberry	-
, Nicholas	1796	York	money only
, Peter	1841	Warrington	-
, Richard	1837	York Boro	-
	1837		vendue
Koeble, George	1838	York	-
Kohl, Valentine	1797	Manchester	German
Kohler, Andrew	1787	"	-
, Baltzer	1820	"	-
, Baltzer	1797	Shrewsbury	-
, John	1813	Paradise	-
, John	1815	Shrewsbury	-
, Joseph	1816	Manchester	-
, Sarah	1829	Newberry	-
Kohr, Mordecai	1833	Fawn	(Corr)
Koil, Joseph	1832	Monaghan	-
Kolb, Peter	1788	(Lanc. Co.)	-

77

File Name	Date	Twp.	Misc. Info.
Kolb, John Nicholas	1833	York Boro	-
Koller, Jacob	1832	Shrewsbury	-
, John	1847	"	-
Kookerly, Jacob	1804	York	German
Koon, John	1804	Chanceford	-
Koons, John	1836	York Boro	-
Kopp, John F.	1837	Manheim	(Copp)
Korbman, Conrad	1785	Shrewsbury	-
, Henry	1809	York Boro	-
Koutz, Peter	1817	Manheim	-
Kraber, Catherine	1847	Warrington	-
, John George	1835	York Boro	Rev.
Kraft, Barbara	1782	Yorktowne	w/o Geo.
, Conrad	1797	Hanover Boro	-
, Frederick	1836	Codorus	-
	1836		vendue
, George	1777	Yorktowne	-
, Joseph	1835	York Boro	-
	1835		vendue
Krall, Ann	1849	Washington	-
, Joseph	1839	"	-
Krantz, Elizabeth	1777	Yorktowne	-
, Elizabeth	1819	Manchester	-
, George	1791	"	-
, Valentine	1755	"	-
Kratzer, Baltzer	1843	Windsor	-
Kraut, Jacob	1841	Springfield	-
Kreamer, Abraham	1821	W. Manchester	-
Kreber, Adam	1801	Manheim	-
, Adam	1815	York Boro	-
, Henry	1795	"	-
, Philip	1785	Yorktowne	-
, Philip	1805	Manchester	-
Krebs, Christina	1792	Germany*	-
, Ludwig	1784	Codorus	-
, Ludwick	1821	"	-
, Margaret	1805	"	German
, Peter	1842	Manheim	-
Kreeger, Elizabeth	1831	Fairview	-
, Henry	1820	Newberry	-
, Jacob	1815	"	-
, Michael	1815	"	-
Kreidler, Christian	1824	York Boro	-
	1837		?
Kreitler, Adam	1835	Windsor	-
, John	1826	"	-
Kriner, John	1823	Dover	-
Kring, Henry	1800	W. Manchester	-
Kroh, Christiana	1840	Hanover Boro	-
Kroll, Barbara	1828	Codorus	-
, Henry	1828	Monaghan	-
, John	1824	Codorus	farmer

File Name		Date	Twp.	Misc. Info.
Krone,	George	1845	Conewago	-
,	Jesse	1846	Newberry	-
,	John	1850	Windsor	-
,	Michael	1843	Newberry	-
,	Michael Sr.	1847	Windsor	-
Krout,	Anna	1817	Shrewsbury	(Kraut)
				w/o Jacob
,	Daniel	1824	"	(Craut)
,	Jacob	1775	?	-
,	Mathias	1828	Heidelberg	money only
,	Michael	1850	(Balt. MD)	-
Kruber,	Mary	1848	Codorus	-
Kuch,	Catharine	1839	Spr. Garden	-
Kuhl,	Peter	1802	York	-
Kuhn,	Catharine	1832	Hanover Boro	-
,	Frederick	1778	Berwick*	-
,	John	1769	Chanceford	-
,	John	1845	Manchester	-
Kunkel,	Gotlieb	1822	Spr. Garden	-
Kuhny,	Henry	1781	Germany*	-
,	John	1790	"	-
Kunkel,	John Henry	1827	Shrewsbury	-
,	Joseph	1850	"	-
Kunkle,	Anna Mary	1825	Spr. Garden	w/o Baltz.
,	Baltzer	1812	Hellam	-
,	Catharine	1846	Spr. Garden	-
,	Elizabeth	1842	"	-
,	Gotlieb	1776	York	-
,	Jacob	1805	Hellam	German
,	John	1790	Dover	-
,	John	1816	Hopewell	-
,	John	1798	York Boro	(Kunkel)
,	Justina	1823	Hopewell	w/o Michael
,	Michael	1788	Shrewsbury	(Conkle)
,	Philip	1829	York Boro	-
Kuntz,	Abraham	1789	Germany*	-
,	Catharine	1758	Heidelberg	w/o Geo.
,	Elizabeth	1781	York	-
,	Francis	1804	York Boro	-
,	George	1826	Windsor	-
,	George	1829	"	-
,	John Jacob	1755	Germany*	-
,	John	1749	?	-
,	John	1753	?	-
		1755		2nd inv.
,	John	1794	Codorus	-
,	John	1826	York Boro	-
,	Michael	1754	York	(Coons)
,	Michael	1795	Germany*	German
,	Philip	1819	Franklin	-
,	William	1781	York	-
Kurtz,	Anna Mary	1806	"	-

File Name		Date	Twp.	Misc. Info.
Kurtz,	Christopher	1777	Fawn	-
,	Martin	1819	Shrewsbury	-
,	Michael	1801	York	-
,	Nicholas	1794	"	Rev.
Kutter,	Peter	1801	Manheim	(Kuder)

-L-

LaBoob,	Michael	1781	Berwick*	-
Lackey,	George	1784	Mt. Pleasant*	-
Laird,	Hugh	1807	Dover	-
,	John	1813	Fawn	-
,	John	1770	Cumberland*	-
,	John	1766	"	-
,	John	1794	Chanceford	-
,	John	1828	Fairview	-
,	Mary	1810	Dover	-
,	Robert	1778	Cumberland*	-
,	Samuel	1833	Monaghan	-
,	Samuel	1763	Fawn	-
,	Washington	1843	Dover	-
Lambert,	Ann	1758	?	-
,	Jacob	1788	Dover	-
,	Mathias	1757	Manchester	-
Lanckert,	George	1815	Hanover Boro	h/o Marg.
Landes,	John	1844	Windsor	-
Landis,	Andrew	1817	Monaghan	-
,	Christian	1827	Windsor	-
,	Christian	1782	"	-
,	Elizabeth	1843	"	-
,	Jacob	1850	Hellam	-
,	Jacob	1764	York	-
,	John	1822	Windsor	-
,	Samuel	1790	"	-
,	Samuel	1833	Spr. Garden	-
,	Stephen	1796	York	-
Lane,	Abraham	1794	Berwick*	-
,	John	1783	"	-
,	John	1840	Lw. Chanceford	-
,	Peter	1795	Berwick*	-
,	Thomas	1795	"	-
Laney,	Isaac	1848	Dillsbg. Boro	-
Lanius,	Barbara (Anna)	1821	York Boro	-
,	Benjamin	1846	"	Esq.
,	Elizabeth	1826	"	-
,	Elizabeth	1815	"	filed w/Henry
,	Henry	1808	York Boro	h/o Eliz.
,	Henry	1817	"	-
,	Jacob	1778	Yorktowne	-
,	Jacob	1847	Hopewell	-

File Name	Date	Twp.	Misc. Info.
Lanius, John	1815	York Boro	-
Lankard, John	1844	Dover	-
Lantsel, George	1839	Heidelberg	-
Lantz, Philip	1802	Windsor	-
Lantzel, George	1804	Heidelberg	-
Larch, John	1812	?	-
Larimer, John	1792	Mt. Joy*	-
, Robert	1772	Berwick*	-
, William	1773	Hanover Boro	-
Lark, Jacob	1850	Manheim	-
Latta, Thomas	1790	Cumberland*	-
Lau, Andrew	1822	Codorus	-
, Anna Mary	1815	W. Manchester	-
, George	1808	Codorus	German
, George	1809	"	s/o Andrew
, Michael	1795	Manchester	-
, Michael	1839	W. Manchester	-
, Peter Sr.	1834	Codorus	-
	1835		vendue
Laub, Conrad	1809	York Boro	-
Lauck, Daniel	1829	Windsor	-
, Susanna	1843	York Boro	-
Laucks, Henry	1806	Windsor	-
, Jacob Sr.	1846	W. Manchester	-
, John	1814	Warrington	-
, John	1818	Codorus	-
Lauer, Abraham	1835	Manheim	-
, Anna	1825	Dover	-
, Daniel	1790	Franklin*	-
, Jacob	1810	Dover	-
, John Mathias	1790	Manheim	-
, Magdalena	1832	Dover	-
, Magdalena	1816	"	-
, Philip	1810	"	-
, Philip Sr.	1802	"	-
Laughlin, Robert	1778	Huntington*	s/o Wm.
Lauman, Anna Maria	1832	York Boro	-
, Christian	1841	Hanover Boro	-
, Susanna	1828	York Boro	-
Laushe, Christina	1816	Reading*	-
, John	1791	"	-
Lautshaw, Joseph	1761	"	-
Lawer, John	1847	Dover	-
Lawson, Joseph	1815	Codorus	-
, Mary	1810	"	-
, Moses	1776	"	-
, William	1808	Chanceford	-
Laxton, Thomas	1830	W. Manchester	-
Lay, John	1844	York Boro	-
Layman, Anthony	1827	Codorus	-
Leader, Jacob	1766	Yorktowne	-
Leas, Franklin W.	1848	Hanover Boro	-

File Name		Date	Twp.	Misc. Info.
Leas,	John	1846	Washington	-
,	Leonard	1782	Reading*	(Lease)
,	Samuel	1821	Franklin	"
Lease,	Abraham	1799	Reading*	-
,	Elizabeth	1844	Franklin	-
,	Stephen	1799	Monaghan	-
,	Leonard	1817	Washington	-
,	Valentine	1806	Paradise	-
Least,	Leonard	1831	Washington	-
,	Philip	1804	"	-
Leathen,	David	1781	Hopewell	-
Leather,	Jacob	1835	Manchester	-
,	John	1831	Dover	-
,	Samuel	1844	"	-
Leatherman,	Conrad	1821	York Boro	-
Leathra,	John	1836	Washington	-
		1836		vendue
Leber,	Conrad	1814	Windsor	-
,	Jacob	1786	"	-
,	Maria	1822	"	-
,	Philip	1845	"	-
,	Samuel	1845	Lw. Windsor	-
Lebezer,	John	1797	Fawn	-
Lebo,	Jacob	1843	Manheim	(Labo)
Lebough,	Abraham Sr.	1775	Germany*	-
Lechner,	George	1790	Manheim	-
,	George Jr.	1806	"	-
Leckrone,	Elizabeth	1849	Dover	-
,	George	1842	"	-
,	Peter	1847	W. Manchester	-
Lecrone,	Barbara	1834	York Boro	(Leckrone)
,	Leonard	1810	W. Manchester	-
Leebenstein,	George	1779	Manchester	-
Leech,	Catharine	1848	Conewago	-
,	James	1793	Tyrone*	-
,	Thomas	1820	Warrington	-
Leeder,	Frederick	1844	York	-
Leedey,	Jacob	1779	Codorus	-
Leedy,	Jacob	1830	Manchester	-
,	John	1760	?	German
		1760		English
,	Mary Magdalena	1809	York Boro	-
Leek,	Jacob	1850	Peach Bottom	-
Lefever,	Catharine	1845	Spr. Garden	-
,	Jacob	1827	"	-
,	John	1844	Newberry	-
,	Peter	1830	"	-
Lefferentz,	Anne	1807	York Boro	d/o Geo.
,	Catharine	1809	"	filed w/Geo.
,	George	1804	"	-
Lehman,	Abraham	1805	Yorktowne	-
,	Anthony	1825	Codorus	German

82

File Name		Date	Twp.	Misc. Info.
Lehman,	Barbara	1759	?	–
,	Christian	1797	Hellam	–
,	Christian	1832	"	–
,	Elizabeth	1846	Windsor	–
,	Frederick	1813	"	–
,	Henry	1829	Hellam	–
,	Jacob	1844	Windsor	–
,	Mary	1773	York	filed w/Peter
,	Peter	1757	"	h/o Mary
,	Rudolph	1770	Hellam	–
,	Ulrich	1738	York	–
		1753		
Lehmer,	Conrad	1790	Warrington	–
,	John	1795	"	–
,	Susanna	1810	(Somerset?)	filed w/Wm.
,	William	1800	Monaghan	h/o Susanna
Lehr,	Casper	1825	Manchester	–
,	Charles	1838	Spr. Garden	–
,	John	1847	Manchester	–
,	John	1828	Spr. Garden	–
,	Mary (Polly)	1841	"	–
,	Peter	1845	"	–
,	Philip	1814	York	–
,	Philip	1819	"	–
,	Rebecca	1829	Spr. Garden	–
Leib,	Abraham	1823	Manchester	–
,	Christian	1817	Dover	German
,	Christian	1796	Manchester	–
,	Henry	1807	Dover	–
,	Henry	1846	"	–
,	Henry	1848	Heidelberg	–
,	Jonas	1763	York	–
,	Nancy	1837	Hopewell	–
Leicht,	Eve	1835	York	filed w/Werner
,	Werner	1831	"	h/o Eve
Leihner,	John	1782	Germany*	–
Leinbach,	Conrad	1781	Dover	(Leinbacher)
Leinbacher,	Felix	1784	"	–
,	Henry	1773	"	–
Leinert,	Alexander	1842	Codorus	–
,	Barbara	1828	Heidelberg	–
,	Henry	1810	Manheim	–
,	Henry	1841	Heidelberg	–
,	Polly	1832	"	see S. Danner
Leininger,	George	1791	Dover	–
,	George	1782	Manheim	–
,	John	1825	Conewago	–
,	Magdalena	1812	Dover	–
		1812		vendue
Leiphart,	Henry	1773	Hellam	–
,	Henry	1796	"	–
,	John Sr.	1821	Windsor	–

File Name		Date	Twp.	Misc. Info.
,	Philip	1823	Hellam	-
Leiss,	Peter	1812	Shrewsbury	German
Leitner,	Adam	1783	Yorktowne	-
,	Elizabeth	1833	York Boro	-
,	Frederick	1811	Newberry	-
,	George Sr.	1807	?	-
,	George	1830	Manchester	-
,	Ignatius	1819	York Boro	h/o Rebecca
,	Ignatius	1828	"	-
,	Peter	1842	Dillsbg. Boro	-
,	Rebecca	1836	York Boro	filed w/Ign.
		1836		vendue
Leivig,	Philip	1806	Washington	(Lewig)
Lemon,	John	1822	New Holland twn.	-
,	Robert	1815	Fawn	
Lenhart,	John	1843	Washington	-
,	Peter	1774	Dover	-
,	William	1819	"	-
Leni,	Abram	1757	?	-
Lentz,	John	1810	Shrewsbury	-
Lepsley,	Jonathan	1765	?	-
Lerew,	Ann	1844	Franklin	filed w/Jacob
,	Jacob	1836	"	h/o Ann
Lesh,	Henry	1807	Manheim	-
Letford,	William	1840	Chanceford	-
Levergood,	Jacob	1850	Wrgvlle. Boro	-
Lewis,	Eli	1807	Newberry	-
,	James	1845	York Boro	-
,	Robert	1846	Dover	-
,	Susanna	1811	York Boro	-
Libhart,	Henry W.	1847	Wrgvlle. Boro	-
,	Jacob	1841	"	-
Lichtenberger,	Adam	1828	Manchester	-
,	Henry	1841	"	-
,	Jacob Sr.	1850	"	-
,	John	1848	"	-
,	Rudolph	1843	"	-
,	Samuel	1837	"	-
		1837		vendue
Lichty,	Abraham	1818	Washington	-
,	Anna Lilly	1787	Berwick*	-
,	Benjamin	1806	Washington	-
,	Christian	1757	Reading*	-
,	Elisabeth	1828	York Boro	-
,	Jacob	1847	Manchester	-
,	John	1804	Washington	-
,	John Sr.	1812	Manchester	-
,	John	1807	Washington	-
Lickway,	Charles	1850	Spr. Garden	(Lieckway)
Lickwig,	Henry	1842	"	-
Lieb,	Christina	1802	York Boro	-
Liebenstein,	George	1808	York	-

File Name		Date	Twp.	Misc. Info.
Liebenstein,	John	1826	York	-
Lieberknecht,	Christina	1800	Windsor	-
,	Daniel	1849	Dover	-
,	Frederick	1798	Windsor	German
,	Henry	1849	Lw. Windsor	-
,	Jacob	1836	Windsor	-
		1836		vendue
,	John	1817	"	-
Liebhart,	Appollonia	1835	Hellam	-
,	Catharine	1838	"	-
,	Moses	1911	Lw. Windsor	-
,	Valentine	1807	Hellam	-
Liggett,	Alexander	1824	Hopewell	-
,	Elenor	1845	"	-
,	George	1766	Windsor	-
,	George	1797	"	-
,	John	1777	"	-
,	John	1763	"	-
,	Joseph	1799	"	-
,	William	1803	Hopewell	-
,	William	1830	"	-
Lilly,	Samuel	1758	Berwick*	-
Lindsey,	Mary Ann	1850	Lw. Chanceford	-
,	Matthew	1825	"	-
Lindt,	Peter	1812	Manchester	-
Lindsy,	John	1793	York Boro	-
Lines,	John	1821	New Holland twn.	-
,	Susannah	1825	Manchester	-
Linewever,	George	1771	Manheim	-
		1771		vendue
Link,	George	1828	Dover	-
,	Michael	1796	Reading*	-
Linn,	Adam	1767	Mt. Joy*	-
,	John	1794	Cumberland*	-
,	John	1777	"	-
,	Robert	1772	"	-
Lint,	Julia Ann	1839	York Boro	-
Lischy,	Jacob	1780	Codorus	Rev.
,	Jacob	1823	"	-
,	Susanna	1794	Warrington	-
List,	Christian	1849	York Boro	-
Little,	Casper	1783	Mt. Joy*	-
,	George	1817	?	-
,	Walter	1778	Chanceford	-
Livingston,	Andrew	1777	Mt. Joy*	-
,	Chauncey	1820	Washington	-
,	George	1847	Paradise	-
,	George	1774	Straban*	-
,	George	1848	Newberry	-
,	Hugh	1824	Monaghan	-
,	John	1792	Fawn	-
,	William	1777	Hamilton Ban*	-

File Name	Date	Twp.	Misc. Info.
Lochner, H. Y.	1810	Yorktowne	-
Logan, Henry	1825	Monaghan	-
, James	1842	Hopewell	-
, John	1796	Monaghan	-
, John	1838	Chanceford	-
Logue, James	1822	Lw. Chanceford	-
Lohr, Abraham	1848	Manheim	-
, John	1804	Hanover Boro	-
Long, George	1767	Dover	-
, Henry	1767	Shrewsbury	-
, Henry	1795	Paradise	German
, Isabella	1818	Chanceford	-
, Jacob	1813	Paradise	-
, James	1773	Windsor	-
, John	1784	Germany*	-
, John	1796	Manheim	-
, John	1789	York	-
, John	1837	Manchester	-
, John	1799	Newberry	-
, Joseph	1808	"	-
, Margaret	1845	Codorus	filed w/Peter
, Margaret	1826	Newberry	-
, Michael	1777	Manchester	-
, Michael	1805	York	-
, Peter	1823	Codorus	h/o Marg.
, Philip	1821	Heidelberg	-
, Samuel Sr.	1842	Manheim	-
, Thomas	1839	Warrington	-
, William	1826	Newberry	-
, William	1792	Chanceford	-
Longenecker, Christian	1814	York	-
, Henry	1836	Spr. Garden	-
Loop, Christian	1785	Newberry	-
Lorch, Michael	1777	Codorus	-
Lori, Henry	1763	Windsor	-
, Melchoir	1762	?	-
, Michael	1768	Dover	-
Lorich, Jacob	1807	Codorus	-
Lorrett, Solomon	1811	York Boro	-
Loser, George	1769	Paradise	-
Lottman, George	1812	York	-
Loucks, Casper	1838	Manchester	-
	1852	W. Manchester	?
, Elizabeth	1849	"	-
, George	1849	Spr. Garden	-
, Peter	1846	W. Manchester	-
Loughery, Jeremiah	1750	Berwick*	-
Loughman, John	1823	Newberry	-
Louis, J.	1780	Berwick*	-
Love, James	1777	Newberry	-
, Thomas	1841	Chanceford	-
, William	1783	Yorktowne	-

File Name	Date	Twp.	Misc. Info.
Low, Caleb	1770	Manchester	-
, Christian	1772	"	-
, Hugh	1762	?	-
, Isaac Sr.	1850	Shrewsbury	-
, Jesse	1816	York	-
, Jesse	1842	Shrewsbury	-
, John Sr.	1848	"	farmer
, John	1794	Manchester	-
, John	1815	Shrewsbury	-
, Joshua	1808	"	-
, Joshua	1762	Manchester	-
, Peter	1806	Codorus	-
, Philip	1781	Manchester	-
Lower, Elizabeth	1838	Dover	-
Lowman, Barnet	1770	York	-
, Catharine	1793	Boro York	-
, Gotlieb	1777	Yorktowne	-
, Henry	1782	?	(Lohman)
, Henry	1771	?	-
Lowmaster, Frederick	1801	York Boro	-
Loyd, Thomas	1817	York	-
, William	1750	?	-
Lucas, Catharine	1838	Shrewsbury	-
Luckas, Adam	1821	"	-
Luckenbauch, Henry	1824	Heidelberg	-
Luckob, Conrad	1785	Chanceford	(Lookup)
Lungren, Edwin	1827	Lw. Chanceford	-
Lupton, Joseph	1834	York Boro	-
	1834		vendue
Lusk, Jean	1826	(Lanc. Co.)	-
, John Jr.	1807	Chanceford	-
, John	1810	Lw. Chanceford	-
, Thomas	1801	Chanceford	-
Luttman, George	1824	York Boro	-
Lutz, Christian	1776	Heidelberg	-
, Christian	1775	Windsor	weaver
, Conrad	1758	?	-
, Emelia	1838	Fairview	w/o James N.
, George	1808	"	-
, James N.	1838	"	-
, John	1810	"	-
, John	1836	Fawn	-
	1836		vendue
, Jonathan	1823	Fairview	-
, Joseph	1843	Shrewsbury	-
Lykes, Philip	1773	Reading*	-
Lynch, Elenor	1850	Dillsbg. Boro	-
Lytle, Rosana	1790	Shrewsbury	(Litel)

File Name		Date	Twp.	Misc. Info.

-M-

File Name		Date	Twp.	Misc. Info.
Machlan,	John	1780	Warrington	-
,	Thomas	1800	Chanceford	-
,	William	1814	"	Blacksmith
Machlin,	George	1845	Newberry	-
,	Solomon	1848	Conewago	-
,	William R.	1846	Fairview	-
Mackaway,	Daniel	1817	Paradise	-
Macklin,	Daniel	1846	Hopewell	-
,	John	1835	Manchester	-
		1836		adtl. inv.
Maffet,	Margaret	1831	Fawn	w/o William
,	William	1831	"	-
Maffit,	James	1825	Hopewell	-
Mahan,	Rebekah	1780	Warrington	clothes only
Maisch,	John	1805	Fairview	-
,	John Sr.	1814	"	-
Maish,	Joseph	1843	"	-
,	Mary	1849	Manchester	-
		1849		vendue
Major,	Isaac	1830	Manchester	-
,	John	1804	Fawn	-
Malaun,	Catharine	1813	Reading*	filed w/Math.
,	Hannah	1784	"	-
,	John	1817	Washington	-
,	John	1798	Reading*	-
		1801		2nd inv.
,	Mathias	1772	Reading*	-
,	Mathias	1798	"	h/o Cath.
Mamber,	Michael	1807	Monaghan	-
Manifold,	Benjamin	1754	?	-
,	Edward	1821	Fawn	-
,	Eleanor	1828	Hopewell	-
,	Elizabeth	1844	"	-
,	Henry	1841	"	-
,	John	1818	"	-
,	John	1837	Fawn	-
,	Lydia	1830	"	-
Manley,	Jacob	1807	Fairview	-
		1807		vendue
Mann,	Appolonia	1799	Hellam	-
,	Jacob H.	1848	Wrgvlle. Boro	-
,	John Jr.	1836	Hellam	-
		1836		vendue
,	John	1839	Hellam	-
,	Magdalena	1832	"	single
,	Martha	1841	Wrgvlle. Boro	-
,	Samuel	1839	"	-
Mansberger,	Joseph	1839	Newberry	(Mansperger)

File Name		Date	Twp.	Misc. Info.
Mansperger,	Daniel	1842	Newberry	-
,	Martin	1775	"	-
,	William	1825	"	-
Manswiller,	Daniel	1831	Warrington	-
Mantle,	Thomas	1822	Fawn	-
,	William	1798	"	-
Mapping,	Moses	1751	Warrington	-
March,	Catharine	1791	Paradise	-
,	George	1791	Dover	-
,	Jacob	1821	"	-
Markel,	Henry	1850	Shrewsbury	-
,	Martin	1838	"	-
Marker,	Mathias	1756	York	poor cond.
Markey,	John Sr.	1832	Shrewsbury	-
Markle,	Catharine	1808	Dover	-
,	George	1777	Monaghan	German
,	Henry	1847	Manheim	-
,	Henry	1783	Codorus	-
,	Jacob	1807	"	German
,	Peter	1850	Paradise	-
,	Susan	1850	Codorus	-
Marks,	David	1832	York	-
,	Jacob	1788	Paradise	h/o Sibella
,	Jacob	1826	York	-
,	John	1766	"	-
,	Sibella	1819	Paradise	-
Marlin,	John	1791	Chanceford	Blacksmith
,	John	1804	"	Tanner
,	John	1804	"	-
,	William Sr.	1781	"	-
,	William Jr.	1782	"	-
,	William	1772	"	-
Marple,	Isaac	1838	York Boro	-
Mars,	Aron	1815	?	-
Marsden,	Edward	1794	Mt. Pleasant*	-
Marsh,	John Sr.	1804	Washington	-
,	John Jr.	1807	"	-
,	Jonathan	1795	Warrington	-
,	Peter	1789	"	-
Marshall,	Elizabeth	1843	Codorus	-
,	Henry	1787	Berwick*	-
,	James	1802	Shrewsbury	-
,	John	1784	Hopewell	-
,	Joshua	1827	Codorus	-
,	Paul	1781	Hamilton Ban*	-
,	William	1818	Shrewsbury	-
,	William	1787	Fawn	-
Marsteller,	John	1821	"	-
Marter,	George	1790	Manheim	(Mortter)
Martin,	Abraham	1826	Fairview	York prop.
		1826		Lanc. prop.
,	Andrew	1805	Hopewell	-

89

File Name	Date	Twp.	Misc. Info.
Martin, Andrew	1801	Newberry	–
, Christian	1800	Hellam	–
, Edward	1769	Newberry	–
, Elizabeth	1838	Spr. Garden	–
, James	1795	Chanceford	–
, Jane	1811	Hopewell	–
, John Sr.	1835	Codorus	–
	1835		vendue
, John	1820	Manheim	–
, Margaret	1825	Hopewell	–
, Margaret	1847	N. Codorus	w/o John
, Michael	1761	Mt. Pleasant*	–
, Peter	1811	Manchester	–
, Robert	1784	Chanceford	–
, Samuel	1783	"	–
, Samuel	1804	Hopewell	–
, Thomas	1783	Cumberland*	–
Masimer, Francis	1842	Shrewsbury	–
Mate, John	1789	Hellam	–
, Philip	1796	"	–
, Philip	1849	"	–
Mather, Jean	1756	York	–
Mathias, Peter	1846	Newberry	–
Matson, Samuel	1826	York	–
, Thomas	1785	Fawn	–
Matteer, Elizabeth	1804	Fairview	Spinster
, James	1804	"	–
, Polly	1824	"	–
, Samuel	1803	Monaghan	–
Matthews, James	1770	Huntington*	–
, William	1792	York Boro	–
Matthias, Henry Sr.	1806	Newberry	German
, John	1817	Hopewell	–
Matz, Henry	1786	"	–
, Jacob	1803	"	–
Maughlin, William	1813	Lw. Chanceford	–
Maul, Bartholomew	1755	York	–
, Conrad	1807	Manheim	German
, Philip	1841	Heidelberg	–
Maurer, Adam	1792	Straban*	–
, Christian	1834	Wrgvlle. Boro	–
	1834		vendue
, Herman	1783	Dover	(Maur)
Maxwell, Henry	1792	Cumberland*	Weaver
, Isabella	1794	Tyrone*	–
, James	1799	"	–
, John	1791	"	–
May, Daniel	1843	York Boro	Printer
, Daniel	1803	Dover	–
, Gibillia (Sibillia)	1814	"	–
, Jacob	1796	"	–
, John	1785	"	–

90

File Name	Date	Twp.	Misc. Info.
, John	1843	"	-
, John	1844	"	-
, John	1822	"	-
Mayes, Charles Sr.	1785	Manallen*	-
, John	1781	"	-

-Mc-

File Name	Date	Twp.	Misc. Info.
McAbee, Dominick	1842	Shrewsbury	-
McAdams, Eleanor	1787	Hamilton Ban*	-
, John	1761	York	-
, Quentin	1768	Hamilton Ban*	-
McAffee, John	1837	Fairview	-
	1837		vendue
McAlister, Charles	1775	Fawn	-
, James	1844	Hopewell	-
, Jenet	1846	"	-
, Samuel R.	1845	York Boro	-
McAllister, Gabriel	1785	Mt. Joy*	-
, James	1782	Hamilton Ban*	-
, John	1846	Hopewell	-
McAlur, Philip	1844	York Boro	-
McBride, Andrew	1759	?	-
, Daniel	1822	Spr. Garden	-
, Hugh	1774	Mt. Joy*	-
McBroom, James	1769	Straban*	-
McCabe, Lawrence	1850	Fairview	-
, Patrich	1837	"	-
McCall, Ann	1837	Lw. Chanceford	-
, James	1781	Chanceford	-
, John	1793	"	-
, John	1755	Tyrone*	-
, Margaret	1810	Chanceford	-
, Matthew	1781	"	-
, Matthew	1836	Lw. Chanceford	-
, Robert	1804	Chanceford	-
, Sarah	1837	Lw. Chanceford	-
McCallister, Richard	1795	Hanover Boro	-
McCally, John	1809	Chanceford	-
McCance, Andrew	1790	Straban*	-
, David	1782	"	-
McCandless, Alexander	1813	Fawn	-
, Alexander	1767	"	-
, James	1789	"	-
, John	1796	Chanceford	-
, Ruthia	1789	Fawn	-
McCann, Charles	1839	York Boro	-
, Henry	1816	Wrgvlle. Boro	-
, Martha	1840	Hopewell	-
, Robert	1817	New Holland twn.	-

File Name		Date	Twp.	Misc. Info.
McCannah,	John	1792	Yorktowne	-
		1792		vendue
McCaon,	Barnard	1849	Hellam	-
McCarrel,	Esther	1773	?	-
,	John	1767	?	h/o Esther
McCarter,	Alexander	1783	Mt. Pleasant*	-
McCarty,	John	1755	?	-
McCaskey,	Neall	1768	Fawn	-
McCauley,	William	1814	Chanceford	-
McClean,	John	1755	(York Co.)	-
,	John	1789	Chanceford	-
,	William	1798	York Boro	-
McCleary,	Andrew	1799	Chanceford	-
,	Ann	1842	Lw. Chanceford	-
,	Elizabeth	1803	Chanceford	-
,	Isabella	1835	Lw. Chanceford	-
,	Isabella	1816	"	-
,	James	1765	Manallen*	-
,	John	1777	"	-
,	John	1770	Hopewell	-
,	John	1806	Chanceford	-
,	John	1811	Hopewell	-
,	Michael	1751	?	-
,	William	1838	Fawn	-
McClelan,	William	1782	Warrington	-
McClellan,	David	1806	Chanceford	-
,	David	1790	Hamilton Ban*	-
,	James	1779	(York Co.)	-
,	John	1809	Warrington	-
,	Robert	1771	Hopewell	-
,	Robert	1794	Chanceford	-
,	William	1755	Cumberland*	-
,	William	1796	"	-
McClellen,	John	1844	Warrington	-
McClintock,	James	1766	Chanceford	-
McClure,	Alexander	1775	(York Co.)	plantation
,	David	1777	?	-
,	James	1788	Cumberland*	-
,	John	1786	Mt. Pleasant*	-
,	Thomas	1782	"	-
McComas,	Thomas	1847	Shrewsbury	Blacksmith
McConaughy,	Oliver	1764	?	-
,	Robert	1750	?	-
McConkey,	Hugh	1837	Peach Bottom	-
		1837		vendue
		1848	Peach Bottom	?
McConnell,	Ebenezer	1774	Hamilton Ban*	-
McCord,	James	1804	Chanceford	-
,	Richard	1779	Fawn	-
		?		vendue
McCormick,	Duncan	1831	Hopewell	-
McCosh,	Mary	1791	(York Co.)	-

File Name		Date	Twp.	Misc. Info.
McCosh,	Nathaniel	1777	Straban*	-
McCourtney,	Ephraim	1826	Peach Bottom	-
McCoy,	Duncan	1752	(Chester Co.)	-
,	John	1810	Fawn	-
,	John	1805	Windsor	-
McCracken,	David	1828	Hopewell	-
McCrea,	John	1778	(York Co.)	-
McCreary,	James	1783	Straban*	Taylor
			(died @ client's	
			house)	
,	John	1766	Newberry	-
,	John	1823	Monaghan	-
,	Robert	1774	Cumberland*	-
,	Robert	1775	"	
,	Thomas	1829	Franklin	-
,	Thomas	1786	Mt. Pleasant*	-
,	William	1795	Straban*	-
McCullough,	Hugh	1778	Reading*	-
,	James	1788	Fawn	-
,	Samuel	1773	Hamilton Ban*	-
,	William	1771	Tyrone*	-
,	William	1784	Newberry	Weaver
McCundy,	Samuel	1850	York Boro	-
McCune,	Thomas Sr.	1788	Mt. Joy*	-
McCurdy,	Elizabeth	1834	Monaghan	-
,	Jennet	1841	"	-
,	John	1785	Reading*	-
,	John	1827	Monaghan	-
,	Mary	1785	Berwick*	-
,	William	1777	Chanceford	-
McDaide,	Hugh	1832	Lw. Chanceford	-
McDermott,	Francis	1835	York Boro	-
,	Patrick	1829	York	-
McDonald,	Aquilla	1850	Hopewell	-
,	Catharine	1775	"	-
,	Jennet	1828	"	-
,	John	1813	York	Captain
,	Margaret	1835	Fawn	-
,	Martha	1781	Cumberland*	-
,	Mary	1798	Hopewell	-
,	Mary	1808	Fawn	-
,	Philip	1788	Hopewell	School Master
,	Richard	1787	"	-
,	Richard	1789	"	-
,	Robert	1826	"	-
McDonaugh,	Henry	1758	Cumberland*	-
,	Joseph	1777	Hopewell	-
McDowell,	Agnes	1838	Spr. Garden	-
,	John	1779	?	-
,	William Sr.	1846	Chanceford	-
McElheany,	Esther	1798	Mt. Joy*	w/o Ezekial
,	Ezekial	1776	"	-

93

File Name	Date	Twp.	Misc. Info.
McElheanny, Robert	1786	Straban*	–
McFadden, Dennis	1815	Newberry	–
	1840		widow
, George	1850	Newberry	–
, Hugh	1823	Peach Bottom	–
McFall, Patrick	1828	Chanceford	–
McFarland, John	1795	Straban*	–
, Peter	1825	Paradise	–
, William	1783	Reading*	–
McFerren, John	1782	Cumberland*	–
McGahey, John	1777	Hamilton Ban*	–
McGarraugh, William	1759	(York Co.)	–
McGarth, Thomas	1841	York Boro	–
McGaughy, James	1798	Hamilton Ban*	–
, William	1750	"	–
McGee, Patrick	1788	Chanceford	–
, William	1771	?	–
McGinney, Michael	1822	York	widow
McGinnis, Dennis	1750	Straban*	from Va.
McGown, Andrew	1777	(York Co.)	–
McGrail, John	1792	Tyrone*	–
McGrew, Alexander	1763	Manallen*	–
, Finley	1767	Tyrone*	–
, James	1793	Manallen*	–
, John	1775	Huntington*	–
, Nathan	1769	Manallen*	–
, Robert	1789	Straban*	–
McGuire, Peter	1818	Monaghan	–
McIlvain, Alexander	1792	Mt. Pleasant*	–
, Jane	1795	Straban*	–
, Moses	1783	Mt. Pleasant*	–
McIntire, John E.	1842	Dillsbg. Boro	–
, John	1758	York	–
McIsaac, Archibald	1819	Chanceford	–
, Robert	1787	Hopewell	–
McKean, Elizabeth	1767	Cumberland*	–
, Hugh	1750	Manchester	–
, John	1763	?	–
, Robert	1790	Cumberland*	–
McKee, Joseph	1792	Hamilton Ban*	–
, William	1757	Cumberland*	–
McKelvey, Agnes	1832	Hopewell	–
, William	1826	"	–
McKesson, Alex	1771	Hamilton Ban*	–
McKinley, Amos	1777	"	–
, Benjamin	1781	Cumberland*	–
, David	1757	?	–
, Elizabeth	1823	Chanceford	–
, Isaac	1788	Manallen*	–
, John	1773	Chanceford	–
, John	1779	Yorktowne	–
, John	1797	Hamilton Ban*	–

File Name		Date	Twp.	Misc. Info.
McKinley,	Stephen	1817	Chanceford	-
,	William	1788	Hamilton Ban*	-
McKinstry,	James	1785	Cumberland*	-
McKnight,	James	1771	Manallen*	-
McLane,	Jacob	1824	Windsor	-
McLaughlin,	John Sr.	1831	Fawn	-
McLeer,	Edward	1773	?	-
McMachan,	James	1803	(York Co.)	-
McMahen,	John	1846	Chanceford	-
McMann,	George	1838	York Boro	-
McMeghen,	Patrick	1756	Hamilton Ban*	-
McMillan,	Ann	1818	Washington	-
,	George	1796	Warrington	-
,	Joanna	1794	"	-
,	John	1791	"	-
,	Joseph	1826	Washington	-
,	Joseph	1843	(Jefferson Co.) Ohio	
,	Michael	1807	?	single
,	Thomas	1831	Warrington	-
McMillin,	George	1846	"	-
McMonagle,	Hugh	1802	Windsor	-
McMordis,	Robert	1796	Franklin*	Rev.
McMullan,	John S.	1849	Carroll	John M.
McMullen,	Anne	1801	Monaghan	-
,	Hugh	1793	"	-
,	James	1818	Fawn	-
,	James	1761	?	-
,	Jennet	1789	Chanceford	-
,	Rebecca	1801	Monaghan	-
,	Robert	1789	Warrington	-
,	Samuel	1805	Monaghan	-
,	Thomas	1754	Warrington	-
,	Thomas John	1807	Newberry	-
,	William	1838	Franklin	Esq.
,	William	1838	Carroll	-
McMullin,	Jacob	1833	Washington	-
McMunn,	Mary	1835	York Boro	-
,	Robert	1827	"	-
McNaive,	Matthew	1772	?	-
McNary,	John	1802	Chanceford	-
McNaughten,	Neal	1779	Tyrone*	(McNaghten)
McNeil,	John	1762	Cumberland*	-
McNutt,	John	1774	Manallen*	-
,	Robert	1775	Cumberland*	-
McPherson,	Frederick	1816	Lw. Chanceford	-
,	Jennet	1767	(York Co.)	-
,	Robert	1749/50	?	-
,	Robert	1789	Cumberland*	Esq.
,	Samuel	1841	Lw. Chanceford	-
,	William Jr.	1810	York Boro	-
McPike,	Daniel	1787	(York Co.)	-
McQuinn,	Josiah	1795	Franklin*	-

File Name	Date	Twp.	Misc. Info.
McQuown, Lawrence	1789	Manallen*	–
McSherry, Edward	1790	Germany*	–
, Patrick	1795	"	–
McSweny, Hugh	1749	Hamilton Ban*	–
McTaggart, James	1797	Berwick*	–
McWhinery, Robert	1812	Hopewell	–
McWilliams, James	1783	Straban*	–

-Me-

File Name	Date	Twp.	Misc. Info.
Meads, Benedict	1840	Hopewell	–
, Washington	1847	"	–
Means, Isaac	1760	?	–
Mearns, William	1762	Windsor	–
Meas, John	1840	Manchester	–
Mease, Anna Maria	1846	"	–
Mechling, John	1835	"	vendue
	1836		"
, Philip	1817	Newberry	German
Meckel, Christian	1764	Windsor	–
, Christian	1800	Codorus	–
Meeds, Langly	1847	York Boro	–
Meem, John	1776	Yorktowne	–
Mehl, Nicholas	1758	?	–
Meily, Martin	1817	Manchester	–
Meinhart, George	1775	Hamilton Ban*	–
, Peter	1801	Manchester	–
Meisenhelter, Barbara	1836	Dover	vendue
, David	1819	"	–
, Henry	1837	Conewago	–
, Jacob	1835	Dover	–
	1835		vendue
, Mary	1840	Dover	–
Melhorn, Andrew	1813	"	–
, Andrew	1847	Manchester	–
, Anna Barbara	1800	McSherry twn.	filed w/ Simon
, Catharine	1822	Manchester	–
, John	1848	Heidelberg	–
, Michael	1836	Manchester	vendue
, Michael	1836	"	–
, Simon	1775	"	–
, Simon	1789	McSherry twn.	h/o Anna
Mellinger, David	1815	Hellam	–
, David	1833	Fairview	–
Melsheimer, Agnes	1842	Hanover Boro	–
, Charles	1826	"	–
, Frederick	1814	"	–
Menchy, John	1797	Germany*	–
Mendenhalt, George	1750	Yorktowne	–

96

File Name		Date	Twp.	Misc. Info.
Mendenhalt,	(George)	1751	Yorktowne	vendue
	, Noah	1820	(York Co.)	-
Menges,	Charles	1786	Windsor	-
	, John	1840	Paradise	-
	, Michael	1802	Manchester	-
	, Peter	1806	W. Manchester	-
	, Peter	1836	Codorus	-
		1837		vendue
Menich,	Michael	1843	York	-
Menke,	Daniel	1806	Hellam	-
Merckly,	Catharine	1806	Codorus	-
Mercky,	Jacob	1810	W. Manchester	-
Meredith,	Israel	1811	Newberry	-
Merkey,	Esther	1839	York	-
Meserli,	Catharine	1833	Dover	-
Messemer,	Yodorus	1796	Manheim	-
Messenhim,	Jonas	1815	"	-
Messerly,	Abraham	1818	Dover	-
	, Daniel	1796	"	-
	, Daniel	1845	"	-
Messersmith,	Elizabeth	1775	Yorktowne	w/o Henry
	, Henry Sr.	1784	"	-
	, Mary Ann	1850	N. Codorus	-
	, Nicholas	1842	"	-
Messing,	John Christian	1806	Hanover Boro	-
Metzel,	George	1803	York Boro	-
	, Geo. Valentine	1839	"	-
Metzer,	Jacob	1843	Hanover Boro	-
Metzger,	George	1811	Manchester	German
	, Paul	1827	Hanover Boro	-
	, William	1823	Manchester	German
Metzler,	Jonas	1835	Paradise	-
	, Thomas	1843	Fairview	-
	, Thomas	1792	Newberry	-
Meyer,	Adolph	1793	Germany*	German
	, Catherine	1796	Newberry	(Miers)
	, Christian Sr.	1779	(York Co.)	-
	, Christian	1806	Hopewell	German
	, Conrad	1830	Codorus	-
	, David	1822	Hanover Boro	16 beds
	, David	1796	Cumberland*	-
	, David	1833	Franklin	-
	, David	1840	Hopewell	-
	, Elias	1805	York	-
	, Frederick	1813	Warrington	-
	, George	1771	(Balt. Co.)	Md.
	, George	1819	Conewago	-
	, George	1810	Franklin	-
	, George	1805	Paradise	-
	, George	1813	Newberry	-
	, George	1813	Windsor	-
	, George	1765	(York Co.)	-

File	Name	Date	Twp.	Misc. Info.
Meyer,	George	1822	Conewago	-
,	George Ernest	1777	Yorktowne	-
,	Henry	1783	York	6 feather beds
,	Henry	1844	Paradise	-
,	Henry	1785	Mt. Joy*	Inn Holder
,	Jacob	1794	York	-
,	Jacob Sr.	1847	Paradise	-
,	Jacob	1789	York Boro	-
,	Jacob	1822	Conewago	-
,	Jacob	1774	Newberry	-
,	Jacob	1814	Shrewsbury	-
,	John	1833	"	-
,	John	1792	Paradise	-
		1795	"	?
,	John	1804	Codorus	German
,	John Sr.	1816	Warrington	-
		1819	"	?
,	John	1806	Windsor	-
,	John	1770	Codorus	-
,	John	1751	Manchester	-
,	John Jr.	1763	Windsor	-
,	Magdalena	1825	"	-
,	Magdalena	1834	York	-
,	Magdalena	1789	Codorus	-
,	Margaret	1825	Paradise	-
,	Margaret	1822	Warrington	-
,	Maria Dorothy	1830	Hanover Boro	-
,	Martin	1785	York	-
,	Mathias Sr.	1843	Manheim	Farmer
,	Mary	1833	?	filed w/Polly
,	Michael	1778	Dover	-
,	Michael	1793	Paradise	-
,	Michael	1799	Mt. Pleasant*	-
,	Nicholas	1787	Huntington*	-
,	Peter	1818	York	-
,	Peter	1795	Codorus	-
		1795		widow
,	Philip	1801	Hanover Boro	-
,	Polly	1833	Washington	-
,	Simon	1804	Windsor	-
Meyers,	Frederick	1837	Monaghan	-
,	George	1838	"	-
,	George	1842	Heidelberg	-
,	John	1841	"	-
,	Michael	1844	Washington	-
,	Paul	1840	York	b/o Magdalena
Michael,	Jacob	1785	Mt. Joy*	-
,	Jacob	1845	Codorus	-
,	John Nicholas	1812	Dover	-
,	John	1814	Hanover Boro	-
,	John	1846	Lw. Windsor	-
,	John	1818	York Boro	-

File Name		Date	Twp.	Misc. Info.
Michael,	Paul	1768	Windsor	-
,	Stophel	1773	Manheim	-
,	Wendell	1812	York Boro	-
Michenfelder,	Casper	1798	Conewago	-
Mickle,	John	1789	Manallen*	-
,	John Jr.	1778	"	-
Mifflin,	Jonathan	1840	Hellam	-
Miles,	Sarah	1845	Peach Bottom	-
		1845		vendue
,	Thomas	1828	Peach Bottom	-
Miley,	Abraham	1815	Warrington	-
,	Catharine	1824	"	-
,	George	1782	"	Money only
Milheim,	George	1840	Heidelberg	-
,	George	1796	Manheim	-
,	Jacob	1835	"	-
		1835		vendue
Millard,	Benjamin	1841	Fairview	-
,	Jane	1832	Monaghan	-
,	Jonathan	1823	Fairview	-
,	Richard	1808	"	-
,	Samuel	1803	"	-
Milleisen,	John	1787	Hanover Boro	Blk.smith
Millen,	John	1826	Shrewsbury	-
Miller,	Abraham	1829	Hopewell	-
,	Abraham	1822	Fairview	-
,	Adam	1782	Newberry	German
,	Adam	1841	Heidelberg	-
,	Adam	1843	Manchester	-
,	Adam	1817	"	German
,	Andrew Sr.	1835	Paradise	-
		1836		vendue
,	Andrew	1779	Manchester	-
,	Andrew	1842	Codorus	-
,	Andrew	1773	"	-
,	Andrew	1825	Shrewbury	-
,	Andrew	1826	Conewago	-
,	Ann	1825	Hanover Boro	-
,	Anna	1817	"	-
,	Barbara	1834	Warrington	-
,	Barbara	1840	Codorus	-
,	Barbara	1843	York Boro	-
,	Barbara	1840	Dover	-
,	Barbara	1797	Heidelberg	w/o Adam
,	Bernard	1801	Dover	-
,	Casper	1784	Yorktowne	-
,	Catharine	1850	Codorus	filed w/Mike
,	Catharine	1768	Yorktowne	-
,	Catharine	1835	Manchester	-
		1835		vendue
,	Catharine	1850	Codorus	-
,	Catharine	1847	York Boro	-

99

File	Name	Date	Twp.	Misc. Info.
Miller,	Catharine	1820	Shrewsbury	-
		1821		2nd inv.
,	Christian	1841	York Boro	-
,	Christian	1794	"	single man
,	Christina	1828	Dover	filed as
				Christian
,	Conrad	1762	?	Rev. ?
,	Conrad	1782	(York Co.)	-
,	Daniel	1842	Dover	-
,	David	1820	New Holland twn.	German
,	Elizabeth	1806	Fairview	-
,	Eve	1845	Hopewell	-
,	Frederick	1803	Shrewsbury	German
,	George	1796	Manheim	-
,	George	1812	Codorus	-
,	George	1819	Manchester	-
,	George	1818	Conewago	-
,	George	1812	Manchester	German
,	George	1795	York Boro	-
,	George	1826	Codorus	-
,	George	1826	Fairview	-
,	George Michael	1815	Dover	Weaver
Miller,	Hannah	1821	Newberry	-
,	Harman	1817	Hopewell	-
,	Henry	1757	Warrington	-
,	Henry	1764	?	Henry & Wm.
,	Henry	1808	Manheim	-
,	Henry	1850	Franklin	-
,	Henry	1842	Monaghan	-
,	Henry	1834	Springfield	-
		1835		vendue
		1836	Shrewsbury	2nd inv.
		1836		vendue
,	Henry	1781	Newberry	-
,	Henry Sr.	1843	Fairview	-
,	Henry	1822	Windsor	-
,	Henry	1819	Conewago	German
,	Henry	1830	"	-
,	Henry Sr.	1821	Shrewsbury	-
,	Herman	1783	Windsor	-
,	Jacob	1822	W. Manchester	-
,	Jacob	1788	Yorktowne	-
,	Jacob	1825	Dover	-
,	Jacob	1822	Heidelberg	-
,	Jacob	1839	Bottstown	Bonds only
,	Jacob	1849	York Boro	-
,	Jacob	1850	Fairview	-
,	Jacob	1831	Windsor	-
,	Jacob	1775	Dover	-
,	Jacob	1803	Newberry	-
,	James	1787	Hamilton Ban*	w/Sam
,	John	1788	Straban*	-

File Name		Date	Twp.	Misc. Info.
Miller,	John	1796	Cumberland*	-
,	John	1818	Shrewsbury	-
,	John	1795	Berwick*	-
,	John	1836	Hellam	-
		1836		vendue
,	John	1805	Hanover Boro	-
,	John	1786	Monaghan	-
,	John	1804	Newberry	-
,	John	1802	"	-
,	John	1838	Manheim	-
,	John	1849	Warrington	-
,	John C.	1824	York Boro	-
,	John	1839	N. Codorus	-
,	Joseph	1769	Huntington*	-
,	Julian	1836	Windsor	-
		1836		items to widow
,	Ludwig	1798	Germany*	-
,	Ludwig	1788	"	-
,	Ludwig	1822	York Boro	-
,	Ludwig	1847	"	-
,	Magdalena	1799	Shrewsbury	-
,	Magdalena	1837	Manheim	-
,	Margaret	1842	Manchester	-
Miller,	Martin	1812	Fairview	-
,	Martin	1831	Heidelberg	-
,	Martin	1790	Shrewsbury	-
,	Mary	1836	Fairview	-
,	Mathias	1812	New Strasbg. twn.-	
,	Mathias	1839	N. Codorus	-
,	Michael	1846	Codorus	h/o Cath.
		1846		vendue
,	Michael	1823	Windsor	-
,	Michael	1796	Hellam	-
,	Michael	1800	Manchester	German
,	Michael	1823	Newberry	-
,	Michael	1784	Huntington*	-
,	Nicholas Sr.	1784	Germany*	-
,	Nicholas	1837	Shrewsbury	-
		1837		vendue
,	Paul	1796	Heidelberg	-
,	Peter	1781	Codorus	-
,	Peter	1791	Tyrone*	-
,	Peter	1826	Codorus	German
,	Philip	1788	Manchester	-
,	Philip	1848	Hopewell	-
,	Philippina	1831	Conewago	-
,	Robert	1797	Newberry	-
,	Robert	1819	Peach Bottom	-
,	Robert	1804	Fairview	-
,	Rudolph	1815	Windsor	-
,	Samuel	1787	Hamilton Ban*	filed w/ James

File Name	Date	Twp.	Misc. Info.
Miller, Samuel	1848	Manheim	-
, Samuel	1820	Paradise	-
, Sarah	1756	Cumberland*	-
, Sarah	1841	York Boro	-
, Solomon	1848	Paradise	-
, Susanna	1839	W. Manchester	-
, Susanna	1829	Hopewell	-
, Susanna	1831	Windsor	-
, Tobias	1810	Shrewsbury	German
, Tobias	1796	"	-
, Tobias	1821	Hopewell	-
	1821		vendue
, Valentine	1803	Dover	-
, William	1791	York Boro	Baker
, William	1764	?	filed w/Henry
Millheim, John	1849	Manheim	-
Milliken, James	1806	Fawn	-
, James Jr.	1807	"	-
Mills, James Jr.	1808	Newberry	-
, James	1816	"	-
, James	1835	Fairview	-
, James	1835	Newberry	vendue
	1836		fruit trees
, John	1790	Newberry	-
, Robert	1809	"	-
, Robert	1777	"	-
, Thomas	1829	"	-
	1829		vendue
Minnich, Elizabeth	1837	York	filed w/Simon
, George	1820	Wrgvlle. Boro	-
, Joseph	1817	Shrewsbury	German
, Sarah	1834	Wrgvlle. Boro	-
, Simon	1795	Shrewsbury	German
, Simon Sr.	1845	Spr. Garden	-
, Simon	1819	York	h/o Eliz.
Minor, Thomas	1751	"	-
Misenhalter, Barbara	1836	Dover	-
Mish, Frederick	1821	Fairview	-
Mitchell, George	1816	Peach Bottom	-
, George	1834	"	Blacksmith
, George	1823	"	Carpenter
, George Sr.	1823	"	-
, James	1833	Warrington	-
, John	1799	Huntington*	single man
			Cobler
, John	1797	Chanceford	Tanner
, John George	1769	(York Co.)	-
, Joseph	1840	Peach Bottom	-
, Joseph	1814	Fawn	-
, William	1797	Monaghan	Esq.
Mitheffer, Rosina	1844	Windsor	-
Mitman, Charles	1829	Dover	-

File Name	Date	Twp.	Misc. Info.
Mittman, Wendel	1763	Dover	German/English
Mitzel, Michael	1845	Windsor	-
, Philip	1832	Chanceford	-
Mitzger, John	1821	W. Manchester	Doctor
Mixell, John	1759	(York Co.)	-
Moatz, Catherine	1815	Dover	German
Mock, Christopher	1752	Berwick*	-
, John Nicholas	1756	?	(Mack)
	1756		vendue
Moffit, Thomas	1821	Windsor	(Moffet)
Mohler, George	1821	Newberry	-
Mohr, Christian	1823	Manchester	German
, Dietrich	1810	"	German
, Nicholas	1796	"	German
Moltzbauch, William	1790	Hanover	clothes only
Monfort, John	1777	(York Co.)	-
, Peter	1783	"	-
, Peter	1769	"	-
Montieth, John	1789	Berwick*	-
Moody, James H.	1842	Shrewsbury	Doctor?
Moore, Alexander	1793	Hopewell	-
, Anthony	1797	Newberry	-
, Anthony	1837	Fairview	-
, Catherine	1805	Dover	-
, Eve	1809	Shrewsbury	German
, Jacob	1822	Washington	-
, James	1783	Manallen*	-
, Jane (Jennie)	1848	Hopewell	-
, Job	1826	Monaghan	-
, John E.	1837	York Boro	-
	1837		vendue
, Mary	1831	Washington	-
, Mordecai	1819	Fairview	-
, Peter	1752	?	-
, Peter	1843	Manchester	-
, Philip Henry	1779	Dover	-
, Robert	1758	Manallen*	-
, Samuel	1756	Cumberland*	(Moor)
, Samuel	1839	Chanceford	-
, Sarah	1850	York Boro	-
, William	1832	Monaghan	crops only
, Yost	1764	Yorktowne	-
Moretz, Nicholas	1785	Mt. Joy*	(Morritz)
	1785		vendue
Morgan, John	1783	Hellam	-
, Thomas	1768	Chanceford	-
, William	1822	"	-
	1822		vendue
, William	1787	Windsor	-
Morifono, Margary	1761	?	-
Morningstar, George	1804	Manheim	s/o Philip
, John	1756	?	f/o Philip

File Name	Date	Twp.	Misc. Info.
Morningstar, Philip	1789	Manheim	f/o Geo.
Morris, Barbara	1832	York Boro	-
, Benjamin	1820	Codorus	Fuller
			"man of coller"
, Jane	1832	Warrington	-
, John Jr.	1810	York Boro	Esq.
, John	1808	"	Doctor
, Joseph	1835	"	-
	1835		vendue
, William	1804	Warrington	-
Morrison, Archibald	1775	Cumberland*	-
, Archibald Jr.	1777	"	-
, Elizabeth	1791	?	-
, Hans	1791	Straban*	-
, James	1825	Fawn	-
, James	1771	Chanceford	-
, Jane	1777	Cumberland*	single
, Janet	1774	"	"
, John	1775	Chanceford	-
, John	1767	?	-
, John	1776	Cumberland*	-
, Martha	1817	Lw. Chanceford	-
, Michael	1838	Hopewell	-
, William	1758	Chanceford	-
, William	1800	"	-
, William	1814	Lw. Chanceford	-
Morrow, Joseph	1846	Chanceford	-
, Thomas	1763	Huntington*	-
Morthland, Charles	1763	Warrington	-
, Hugh	1760	"	-
, Hugh	1812	Washington	-
, Michael	1815	Warrington	-
, Robert	1822	Washington	-
, William	1786	Warrington	-
Mortimore, Thomas	1788	Chanceford	Pa. line
Moser, Christian	1789	Hellam	-
, Henry	1822	Fairview	-
, Samuel	1796	York	-
, Samuel	1816	"	-
Mosser, Christian	1835	Fairview	-
	1835		vendue
, Jacob	1836	Warrington	-
	1836		two vendues
, John	1829	Fairview	Doctor
Moul, Elizabeth	1846	Heidelberg	-
Moyer, David W.	1847	Manheim	-
, Jacob	1845	Fairview	-
, Jacob	1827	Monaghan	money only
, Magdalena	1831	Codorus	w/o Conrad
Muhlheim, Christian	1803	Hanover	-
, Nicholas	1804	Manheim	single
Mullen, John	1781	Berwick*	shoemaker

File Name	Date	Twp.	Misc. Info.
Muller, Jacob	1767	Newberry	-
Mullochory, Daniel	1749	?	-
Mummert, Christian	1835	Paradise	-
	1835		vendue
, Ditrik	1770	Reading*	-
, Jacob Sr.	1830	Codorus	-
, Richard	1820	Paradise	-
	1835		widow
	1835		widow vendue
, William	1822	Heidelberg	-
Mumper, Michael	1837	Franklin	-
	1837		vendue
, Samuel	1824	Franklin	-
Mundorf, John	1832	Chanceford	-
, Peter	1813	York Boro	-
	1824		?
, Peter Sr.	1831	York Boro	-
Munn, John	1799	Fawn	-
Murdock, Robert	1786	Tyrone*	-
Murphy, Alexander	1759	Straban*	-
, Barbara	1848	Chanceford	-
, James	1825	"	-
, James	1839	"	-
, James	1777	Cumberland*	-
, James	1800	Newberry	-
, John	1809	Chanceford	-
, John	1798	Cumberland*	-
, Joseph	1838	Chanceford	-
Murray, Duncan	1785	Hamilton Ban*	-
, Francis	1803	Chanceford	-
	1803		vendue
, John	1784	Hamilton Ban*	Rev.
Muse, Daniel	1816	Manheim	-
Musser, Elizabeth	1845	Fairview	-
, Henry	1832	Hellam	-
, John B.	1848	Fairview	-
Myers, Mary	1838	Hopewell	-
, Peter	1816	Newberry	-
Myrise, George	1799	Germany*	-

-N-

Nace, Adam	1816	Codorus	-
, Elizabeth	1829	"	-
Nagel, Jacob	1850	Paradise	-
, John Sr.	1771	"	-
Nailor, Jacob	1844	W. Manchester	-
, James	1779	Newberry	-
, William	1847	Carroll	-
Narragana, Peter	1789	Paradise	German

File Name	Date	Twp.	Misc. Info.
Nass, Mathias	1799	Manheim	-
Nau, John	1844	Springfield	-
Neal, Grizel	1834	(Lanc. Co.)	(Neil)
, John	1802	Hellam	Shoemaker
Neale, Letiss	1774	Manallen*	-
, Thomas	1808	York Boro	(Neill)
Neas, Mathias	1815	Hanover Boro	-
Neavius, Martin	1790	Mt. Pleasant*	(Neavous)
Nebinger, Andreas	1779	Yorktowne	-
, Ann	1827	Newberry	w/o Geo.
, George	1796	"	-
Neely, Jackson	1792	Yorktowne	-
, Joseph	1786	"	-
, Margaret	1774	Tyrone*	-
, Samuel	1775	"	-
, Thomas	1756	?	-
Neeper, Elizabeth	1832	Peach Bottom	-
, James	1831	"	-
, John	1829	"	-
Neff, Henry	1833	York Boro	-
, Henry	1792	Codorus	German
	1800		plantation
, Jacob	1792	Windsor	-
, Joseph	1840	York	-
, Peter	1768	Newberry	-
, Peter	1802	Manheim	-
, Ulrich	1832	York	-
Nehrbass, Francis	1790	Dover	-
Neidig, Christina	1814	Hanover Boro	-
, Jacob	1801	"	-
, John	1799	Heidelberg	-
Neil, William	1836	Lw. Chanceford	-
	1837		vendue
Neiler, George	1828	W. Manchester	-
Neiman, Andrew	1828	York Boro	-
, Charles	1844	Newberry	-
, Elizabeth	1827	Conewago	-
, Elizabeth	1838	"	-
, Magdalena	1837	Manchester	-
	1837		vendue
, Mary	1844	Newberry	-
, Michael	1828	Manchester	-
Nelig, Henry	1839	York	-
Nellinger, Jacob	1837	Heidelberg	-
	1837		vendue
Nelson, Alexander	1750	?	-
, Daniel	1838	Monaghan	-
, Hugh	1778	Hopewell	-
, James	1795	Warrington	-
, Jane	1849	Monaghan	-
, John	1800	Newberry	-
, John	1849	Fairview	shoemaker

106

File Name		Date	Twp.	Misc. Info.
Nelson,	John	1754	?	-
,	Joseph	1781	Warrington	-
,	Mary	1828	Monaghan	-
,	Robert	1823	Warrington	-
,	Samuel	1799	Newberry	-
,	Samuel	1802	Monaghan	-
,	Thomas	1813	Warrington	-
,	William	1835	Monaghan	-
,	William	1766	Warrington	-
Nes,	Elizabeth	1841	York Boro	-
Nesbitt,	Jane	1805	Warrington	-
,	John	1802	"	-
Ness,	Daniel	1848	Springfield	-
,	Jacob	1782	Shrewsbury	-
,	Jacob	1818	"	-
,	Jacob Jr.	1817	"	-
,	Mathias	1767	Manchester	-
,	Peter	1767	Shrewsbury	-
Neucomer,	Baltzer	1822	Hellam	-
,	Christian	1814	"	Shoemaker
,	John Jr.	1812	"	-
,	Michael	1848	Heidelberg	-
Nevitt,	Hannah	1806	Washington	-
,	William	1800	"	h/o Hannah
Newcomer,	Abraham	1818	Hellam	-
,	Christian	1833	Washington	-
		1839		?
,	Christian	1825	Hellam	-
,	Christian	1782	"	-
,	Christian	1785	Warrington	Carpenter
,	George	1821	Washington	-
,	Jacob	1831	Manheim	-
,	John	1840	Hellam	-
,	John	1821	"	-
,	Magdalena	1790	"	filed w/Ulrich
,	Martha	1825	"	-
,	Mary	1837	"	-
		1837		vendue
,	Ulrich	1787	Hellam	h/o Magdal.
,	William	1770	Manallen*	-
Newman,	David	1804	Hanover Boro	-
,	George	1839	Conewago	-
,	Henry	1814	York	German
,	Michael	1778	Codorus	-
,	Michael	1810	Manheim	-
		1810	Dover	2nd inv.
,	Nicholas	1842	Hanover	-
,	Sophia	1829	Heidelberg	-
Newswanger,	Joseph	1777	Codorus	-
,	Peter	1775	Shrewsbury	-
Neyman,	Michael	1842	Heidelberg	(Newman)
Nichol,	George	1832	Peach Bottom	-

107

File Name	Date	Twp.	Misc. Info.
Nichols, Anthony	1824	Chanceford	bellows
, James	1816	Newberry	-
, John	1823	Fawn	-
, Marg	1817	Newberry	-
, William	1773	Chanceford	-
Nickey, Daniel	1846	Washington	-
, Johs	1845	"	filed w/Daniel
	1847		"
Niemand, Jacob	1813	Freystown	-
Nipman, Barbara	1844	Springfield	-
Noblit, Abraham	1764	Newberry	-
, Ann	1796	"	-
Noel, Jacob	1825	Paradise	(Noell)
, James	1846	"	-
, John	1847	"	-
, Mary	1841	"	-
Noell, Christopher	1819	Hellam	-
, John	1766	Paradise	Shoemaker
, Peter	1771	"	-
	1777		2nd inv.
, Susanna	1800	Codorus	German
Noll, Francis	1772	Heidelberg	-
, Johann Yost	1784	Berwick*	-
, Philip	1785	"	-
Nonemacher, Gotlieb	1834	Manheim	-
	1834		vendue
Nonemaker, Abraham	1791	York Boro	loom
, Anna Maria	1813	Shrewsbury	filed w/Sol
, Soloman	1810	"	h/o Anna
Norris, Alexander	1810	Fawn	-
, Thomas	1808	Hopewell	-
, William	1837	York Boro	-
Norton, John (Johannes)	1768	Shrewsbury	-
Nunnemaaker, George Sr.	1845	Manheim	-
, George	1845	Heidelberg	-

-O-

Oberdier, Franey	1819	Dover	filed w/John
, Jacob	1774	"	-
, Jacob	1827	"	-
, John	1812	"	h/o Fran
, Ludwig	1815	Manheim	-
Oberdorff, Casper	1768	Hellam	-
, George Sr.	1828	Windsor	-
, George	1845	Lw. Windsor	beehives
Oberholtzer, Martin	1749	?	-
Oberlander, Jacob	1816	Chanceford	-
Oberlin, Christopher	1811	Paradise	-
, John	1848	"	-

File Name	Date	Twp.	Misc. Info.
Ocker, John	1761	Warrington	-
Oderman, George	1826	Paradise	-
O'Hail, Daniel	1783	Monaghan	-
, Hugh	1815	"	-
, James	1843	Carroll	Esq.
, Jane	1818	Monaghan	-
O'Hara, Charles	1770	Chanceford	-
, Patrick	1776	"	-
Oldham, William	1758	?	-
Oldweiler, Maria	1839	Windsor	-
Oledweiler, Leonard	1846	"	-
Olewiler, George	1818	"	-
, Jacob	1803	"	-
, Jacob	1823	"	-
, Philip	1805	"	-
Ollinger, Adam	1816	Shrewsbury	-
, John	1768	?	-
, John	1815	Shrewsbury	-
, Peter	1801	"	-
Olp, John	1812	"	(Olbs)
Oment, John	1823	Windsor	-
Opp, Jacob	1794	Dover	-
, Nicholas	1754	Manchester	-
, Peter	1807	Dover	-
, Peter	1772	"	(Obb)
Opperman, Casper	1787	Codorus	-
Orbison, Thomas	1785	Hamilton Ban*	-
Orin, Benjamin	1792	Monaghan	Carpenter
, Joseph	1836	Newberry	-
	1836		vendue
Orme, Samuel	1823	Chanceford	-
Orr, Robert	1780	Cumberland*	-
Orson, George	1802	Chanceford	-
Ort, Barbara	1842	Newberry	-
, Catharina	1817	Manchester	German
, Henry	1813	"	"
, John S.	1850	Newberry	-
, Melchoir	1788	Windsor	shoemaker
Ortt, Eve	1822	Manchester	German
Orwick, Frederick	1839	Hopewell	-
Orwig, Joseph	1850	Shrewsbury	wife gets all if single
Osborn, Samuel	1840	York	-
Osborne, Robert	1815	Hopewell	-
, Thomas	1751	Mt. Pleasant*	-
Otslott, Frederick	1850	Fairview	-
Ott, John Diettrich	1755	Yorktowne	-
Ottinger, Henry	1786	Dover	-
, Jacob	1781	Manchester	Carpenter
Ottman, Henry	1782	Windsor	-
Overdeer, Christiana	1848	Dover	-
, Henry	1839	Hanover Boro	-

File Name		Date	Twp.	Misc. Info.
Overdeer,	Jacob	1842	Hanover Boro	168 skins
,	Peter	1843	Manheim	Esq.
Overdier,	Henry	1833	Dover	-
,	Lewis	1834	Washington	-
Overdorf,	John	1833	Windsor	-
Overholser,	Benjamin	1830	"	-
,	Solomon	1832	Heidelberg	-
Overmiller,	Catharine	1844	Loganville twn.	-
,	Christina	1823	Hopewell	-
,	Martin	1803	"	-
Owen,	Thomas	1830	York Boro	-
Owings,	John	1780	Hamilton Ban*	(Owns)
		1781		2nd inv.
,	Joshua	1782	Hanover twn.	-
,	Robert	1759	Heidelberg	Taylor

-P-

Packer,	Moses	1797	Warrington	-
Painter,	Valentine	1784	Mt. Joy*	-
Park,	William	1752	Manallen*	-
Parke,	John	1750	?	-
		1750		vendue
,	John	1773	Hellam	-
,	John	1777	Warrington	2 inv.s
,	John	1786	Fawn	-
,	William	1806	?	-
Parker,	Rebecah	1767	Cumberland*	-
Parr,	John	1794	Germany*	German
,	John	1845	Heidelberg	-
Parry,	John	1836	Spr. Garden	-
		1836		vendue
Patterson,	David R.	1842	Chanceford	-
,	Elizabeth	1839	York Boro	-
,	James	1770	York	-
,	James	1795	Berwick*	-
,	James	1769	?	-
		1772		?
,	James	1845	Chanceford	-
,	James	1773	"	-
,	John	1817	"	-
		1818		Brogue tavern
,	John	1825	Chanceford	-
,	Mary	1805	"	-
,	Nathan	1771	Straban*	-
,	Rebecca	1785	Mt. Joy*	-
,	Thomas	1800	Hamilton Ban*	-
Patton,	Elisabeth	1783	Monaghan	clothes only
,	Jane	1828	Chanceford	-
,	William	1788	Monaghan	-

File Name		Date	Twp.	Misc. Info.
Paules,	Adam	1822	Windsor	-
,	Michael	1782	"	-
Paulis,	Jacob	1849	Lw. Windsor	(Paules)
Paup,	Jane	1822	Dover	w/o Val.
,	Jacob	1844	"	Weaver
,	Valentine	1815	"	f/o Jacob
Paxton,	Andrew	1792	Chanceford	-
,	John	1792	Mt. Joy*	Alleg. Co.
,	John	1784	"	-
,	Nathaniel	1760	?	-
,	Samuel	1793	Cumberland*	-
Payne,	Eleasor	1775	?	-
,	John	1776	York	-
,	John	1818	Fawn	-
Pearson,	Elizabeth	1846	Newberry	-
,	Joseph W.	1842	"	-
,	William	1822	?	-
Pedan,	Benjamin	1813	Chanceford	-
,	Benjamin Martin	1814	Lw. Chanceford	-
,	David	1803	Chanceford	Carpenter
,	Stephan	1827	"	-
,	Susanna	1829	"	-
Peifer,	Christopher	1832	W. Manchester	Smith
Pences,	Joseph	1785	Warrington	-
Pennington,	Ephraim	1815	York Boro	Esq.
,	George	1811	?	-
Penrose,	William	1785	Huntington*	-
Penry,	Robert	1786	?	-
Pentz,	Catharine	1845	Carroll	-
,	Elizabeth	1826	York Boro	-
,	John	1841	Carroll	-
,	John	1804	Washington	-
Peter,	George Michael	1825	Yorktowne	-
,	Peter	1790	York	-
,	Philip	1772	Yorktowne	-
Peterman,	Christina	1817	Manheim	-
,	Daniel	1815	Shrewsbury	-
,	Daniel	1814	Manheim	-
,	Dorothea	1790	Yorktowne	-
,	John	1827	Shrewsbury	-
,	Peter	1778	Windsor	h/o Dorothea
Petry,	George	1823	Codorus	-
Pettery,	Stephen	1793	"	-
Pettit,	James	1771	Berwick*	h/o Precila
,	Precila	1771	"	filed w/James
,	Thomas Sr.	1790	Dover	-
Pew,	Elisha	1827	Hopewell	-
Pfaff,	George	1819	Windsor	-
Pflieger,	Frederick	1791	York	-
,	George	1821	Codorus	-
,	Jacob	1829	York Boro	-
,	Jacob	1800	York	-

File Name	Date	Twp.	Misc. Info.
Pflieger, Maria Marg.	1816	York	w/o Fred.
, Philip	1791	"	-
Phillips, Edmond	1775	Warrington	-
, George	1784	Newberry	-
, Jacob	1837	Fawn	-
	1837		vendue
, John Sr.	1806	Fawn	-
, John Jr.	1819	Windsor	-
, Nathan	1811	Warrington	-
, Peter	1834	Chanceford	-
	1834		vendue
, Pricilla	1794	York Boro	-
, Thomas	1842	Warrington	-
Pickel, Francis	1773	Manchester	-
Picking, Elisabeth	1814	Washington	-
, John Sr.	1813	"	-
Pike, Ann	1791	Newberry	-
, Elizabeth	1809	Fairview	-
, John	1791	Newberry	-
, John	1814	Fairview	-
Plough, Anna	1837	Newberry	-
, John	1840	"	-
Plowman, William	1830	Monaghan	-
Pocter, Richard	1838	York Boro	-
Poe, Alexander	1788	Franklin*	-
, Margaret	1790	Cumberland*	-
, Philip	1804	Manheim	-
Pohl, Henry	1800	Windsor	-
Pohlman, Henry	1845	York Boro	-
Poke, David	1761	Newberry	-
, James	1799	Reading*	(Pollack)
Polinger, John	1844	Monaghan	-
Pollack, William	1794	Chanceford	single
Poor, Charles M.	1832	Newberry	-
	1836		vendue
Porch, John	1806	Chanceford	-
Porter, Caroline	1847	Carroll	-
, Charles William	1814	Lw. Chanceford	-
, David	1775	Cumberland*	-
, John	1773	Hamilton Ban*	-
, John	1770	Cumberland*	-
, John	1820	Monaghan	-
, Nathaniel	1766	Cumberland*	-
, Ross	1832	Monaghan	-
, Thomas	1822	"	-
, William	1777	Mt. Joy*	-
, William	1786	Straban*	-
, William	1824	Monaghan	-
Porterfield, Samuel D.	1833	Codorus	-
Posey, Frederick	1808	Shrewsbury	-
Potterfeld, Susanna	1833	Manheim	-

File Name		Date	Twp.	Misc. Info.
Potts,	George	1845	Newberry	–
,	Nathan	1836	"	–
Poulton,	Smith	1847	Fairview	–
Powell,	John	1774	Newberry	–
Prall,	Cornelius	1834	Hopewell	–
Prem,	Jacob	1839	Warrington	–
,	Peter	1750	Manchester	–
,	Samuel	1800	Warrington	–
Pressel,	David	1787	Berwick*	–
,	Margaret	1835	Carrol	–
		1835		vendue
,	Richard Sr.	1782	Berwick*	Smith
,	Sarah	1794	"	–
,	Valentine	1807	Washington	–
,	Valentine	1835	"	–
Price,	Joseph	1769	Fawn	–
Pritz,	Adam Sr.	1836	Hanover Boro	–
,	Susanna	1849	Heidelberg	–
Probst,	Jacob	1781	Yorktowne	–
Proudfit,	Sarah	1814	Hopewell	w/o Andrew
Proudfoot,	Andrew	1807	"	–
,	David	1822	"	–
,	James	1811	"	–
,	Mary	1802	"	–
,	Robert	1802	"	h/o Mary
Prowell,	James	1849	Fairview	–
,	Joseph	1838	"	–
,	William	1811	"	–
Prunk,	David	1842	Newberry	–
,	Jacob	1842	"	–
Pugh,	Mordicai	1803	Warrington	–
Pupp,	Elizabeth	1845	Franklin	–
Purdy,	Archibald	1804	Hopewell	–
,	Hugh	1766	Shrewsbury	–
,	William	1814	Lw. Chanceford	–
Pusey,	John	1829	York Boro	–
Pyle,	Enoch B.	1850	"	–
,	Nicholas	1850	"	–

-Q-

Quickel,	Barbara	1802	Dover	German
,	Catharina	1822	Conewago	filed w/Phil
,	George	1784	Dover	–
,	George	1845	Manchester	–
,	John Sr.	1831	"	loom
,	Michael	1788	Dover	–
,	Peter	1776	"	–
,	Philip Sr.	1821	Conewago	h/o Cath.
,	Philip Jr.	1818	"	–

File Name	Date	Twp.	Misc. Info.
Quickel, Richard	1846	Conewago	-
Quigley, James	1817	Newberry	-
Quiner, John	1760	?	-

-R-

Raab, Catharine	1840	York	-
, Peter	1831	Windsor	-
Raber, John	1760	Codorus	(Raver)
, Philip	1846	W. Manchester	-
Rackey, Henry	1785	Dover	-
Raffensberger, Catharine	1806	Paradise	-
, Christian	1836	"	-
	1836		vendue
, Christian	1802	Paradise	h/o Cath.
, Elias	1813	"	-
, John	1784	Mt. Pleasant*	-
, Martin	1822	Paradise	-
, Peter	1839	Dover	-
, Peter M.	1846	Washington	-
Ragen, Daniel	1814	York Boro	-
Rahauser, John	1843	Conewago	-
Raise, John	1836	Codorus	-
Ralston, Alice (Else)	1782	Cumberland*	-
, John	1796	Fawn	-
, John	1774	Hamilton Ban*	-
, Mary	1808	Fawn	-
Ramer, Peter	1842	York	-
Ramsay, David	1802	Fawn	-
, James	1757	York	-
, James	1808	Fawn	-
, John	1797	"	h/o Marg.
, Samuel	1825	Newberry	-
, Thomas	1780	Dover	h/o Mary
, William	1777	Hamilton Ban*	-
Ramsey, Alexander	1815	Dover	-
, David	1822	Conewago	-
, James	1826	Fairview	-
, Samuel	1841	Newberry	-
, William	1841	Peach Bottom	-
, William	1831	Fairview	-
Randels, William	1792	Newberry	-
Raney, Elizabeth	1763	?	-
, William	1762	Chanceford	h/o Eliza.
Rankin, Abraham	1806	Newberry	-
, John	1785	Yorktowne	Esq.
Rapp, Margaret	1823	Dover	-
Rathfon, Christian	1824	Windsor	-
, Frederick	1793	"	-
, Jacob	1824	"	-

114

File Name	Date	Twp.	Misc. Info.
Rathfung, Leonard	1842	Lw. Windsor	-
Raudenbush, Henry	1784	Berwick*	h/o Anna M.
, Mary	1786	"	-
Rauhauser, Daniel	1818	Dover	Eng/German
, George	1843	Conewago	-
, Henry	1761	?	-
, Henry	1809	Dover	-
, Jacob	1822	"	-
, Mary	1823	"	filed w/Jacob
Raver, John	1800	Codorus	-
Rawenzawen, Ludwig	1778	Germany*	-
Rawhauser, Mary	1830	Dover	-
, Samuel	1850	Conewago	-
Raymer, Barnet	1815	Hopewell	-
, Frederick	1784	Manchester	-
, Richard	1816	Shrewsbury	-
Reabert, John	1843	Hanover Boro	-
Reachard Julian	1848	Manheim	-
Reary, Jacob	1782	Dover	-
Reber, Catharine	1820	Codorus	-
Rebert, Christina	1836	"	-
	1836		vendue
Rebman, George	1823	Newberry	-
Reck, Christian Sr.	1789	Germany*	Petersburg
, Joseph	1839	Paradise	-
Recks, George	1790	Manallen*	-
Redick, Andrew	1776	Berwick*	-
, John	1773	Germany*	-
Reeber, Peter	1816	Hopewell	-
Reed, Henry D.	1850	Monaghan	-
, Hugh	1778	(York Co.)	-
, James	1759	Cumberland*	-
	1763	Chanceford	?
, Jennet	1790	"	-
, John	1828	Lw. Chanceford	-
, John	1773	Mt. Pleasant*	-
	1773		2nd inv.
, John	1781	Straban*	-
, John	1790	Tyrone*	-
, John	1780	Cumberland*	-
, Joseph	1782	Chanceford	-
, Joseph	1804	"	Esq.
, Joseph	1848	"	-
, Leonard	1848	Paradise	-
, Margaret	1793	Tyrone*	-
, Mary	1789	Straban*	-
, Thomas	1804	Monaghan	-
, Thomas	1763	Newberry	-
, William	1781	Chanceford	-
, William	1846	"	-
, William	1790	Mt. Pleasant*	-
Reep, Christian	1761	?	-

115

File Name	Date	Twp.	Misc. Info.
Reep, Yost	1789	Hellam	-
Reese, Benjamin	1832	Warrington	-
, Joseph	1798	"	-
Reeser, Margaret	1831	Conewago	-
Reib, Stephan	1819	Hellam	-
Reibolt, Andrew	1803	Codorus	-
Reichly, Mathew	1848	Warrington	-
Reider, Frederick	1811	Washington	-
, Frederick	1831	"	-
, Laurence	1786	Windsor	-
Reiff, Henry	1784	Dover	-
, Jacob	1839	Fairview	-
, Jacob	1804	"	-
, Joseph	1806	Newberry	-
Reifsnider, Aron	1765	?	-
Reigert, Henry	1832	Spr. Garden	-
Reighart, William	1788	York	German
Reily, James R.	1844	York Boro	-
, Thomas	1753	?	-
Reiman, John	1841	York Boro	-
Reinberger, Philip	1815	Newberry	-
, Stephen	1815	Manchester	-
Reinecker, Casper	1790	Heidelberg	Innkeeper
Reinholt, Samuel	1825	Dover	-
Reinlefs, James	1756	York	-
Reipe, Henry	1844	Hopewell	-
Reis, Philip	1823	Codorus	-
Reisinger, Conrad	1800	W. Manchester	-
, Daniel	1823	Hellam	-
, Eve	1808	Windsor	filed w/Peter
, George	1846	W. Manchester	-
, George	1849	Lw. Windsor	-
, Henry	1814	W. Manchester	-
, John	1815	York Boro	-
, John	1805	Hanover	-
, Martin	1814	Dover	-
, Nicholas	1784	Manchester	-
, Peter	1801	Windsor	h/o Eve
Reist, John	1759	?	-
Reitinger, Anna	1810	W. Manchester	-
, Stephen	1801	"	-
Reitz, Elizabeth	1848	Codorus	-
Remby, Israel	1814	Manheim	-
Renchman, James	1767	York	-
Renoll, Christian Sr.	1850	N. Codorus	-
, Christian	1837	Codorus	-
	1837		vendue
, Daniel	1800	Codorus	-
, Elizabeth	1821	"	-
, Henry	1824	"	-
, Jacob	1829	"	-
, John	1824	W. Manchester	-

File Name		Date	Twp.	Misc. Info.
Renoll,	Magdalena	1824	W. Manchester	-
Renshaw,	John	1750	?	-
Renthrew,	Mary	1844	?	-
Rentzel,	Jacob	1836	Paradise	-
,	John	1846	Dover	-
,	Justus	1784	Paradise	-
,	Henry	1815	"	-
Repman,	Ann	1845	Newberry	-
,	Charles	1849	"	-
,	George	1795	Dover	German
Resch,	Christian	1783	York	-
Ressler,	Mathias	1787	Newberry	-
Reynolds,	Samuel	1758	Cumberland*	-
Rhea,	Joseph	1750	Berwick*	-
Rheal,	William	1784	Yorktowne	-
Rhine,	Martin	1758	Manchester	-
Rhode,	Abraham	1826	"	-
,	Anthony	1785	"	-
,	Jacob	1784	Paradise	-
Rhodes,	Jacob	1837	Manchester	-
Ribold,	Henry	1839	Codorus	-
Rice,	John	1836	"	vendue
,	Philip	1791	Hellam	-
Richards,	Barshaba	1836	Fawn	-
		1836		vendue
,	Benjamin	1831	Manchester	-
,	Catharine	1835	"	-
		1835		vendue
,	Lewis	1818	York	-
Richardson,	Thomas	1774	?	-
,	William	1837	Chanceford	-
Richcrick,	John Sr.	1822	Conewago	-
Richey,	Elizabeth	1816	Newberry	-
Richler,	Frederick	1779	Codorus	-
,	George	1782	Dover	-
Riddle,	Dominicus	1764	Germany*	-
,	James	1789	Franklin*	-
Rieb,	Nicholas	1816	Shrewsbury	-
Riebold,	John	1849	Codorus	-
Rieder,	Jacob	1820	Hanover Boro	-
,	Joseph	1849	Wrgvlle. Boro	-
Riegel,	John	1785	Germany*	-
,	Ludwig	1809	Codorus	-
,	Peter	1818	"	-
Rieley,	Michael	1820	York	-
Rieman,	Anna	1831	Windsor	-
,	Jacob	1815	York	-
Riemar,	John	1832	Shrewsbury	-
Rieser,	William	1815	Dover	-
Riesser,	George	1825	Warrington	-
Riffel,	Mathias	1792	Mt. Joy*	-
Rightsline,	Conrad	1824	Newberry	-

117

File Name	Date	Twp.	Misc. Info.
Rineamon, Wilhelm	1834	Manheim	-
	1834		vendue
Rinebine, Jacob	1823	Wrgvlle. Boro	-
Rinehart, George	1801	Manheim	-
, George	1780	Windsor	-
, Yost	1834	Dover	-
	1835		vendue
Ringer, George	1790	Manchester	-
, John	1801	"	-
Ritchey, David	1797	Huntington*	-
Ritter, Frederick	1787	Tyrone*	-
, Jacob	1831	Heidelberg	-
	1831		vendue
, Jacob	1849	Carroll	-
, John F.	1848	Manheim	-
Ritz, Anthony	1814	York Boro	-
, Jacob	1823	Hanover Boro	-
, John	1783	York	-
, Mathias	1835	Shrewsbury	-
Roberts, John	1797	"	vendue
, Joseph	1781	Manchester	-
, Patrick	1778	Hopewell	-
Robeson, James	1752	(Lancaster Co.)	-
Robinson, Andrew	1805	?	Esq.
, George	1820	Newberry	-
, Henry	1772	Chanceford	-
, Issac	1796	Hamilton Ban*	-
, James	1815	Chanceford	-
, James	1767	York	-
, James	1842	Peach Bottom	-
, James Sr.	1822	"	-
, John	1763	?	-
, John	1822	Hopewell	-
, Penrose	1846	York Boro	-
, Sarah	1818	Lw. Chanceford	-
, Thomas	1751	Mt. Joy*	-
, Walter	1841	Peach Bottom	-
, William	1806	Fawn	-
, William	1841	Peach Bottom	-
Roch, Johannes	1782	?	-
Rockenback, Peter	1805	Hellam	-
Rockenbaugh, Mathias	1773	Yorktowne	-
Rockey, Elizabeth	1828	Newberry	-
Rode, Christian	1838	Manchester	-
, John	1835	"	-
, John	1837	"	-
, Sarah	1838	"	-
Rodney, James		Wrgvlle. Boro	-
Roebach, Michael	1791	Germany*	-
Rogers, John	1761	?	-
Rohler, Philip	1832	Warrington	-
Rohrbach, Amos H.	1850	N. Codorus	single

File Name		Date	Twp.	Misc. Info.
Rohrbach,	David	1850	N. Codorus	-
,	John	1818	Manheim	-
Rohrbauch,	George	1842	N. Codorus	-
,	John	1844	"	-
,	John	1841	Codorus	-
Rohrbaugh,	Anna M.	1850	Heidelberg	-
,	Christian	1827	Codorus	-
,	Christian	1789	"	-
,	Henry	1850	Heidelberg	-
,	Jacob	1821	Codorus	-
,	Jacob	1767	Mt. Joy*	-
,	Lorentz	1795	Codorus	-
,	Zachariah	1794	Mt. Joy*	-
Rolay,	John	1805	Washington	-
Roller,	George	1834	Manchester	-
,	Jacob	1820	Dover	-
,	Jacob Sr.	1817	"	-
,	Samuel	1826	Washington	-
Romer,	Frederick	1831	W. Manchester	-
Romig,	Jacob	1795	Manchester	-
,	Michael	1793	"	-
Roseborough,	Joshua	1775	Monaghan	-
,	Robert	1775	(Cumberland Co.)	Allen
Rosensteel,	John	1758	?	-
Roser,	Adam	1794	Shrewsbury	-
,	Lorentz	1850	"	-
Ross,	Alexander	1816	Warrington	-
,	Allen	1840	Fairview	-
,	George	1804	Warrington	-
,	Hugh	1780	Chanceford	-
,	James	1757	Warrington	-
,	James	1820	"	-
,	Jane	1820	"	-
,	Martha	1820	"	-
,	William	1797	Straban*	-
,	William	1821	Fairview	-
,	William	1818	Chanceford	Esq.
,	William	1777	Warrington	-
Rossenbaum,	John	1790	Newberry	-
Rosser,	Philip	1845	Springfield	-
Roth,	Christian	1840	Spr. Garden	-
,	Henry	1831	Manheim	-
,	John	1827	Spr. Garden	-
,	Julianna	1821	Codorus	-
,	Susanna	1815	"	-
Rothrock,	Barbara	1799	Newberry	-
,	John	1805	York Boro	-
,	Mary	1820	Hanover Boro	-
,	Philip	1803	York Boro	-
Rotz,	Henry	1773	Paradise	-
Rouse,	Frederick	1785	Warrington	-
,	Lucas	1788	Yorktowne	Rev.

File Name	Date	Twp.	Misc. Info.
Row, Ernst	1820	Fairview	–
Rowland, Robert	1779	Fawn	–
Rowmans, Andrew	1770	"	–
Ruble, Anna	1849	Hellam	–
, Christian	1817	Codorus	–
, Esther	1819	"	–
, Peter	1773	"	–
Ruby, Casper	1776	Windsor	–
, David Sr.	1849	Lw. Windsor	–
, David K.	1847	"	–
, Frederick	1842	"	–
, George	1821	Windsor	–
, Henry	1780	"	s/o Magdal.
, John	1843	Hellam	–
, John Sr.	1826	Windsor	–
, Magdalena	1795	"	–
, Michael	1848	Lw. Windsor	Esq.
Ruch, John	1828	Heidelberg	–
Rudisill, Adam	1818	Codorus	Rev./½ Ger.
, Catharine	1803	Dover	–
, John	1816	York Boro	–
, John Sr.	1823	Codorus	–
, John	1844	N. Codorus	–
, Lewis	1829	Codorus	Jefferson
, Ludwig	1825	"	–
	1837		vendue
Rudisille, Jacob	1787	Manchester	–
, Jacob	1810	Hanover Boro	Esq.
, Jacob	1776	Yorktowne	(Rudisilly) Wheelwright
, Jonas	1799	Manchester	–
Rudy, Anna Mary	1840	Hellam	–
, Catharine	1846	Manchester	–
, Henry	1804	Dover	h/o Barb.
, Henry	1817	"	–
, Jacob	1834	Manchester	–
, Martin	1837	"	–
	1837		vendue
, Michael	1801	Hellam	–
, Michael	1845	Spr. Garden	–
Ruhl, Clements	1778	Codorus	–
, Frederick	1815	Shrewsbury	–
, Jacob	1847	"	–
, John	1825	Codorus	–
	1826	"	widow (Rule)
, Michael	1812	"	–
, Peter	1835	Shrewsbury	–
, William	1828	"	–
, William	1815	Codorus	–
Ruhle, Jacob	1815	"	–
Ruhlman, Christian	1829	Manheim	–
, George	1840	"	–

File Name	Date	Twp.	Misc. Info.
Ruhlman, George	1827	Manheim	-
, Jacob	1809	"	-
Rummel, John	1800	York Boro	Plasterer
, Mary	1828	"	-
, Peter	1812	"	-
, Richard	1835	Manchester	-
	1836		vendue
Runck, Peter	1772	?	-
, Yost	1826	Codorus	-
Runckel, Jacob	1794	Manheim	-
, John	1791	"	-
Runk, John	1845	Spr. Garden	-
, Valentine	1844	N. Codorus	-
Runkel, Anna Mary	1821	Manheim	-
, Anna Mary	1842	Heidelberg	-
Runkle, John	1833	Manheim	-
Rupp, Baltzer	1796	Hellam	-
, Christian	1821	York Boro	-
, Gotlieb	1830	"	-
, John	1826	Windsor	-
	1836		vendue
, John	1835	Wrgvlle. Boro	-
	1835		vendue
, John	1848	Newberry	-
, Margaret	1813	York Boro	-
, Mary	1836	Windsor	-
	1836		vendue
, William Henry	1765	Windsor	-
Ruppert, Adam	1781	Manchester	-
, Adam	1844	Dover	-
, Dietrich	1820	W. Manchester	German
Ruse, Jacob	1774	Reading*	(Roose)
Russell, James	1775	?	-
Ruth, Catharine	1836	Codorus	-
, James	1826	"	-
, Samuel	1849	N. Codorus	-
Rutter, Adam	1822	Manchester	-
, Andrew	1824	York Boro	-
, Samuel	1832	"	-
Ryland, Arther	1820	Lw. Chanceford	-

-S-

Sable, Adam	1826	Manheim	now Ohio
, Peter	1831	"	-
Sadler, Isaac	1795	Huntington*	-
, Mary	1796	"	-
, Richard	1765	"	-
, William	1765	"	-
Sagmiller, Frederick	1818	Chanceford	-

File Name	Date	Twp.	Misc. Info.
Sakemiller, Elizabeth	1837	Hellam	-
Saltzgeber, Deeter	1762	Paradise	-
Sample, Cunningham	1803	Fawn	-
, John	1823	Peach Bottom	-
, John	1841	"	-
Sanders, Philip	1847	York Boro	-
Sanderson, Elizabeth	1803	Warrington	-
, John	1803	"	-
Sangrey, Charlotte	1811	Chanceford	-
, Christian	1759	?	-
Sangry, John	1840	Chanceford	-
	1840		2nd inv.
, Peter	1809	Chanceford	(Sangoree)
Sank, George	1782	Yorktowne	-
Sankey, William	1757	?	h/o Eliz.
Sarbach, Catharine	1795	Berwick*	-
, David	1816	Washington	-
, Jacob	1787	Berwick*	-
Saurbaugh, Jacob	1848	Washington	-
, Jacob	1849	"	-
Sauter, John A.	1848	Paradise	-
Savage, Joseph	1773	Manallen*	-
Sax, Nicholas	1796	Huntington*	-
Saxhor, Jacob	1757	?	(Sausser)
Saylor, Benjamin	1754	?	-
, Casper	1804	Chanceford	-
, Conrad	1809	Fairview	-
, Eleanor	1795	Manchester	-
, Hans	1761	?	-
, Isaac	1790	Manchester	-
, Ulrich	1771	?	-
Scannal, Lawrence	1785	Germany*	-
Scantling, Michael	1831	Windsor	-
Scarborough, James	1827	Manchester	-
Schaum, John	1766	Germany*	-
Scheets, Jonas	1848	Carroll	-
Schemberger, John	1848	Lw. Windsor	-
Schertz, Samuel	1826	Franklin	-
Schleby, Adam	1775	?	(Sleepy)
Schlosser, George	1815	York Boro	-
Schmidt, Henry	1850	Shrewsbury	-
Schmuck, John	1839	Windsor	-
, Mary	1841	"	-
Schnell, Frederick	1841	"	-
Schrack, Philip	1844	York	-
Schrantz, Henry	1848	Windsor	-
Schreid, Casper	1798	Chanceford	-
Schriver, Andrew	1850	Manchester	-
, Elizabeth	1834	"	-
, Susanna	1825	?	w/o Peter
Schroll, Philip	1848	Hellam	-
Schroyer, George	1819	Hanover Boro	-

122

File Name	Date	Twp.	Misc. Info.
Schulthower, John	1840	Washington	-
Schultz, Conrad	1851	York Boro	-
, Rebecca	1841	Hanover Boro	(Shultz)
Schutz, John	1841	Manheim	-
Schwartz, Catharine	1820	?	-
, John	1838	Springfield	-
Schweigert, Samuel	1840	Paradise	-
Schweisgood, Lawrence	1799	"	German
Schweiszgood, Andrew	1796	Newberry	-
Schweitzer, Andrew	1818	Fawn	-
	1831	"	widow
Schy, Simon	1779	?	-
Scoggins, John	1774	?	-
Scott, Allen	1799	Chanceford	-
, Cunningham	1825	Lw. Chanceford	-
, Gavin	1822	"	-
, James K.	1831	York Boro	-
, John	1821	W. Manchester	-
, John	1825	Chanceford	-
, John	1785	Cumberland*	-
, John	1758	Straban*	-
	1761		2nd inv.
, Patrick	1825	Peach Bottom	-
, Robert	1790	Straban*	-
, William	1784	Hamilton Ban*	-
, William	1771	Cumberland*	-
Sealy, Henry	1798	Berwick*	-
Sechrist, Adam	1809	York Boro	German
, Catherine	1820	York	-
, Francis	1819	Hopewell	(Siegrist)
, John	1763	York	German/Eng.
, Michael	1832	Hopewell	(Segrist)
, William	1830	"	-
Seftel, Valentine	1759	?	-
Segmiller, Frederick	1817	Hellam	-
, John	1825	Chanceford	-
Seib, Andrew	1794	Dover	German
Seichrist, Jacob	1841	York Boro	-
Seifert, Adam	1821	Dover	(Syfort)
, Anna Mary	1805	"	-
, John	1834	Paradise	-
, Magdalena	1820	Dover	-
, Philip	1850	"	-
Seiffert, John	1842	"	-
Seiger, Casper	1840	Windsor	-
Seip, Charles	1850	Newberry	-
, Emanuel	1824	Conewago	-
, Emanuel	1850	Newberry	-
, George	1831	Conewago	-
, Philip	1831	"	-
Seipe, Charles	1768	Dover	(Seib)
Seiple, Anthony	1838	?	(Sipel)

123

File Name		Date	Twp.	Misc. Info.
Seitz,	Benjamin	1792	Heidelberg	(Sids)
,	Casper	1776	?	-
,	Catharine	1820	Shrewsbury	-
,	Charles	1848	Springfield	-
,	Henry	1841	Newberry	-
,	Jacob	1821	Hanover Boro	-
		1822		
,	John	1824	Shrewsbury	-
,	John	1793	"	German
,	Joseph	1811	"	"
,	Mary	1842	York Boro	-
,	Michael	1834	York	-
,	Peter	1847	Manchester	-
Sell,	Abraham	1786	Germany*	-
,	Isaac	1799	"	-
Senft,	Andrew	1844	N. Codorus	-
		1837	Codorus	vendue
		1836		
		1836		vendue
,	Peter	1838	Heidelberg	-
,	Philip	1798	Codorus	German
,	Philip	1833	Paradise	-
Sentz,	Peter	1798	Hopewell	(Sintz)
Shadden,	Robert	1765	Manallen*	-
Shade,	George	1775	?	-
Shadley,	Adam	1765	Manchester	-
Shadow,	Detlove	1825	Paradise	-
Shafer,	Abraham	1825	Dover	-
,	Anna Margaret	1785	Yorktowne	-
,	Barnhard	1750	?	-
,	Catherine	1797	Shrewsbury	-
,	Cathrine	1796	Dover	-
,	Charles	1760	?	German/Eng.
,	Christiana	1830	York Boro	-
,	Christofel	1788	Windsor	-
,	David	1770	?	-
,	David	1823	Shrewsbury	-
,	Frederick	1776	Paradise	-
,	Frederick	1800	Dover	German
,	Frederick	1801	Newberry	-
,	George	1845	Dover	-
,	Hannah	1830	Manchester	-
,	Henry	1835	Codorus	(Sheffer)
,	Henry	1835	Shrewsbury	vendue
,	Henry	1826	"	-
,	Henry	1788	Windsor	German
,	Jacob	1784	Codorus	-
,	Jacob	1793	Huntington*	-
,	Jacob	1794	Dover	(Sheaffer)
,	Jacob	1810	W. Manchester	-
,	Jacob	1818	Shrewsbury	-
,	Jacob	1803	Hopewell	-

File Name		Date	Twp.	Misc. Info.
Shafer,	John	1790	York Boro	Wagonmaker
,	John Adam	1827	Manchester	-
,	John	1835	York	-
		1835		vendue
,	John	1802	Newberry	-
,	Nicholas	1776	Yorktowne	-
,	Nicholas	1810	Codorus	-
,	Paul	1784	Windsor	h/o Anna E.
		1807	"	widow
,	Philip	1791	Franklin*	-
,	Philip	1824	Shrewsbury	-
,	Serenus	1770	Manchester	-
,	Susanna	1817	Dover	-
Shaffer,	Adam	1834	Shrewsbury	-
,	Charles	1834	Warrington	-
,	Daniel	1832	Dover	-
,	Elizabeth	1820	York	German
,	Elizabeth	1850	Manchester	-
,	Henry	1835	York	-
,	John	1823	"	-
,	John	1848	Warrington	-
Shall,	Catherine	1825	Chanceford	(Schaull)
,	George	1819	York Boro	-
Shaller,	George	1803	Monaghan	-
,	Samuel	1819	Wrgvlle. Boro	-
Shank,	Andreas	1762	York	(Schenck)
Shanks,	Sarah	1836	Warrington	-
Shannon,	Andrew	1763	?	-
		1762		vendue
,	Thomas	1797	Hamilton Ban*	-
Shantz,	Jacob	1795	Berwick*	-
,	John	1786	Windsor	-
Sharp,	George	1816	Dover	-
,	James	1780	Newberry	-
,	John	1816	?	w/Jane's inv.
,	John	1843	York Boro	-
,	Margaret	1824	Fairview	-
,	Walter	1780	Hamilton Ban*	-
Shaull,	Feutt	1757	Yorktowne	-
,	Frederick	1774	Warrington	-
,	George	1767	Hellam	-
,	Henry	1816	Lw. Chanceford	-
,	Jacob	1823	"	-
,	James	1845	York Boro	(Schall)
,	John	1770	Manheim	-
,	John	1814	Lw. Chanceford	-
,	John	1831	York Boro	(Schall)
,	John	1823	"	-
,	John Jacob	1780	Codorus	-
,	Lewis	1814	Manheim	-
,	Michael	1778	?	(Sholl)
Shaw,	Charles	1842	Spr. Garden	-

File Name	Date	Twp.	Misc. Info.
Shaw, Daniel	1781	?	-
, John	1762	Chanceford	-
Shawman, John	1761	?	-
Shearer, Abraham	1825	Windsor	(Scherer)
, Andrew	1846	Washington	-
, Catharine	1795	York	German
, David	1827	Warrington	-
, Henry	1781	Germany*	-
, Jacob	1791	Codorus	(Sherrer)
, Philip	1850	Washington	-
Shebp, John Simon	1816	?	-
Sheely, Catharine	1838	York Boro	-
, Christopher	1800	"	-
, George	1779	?	-
Sheepshanks, Nancy	1845	Warrington	-
Sheffel, George	1822	York Boro	-
Sheffer, Barbara	1848	Springfield	-
, John	1821	Windsor	(Scheffer)
, John	1820	York Boro	-
Sheiner, Daniel	1821	Shrewsbury	(Sheyre)
Shelaberger, Elizabeth	1839	Dover	-
Shellenberger, John	1831	"	-
Shelley, Abraham	1812	Newberry	-
	1808	"	?
, Daniel	1827	"	-
, Jacob	1775	"	-
, John	1814	Paradise	-
, Mary	1828	"	-
, Peter	1769	Newberry	-
Shelly, Daniel	1822	"	-
, George	1850	York Boro	-
, John	1849	Paradise	-
Shenberger, Adam	1815	Windsor	-
, Adam	1847	Lw. Windsor	-
, Adam	1822	Windsor	-
	1822		vendue
, Baltzer	1751	Hellam	-
, Baltzer	1805	Hopewell	-
, Frederick	1847	Chanceford	-
, Henry	1848	Windsor	-
, Jacob	1819	"	-
, Jane	1834	"	(Shinberger)
	1834		vendue
, John	1837	Windsor	-
, John	1799	"	-
, Joseph	1813	"	-
, Margaret	1823	York	-
, Margaret	1809	"	-
, Margaret	1803	Windsor	-
, Susanna	1809	"	-
Shenck, Elizabeth	1820	Codorus	(Schenck)
Shenk, Christian	1798	Newberry	-

File Name		Date	Twp.	Misc. Info.
Shenk,	Henry	1805	Codorus	(Schenck)
,	John	1791	Franklin*	(Shanks)
,	John	1832	Codorus	-
,	Joseph	1789	Yorktowne	-
,	Magdalena	1811	Codorus	d/o Henry
,	Mary	1815	"	-
,	Thomas	1806	Warrington	(Shanks)
Shephard,	William	1757	Manallen*	-
Shepp,	Abraham	1837	Spr. Garden	-
		1837		vendue
Sherbaum,	Conrad	1826	Spr. Garden	-
Sherer,	Jacob	1784	York	h/o Rosanna
,	Rosanna	1836	Warrington	filed w/Jac.
,	Theobald	1826	Shrewsbury	-
Sheretz,	Arnold	1786	Manheim	-
,	Jacob	1793	"	-
,	Ludwig	1799	"	-
Sherich,	Ann	1843	Lw. Windsor	-
Sherman,	Conrad	1823	Manheim	General
,	Jacob	1846	Codorus	-
,	John	1825	Heidelberg	-
Sherp,	Adam	1798	Manheim	(Schorp)
,	George	1800	Manchester	-
,	John	1789	"	-
Shertley,	John	1771	Dover	-
Shertz,	Mary	1846	Franklin	-
Shetler,	Andrew	1807	Codorus	-
,	Christian	1778	York	-
,	Mary	1789	Yorktowne	-
Shetley,	Frederick	1789	York Boro	-
Shetrone,	Abraham	1759	?	-
,	Henry	1772	Shrewsbury	-
,	Jacob	1807	Newberry	-
,	Leonard	1768	(York Co.)	Blacksmith
Shettel,	George	1840	Conewago	-
,	Philip	1823	Newberry	-
Shetten,	Jacob	1841	Paradise	-
Shetter,	Jacob	1846	N. Codorus	-
,	Jacob Jr.	1777	(York Co.)	-
,	John	1786	Newberry	(Shitter)
,	Martin	1794	"	-
,	Mary	1849	W. Manchester	-
Shettle,	George	1810	Dover	-
,	Michael	1829	Conewago	-
Shettley,	Jacob	1795	York Boro	-
Shields,	John	1783	Cumberland*	-
Shiely,	Jacob	1787	Mt. Joy*	-
Shier,	John	1812	?	-
Shiery,	Michael	1838	Springfield	-
Shiley,	Samuel	1848	Fairview	-
Shimp,	John	1847	Lw. Chanceford	-
Shindle,	Frederick	1816	Manchester	German

File Name	Date	Twp.	Misc. Info.
Shindle, Gertrude	1845	Manchester	German
Shinleber, Frederick	1777	Codorus	-
Shireman, Dewald	1833	Paradise	-
, John	1827	"	-
Shirey, George	1831	Shrewsbury	-
, John	1812	Manheim	-
Shirk, Barbara	1831	Windsor	-
, John	1783	Paradise	-
, Samuel	1830	Windsor	-
Shiry, George	1843	Fawn	-
Shisler, Henry	1818	Paradise	-
Shissler, John	1824	Shrewsbury	-
, Nancy	1824	Codorus	-
Shitz, Frederick	1750	Heidelberg	-
, John	1817	Newberry	-
, Michael	1835	Windsor	-
	1835		vendue
Shively, Christian	1774	York	-
, Esther	1804	Monaghan	-
Shlotterbeck, Henry	1817	York Boro	-
Shock, Michael	1807	Manheim	-
Shoemaker, Elizabeth	1840	York	-
Shoeman, John	1828	Newberry	-
, John Jr.	1808	"	-
Shoff, Jacob	1828	Chanceford	-
Sholl, John	1845	Hanover Boro	-
Shollas, Magdalena	1789	Mt. Pleasant*	-
, Thobal	1788	"	-
Shorb, Anthony	1800	Heidelberg	-
, John	1815	Manchester	German
Short, James	1797	York Boro	Merchant
Shortledge, Thomas	1848	Chanceford	-
Shotter, Henry	1797	York Boro	-
Shram, Jacob	1808	"	-
, John	1808	Dover	-
Shreiner, Michael	1815	Fairview	-
	1815	(Lanc. Co.)	2nd inv.
, Philip	1803	Fairview	-
Shriver, Adam	1816	Manchester	-
, Conrad	1794	Germany*	German
, Henry	1794	Newberry	-
, Jacob	1798	York Boro	-
, Jacob	1784	Germany*	-
, John	1824	Manchester	-
, John	1816	Franklin	-
, Ludwig Sr.	1796	Heidelberg	-
, Michael	1804	Manchester	-
, Peter	1795	"	-
, Peter	1819	W. Manchester	-
, Peter	1831	Manchester	-
Shroll, Catharine	1819	"	-
	1836		vendue names Eve

File Name		Date	Twp.	Misc. Info.
Shroll,	Christian	1803	Hellam	-
,	Eve	1835	Manchester	-
,	John	1810	Hellam	-
Shrom,	Anna Maria	1754	Manchester	-
,	Elizabeth	1798	"	-
,	George	1772	"	-
,	Jacob	1748	?	-
Shue,	Elizabeth	1825	Codorus	filed w/Zach
,	Isaac	1843	Springfield	-
,	Jacob	1844	Windsor	-
,	Jacob	1824	Hanover Boro	-
,	John	1836	Codorus	-
		1836		vendue
,	Zacharias	1812	Codorus	h/o Eliz.
Shuh,	Henry	1785	Berwick*	(Shoe)
,	John	1819	Chanceford	-
Shuler,	Adam	1802	Dover	German
,	Andrew	1817	Manchester	"
,	Andrew	1778	Newberry	-
,	Elizabeth	1850	(Gallie Ohio)	-
,	Joel	1828	Fairview	-
		1828		vendue
,	John	1845	Conewago	-
,	John Adam	1794	Newberry	German
,	Margaret	1838	Manchester	-
,	Martin	1764	?	-
		1764		vendue
,	Mary	1807	"	German
,	Peter	1794	Manchester	-
Shultz,	Frederick	1830	Hanover Boro	-
,	Henry	1816	Newberry	-
,	Henry	1757	?	-
,	Jacob Jr.	1829	York Boro	-
,	Jacob	1822	Heidelberg	-
,	Jacob Sr.	1794	Hellam	-
,	James	1842	"	Blacksmith
,	John	1804	Monaghan	-
,	Lorentz	1826	York	-
,	Martin	1761	Hellam	-
,	Michael	1834	Codorus	-
		1834		vendue
,	Peter Sr.	1815	Hanover Boro	-
,	Peter Jr.	1811	Heidelberg	-
,	Peter	1755	?	-
		1757		vendue
,	Peter	1784	Manchester	-
,	Peter	1809	"	-
,	Peter	1843	W. Manchester	-
,	Samuel	1770	Yorktowne	-
,	Valentine	1814	Newberry	German
,	Yost	1750	Hellam	-
Shuman,	John	1815	Newberry	-

File Name		Date	Twp.	Misc. Info.
Shupp,	Andrew	1790	Warrington	-
,	Casper	1817	Fairview	-
,	Jacob	1784	Mt. Pleasant*	f/o Lov.
,	Lovina	1797	(Lw. Paxton)	w/o Geo.
,	Martin	1796	Mt. Pleasant*	-
Shurr,	Philip	1817	Fairview	-
Shyrock,	John	1788	Manchester	(Shirock)
Sibert,	Peter	1833	Windsor	-
Siddons,	John	1837	Fairview	-
Sidle,	George	1848	Monaghan	-
Siechrist,	John	1841	Shrewsbury	-
Siegle,	Jacob	1800	Hopewell	-
Sigler,	Joseph	1818	Peach Bottom	-
Siglor,	Michael	1826	Hopewell	-
Silicks,	Thomas	1790	Manallen*	-
Sille,	Elizabeth	1847	Hopewell	-
,	John	1835	"	-
		1835		vendue
Simers,	Robert	1767	Chanceford	-
Simmon,	John	1825	Codorus	-
Simmons,	Philip	1761	Hamilton Ban*	Ger/Eng
Simon,	Casper	1794	Codorus	-
,	Christina	1793	Manallen*	-
,	Jacob	?	(Va.)	-
Simpson,	James	1784	Cumberland*	-
,	James	1797	Franklin*	-
Sinclair,	John	1834	Lw. Chanceford	-
		1834		vendue
Singer,	John	1793	Newberry	-
,	Peter	1829	Yorktowne	-
,	Peter Jr.	1844	York	-
Singhaus,	Elizabeth	1821	?	-
Single,	Michael	1821	Paradise	-
Sinker,	James	1807	Hopewell	-
Sinn,	Christian	1804	York Boro	Slaughterer
,	George	1786	Yorktowne	-
Sinnard,	Elinor	1780	Hopewell	-
Sipe,	Charles	1846	Newberry	-
,	Eva Elizabeth	1822	Dover	-
,	George	1780	Cumberland*	-
,	George	1849	York	-
,	George	1850	Lewisbury Boro	-
,	Jacob	1844	W. Manchester	-
,	John	1756	Manchester	-
,	John	1833	"	-
,	Joseph	1827	Spr. Garden	Carpenter
,	Joseph Sr.	1847	Conewago	filed w/above
		1847		vendue
,	Tobias	1839	Spr. Garden	-
,	Tobias	1846	"	-
Skiles,	Henry	1782	Codorus	-
Skinner,	Luther H.	1848	Hanover Boro	-

File Name		Date	Twp.	Misc. Info.
Slagle,	Christian	1842	Codorus	–
,	Christopher	1772	Berwick*	–
,	Daniel Sr.	1793	"	–
,	George	1831	Manheim	–
,	Jacob Sr.	1790	Berwick*	–
,	William	1829	Bottstown	–
Slaybaugh,	Henry	1783	Manallen*	–
Sleeger,	Daniel	1847	Spr. Garden	–
Slemons,	James	1799	Hamilton Ban*	–
Slenker,	Andrew	1793	Windsor	–
,	Franey	1850	"	–
,	Martin	1826	"	–
Slentz,	John	1796	Mt. Joy*	–
,	Philip	1796	Heidelberg	–
Slessman,	Paul	1777	Codorus	–
Slider,	Henry	1833	Washington	–
,	Jacob	1832	"	–
,	Philip	1814	Manheim	–
Sloat,	Adam	1833	Windsor	–
,	Michael	1805	"	–
Slothower,	Elizabeth	1792	Manheim	German
,	Nicholas	1780	"	–
Slough,	Jacob	1789	Straban*	–
Slyder,	Adam	1823	Manheim	–
Small,	George	1839	York Boro	–
,	Jacob Sr.	1817	Spr. Garden	–
,	John	1799	Heidelberg	h/o Mary
,	John	1846	Newberry	–
,	John	1810	York Boro	–
,	Joseph	1845	"	–
,	Killian	1815	"	–
,	Lawrence	1832	"	–
,	Lawrence	1749	Hellam	–
,	Mary	1811	?	filed w/John
,	William	1845	(Fred. Md.)	–
Smeltzer,	Anna Maria	1832	Lw. Chanceford	German
,	Catharine	1845	Chanceford	–
,	George	1849	Lw. Windsor	–
,	Michael	1830	Chanceford	–
,	Michael	1838	"	–
,	Philip	1792	Windsor	–
,	Valentine	1773	?	–
Smeltzmoyer,	Henry	1849	York	–
Smeych,	Simon	1849	Chanceford	–
Smich,	Philip	1815	Manheim	(Smick)
,	Mary (Polly)	1826	Heidelberg	–
,	Mary	1822	"	–
Smiley,	Joseph	1767	Manheim	(Smilie)

-Smith-

131

File	Name	Date	Twp.	Misc. Info.
Smith,	Abraham	1822	Washington	–
,	Adam	1830	Shrewsbury	–
,	Adam	1845	Codorus	–
,	Alexander	1764	?	–
,	Alexander	1804	Chanceford	–
,	Andrew	1826	Manchester	–
,	Andrew	1812	"	–
,	Andrew	1834	"	–
,	Anna Maria	1755	?	–
,	Anna Mary	1837	Paradise	filed w/Geo.
		1837		vendue
,	Arthur	1809	Hopewell	–
,	Baltzer	1802	Warrington	–
,	Barbara	1798	York Boro	–
,	Barbara	1826	Manchester	–
,	Barnet	1798	"	–
,	Benjamin	1841	Conewago	–
,	Catharine	1815	Codorus	–
,	Charles	1801	Manheim	–
,	Charles	1825	Chanceford	–
,	Christian	1808	Windsor	–
,	Christian	1820	Chanceford	–
,	Christina	1828	York	–
Smith,	Daniel	1837	Windsor	–
		1837		vendue
,	Elizabeth	1844	Washington	–
,	Emanuel	1821	"	–
,	George	1820	Chanceford	–
,	George	1844	Codorus	–
		1824	Paradise	h/o Anna
,	George	1812	York	–
,	George	1806	Codorus	–
,	George	1836	Washington	–
,	Henry	1771	Hellam	–
,	Henry	1817	Washington	–
,	Henry	1779	Dover	–
,	Jacob	1824	Conewago	–
,	Jacob	1830	Codorus	–
,	Jacob F.	1833	"	f/o Marian
,	Jacob	1794	Dover	–
,	Jacob	1784	York	–
,	Jacob	1773	Dover	–
,	Jacob	1828	Washington	–
,	Jacob	1834	York Boro	–
,	Jacob	1817	Bottstown	–
,	James S.	1841	Chanceford	–
,	James	1795	Fawn	–
,	James	1770	Manallen*	–
,	James H.	1848	Lw. Chanceford	–
,	James	1807	York Boro	Esq.
,	Jeremiah	1842	Springfield	–
,	John	1843	Lewisbury Boro	–

132

File Name		Date	Twp.	Misc. Info.
Smith,	John Sr.	1845	Manchester	-
,	John	1849	Wrgvlle. Boro	-
,	John	1777	Manallen*	German
,	John	1835	Hopewell	vendue
,	John	1803	Codorus	German
,	John L.	1834	"	-
		1834		vendue
,	John	1788	Hopewell	-
,	John	1832	(York Co.)	-
,	John Sr.	1758	Manchester	-
,	John	1836	Codorus	-
		1836		2 vendues
,	John	1785	Huntington*	-
,	John	1828	Chanceford	-
,	John	1831	Washington	-
,	John S.	1832	Carroll	-
,	John	1834	Hopewell	Esq.
,	John	1835	York Boro	(Schmidt)
,	John	1783	?	-
,	John	1786	Warrington	-
,	John	1792	Berwick*	Captain
,	Joseph	1847	Lw. Chanceford	-
,	Joseph	1784	Yorktowne	-
Smith,	Joseph	1835	Washington	-
		1836		vendue
,	Killyan	1763	Manchester	-
,	Lewis	1831	York Boro	-
,	Magdalena	1838	Manheim	-
,	Margaret	1778	?	-
,	Margaret	1801	?	-
,	Michael	1808	Dover	-
,	Peter	1812	Washington	-
,	Peter	1825	Manchester	-
,	Peter	1786	Shrewsbury	-
,	Philip	1822	York	-
,	Rebecca	1818	Washington	-
,	Richard	1821	Hopewell	-
,	Robert	1789	Hamilton Ban*	-
,	Robert	1823	Chanceford	-
,	Ruth	1831	Spr. Garden	-
,	Samuel	1823	"	-
,	Samuel	1832	York	-
,	Samuel	1844	Franklin	-
,	Samuel	1846	Paradise	-
,	Samuel	1846	Lw. Chanceford	-
,	Steven	1761	?	-
,	Susannah	1845	Manchester	-
,	Thomas	1773	Newberry	-
,	Thomas	1751	"	-
,	Valentine	1798	Dover	-
,	William	1813	Manheim	-
,	William	1777	Huntington*	-

File Name		Date	Twp.	Misc. Info.
Smith,	William	1796	Cumberland*	-
,	William	1810	Hopewell	Esq.
,	William	1847	Chanceford	Doctor
,	William	1825	Hopewell	-
,	William	1822	Dover	-
,	William	1841	Chanceford	-
,	William	1836	York Boro	-
		1836		vendue
,	William	1820	Dover	-
Smuck,	Catharine	1803	Windsor	-
,	Elizabeth	1800	York Boro	-
,	George	1804	"	-
,	Jacob	1789	Windsor	-
,	John	1782	"	-
,	Joseph	1829	Hanover Boro	-
,	Peter	1798	York Boro	-
Smyser,	Anna Maria	1826	W. Manchester	-
,	Barbara	1841	"	-
,	Elizabeth	1841	Hanover Boro	-
,	Elizabeth	1849	York Boro	-
,	Israel	1848	"	-
,	Jacob	1841	(Wayne Co.)	Ohio
,	Jacob	1850	York Boro	-
,	Jacob	1794	Manchester	-
,	Jacob	1834	"	-
,	John	1842	Springfield	-
,	Martin	1807	York Boro	-
,	Matthias	1778	Manchester	-
,	Matthias	1843	York Boro	-
,	Matthias	1829	W. Manchester	-
,	Michael Sr.	1845	"	Tavern
,	Michael	1826	Bottstown	-
Sneidman,	Daniel	1790	Hellam	-
,	Sebastian	1787	"	-
Snell,	Catherine	1797	Dover	-
,	Christian	1833	Fairview	-
,	Michael	1849	"	-
Snellbaker,	George	1833	Dover	-
,	Jacob	1781	"	-
Snerr,	Casper	1790	Manallen*	-
Snodgrass,	James	1793	Franklin*	-
Snyder,	Adam	1782	Manallen*	-
,	Barbara	1829	Hellam	-
,	Christian	1839	Manchester	-
,	Conrad	1807	Fairview	-
,	Conrad	1801	Manchester	-
,	Dewalt	1821	Codorus	-
,	Elizabeth	1805	(York Co.)	-
,	Elizabeth	1837	Hanover Boro	filed w/Jb
		1837		vendue
,	George	1829	Conewago	-
,	George	1805	York Boro	-

File Name		Date	Twp.	Misc. Info.
Snyder,	Henry	1806	Manheim	-
,	Jacob	1840	Peach Bottom	-
,	Jacob	1819	Hanover Boro	h/o Eliz.
,	Jacob	1821	Shrewsbury	-
,	Jacob	1817	Manchester	-
,	John	1826	Hopewell	-
,	Lorentz	1806	Monaghan	-
		1806		2nd inv.
,	Margaret	1840	Codorus	-
,	Martin	1813	Manheim	-
,	Michael	1837	Peach Bottom	-
,	Philip	1802	Manchester	-
,	Siegfried	1833	W. Manchester	-
,	Theobald	1776	Manheim	-
,	Zigfried	1765	Germany*	-
Sohn,	George	1761	Yorktowne	-
Soll,	Henry	1749	?	(Coll)
Sollenberg,	Samuel	1820	Windsor	-
Sollt,	Philippina	1802	Chanceford	-
Sonday,	Henry	1843	Heidelberg	-
Souder,	Christian	1829	Hopewell	-
,	Rudolph	1848	"	-
Souerman,	Peter	1754	?	German
Sowden,	James	1756	?	-
Sower,	Adam	1782	Berwick*	-
,	Casper	1843	York Boro	-
Sowers,	Jacob	1841	Washington	-
Spahr,	Dorothy	1822	Warrington	-
,	Elijah	1849	Dover	-
,	George	1830	"	-
,	Johan Michael	1804	Washington	-
,	John	1806	Dover	-
,	John	1846	Washington	-
,	Michael	1778	Dover	-
,	Moses	1840	"	-
,	Peter	1841	Carroll	-
,	Peter	1846	Warrington	-
,	Philip Adam	1806	Dover	German
,	Philip	1802	"	"
,	William	1840	"	-
Spangler,	Adam	1825	Monaghan	-
,	Anna Mary	1844	York Boro	-
,	Baltzer	1770	"	-
		1801	"	?
,	Bernhard	1804	Paradise	-
,	Bernhart	1828	Manchester	-
,	Casper	1807	York Boro	-
,	Catharine	1850	Paradise	-
,	Charles	1832	York Boro	-
,	Christian	1821	Yorktowne	-
,	Daniel	1780	Paradise	-
,	Daniel	1850		-

File Name		Date	Twp.	Misc. Info.
Spangler,	Daniel	1813	York Boro	-
,	Dorothy	1835	"	-
		1835		vendue
,	Emanuel	1846	Wrgvlle. Boro	-
,	Eva	1819	Paradise	-
,	Ferdinand	1836	York Boro	-
		1837		2 vendues
,	George	1754	Manchester	-
,	George	1797	York	-
,	George	1832	York Boro	-
,	George	1810	York	-
,	George M.	1827	York Boro	-
,	George M.	1823	Paradise	-
,	Henry	1791	"	-
,	Henry	1776	York	-
,	Henry	1826	Paradise	-
,	Jacob	1842	York Boro	Esq.
,	Jacob Sr.	1847	Paradise	-
,	John	1820	Warrington	-
,	John	1850	"	-
,	John	1796	York	-
,	John	1831	York Boro	Doctor
,	Jonas	1836	Springfield	vendue
,	Jonas	1821	Yorktowne	-
,	Jonas	1762	?	-
,	Joseph	1802	Dover	-
,	Margaret S.	1813	York Boro	-
,	Margaret	1804	"	-
,	Margaret	1845	"	-
,	Mary Magdal.	1784	York	w/o Baltzer
,	McConolless	1850	York Boro	-
,	Michael H.	1834	"	-
,	Michael	1834	Paradise	-
,	Peter	1792	Tyrone*	-
,	Peter	1823	York Boro	Esq.
,	Philip Casper	1782	York	-
,	Rebecca	1848	Paradise	-
,	Rosina	1767	Manchester	-
,	Rudolph	1763	York	-
,	Rudolph	1816	"	-
,	Rudolph	1834	York Boro	-
,	Rudolph	1784	Paradise	-
,	Samuel	1839	Springfield	-
,	Sarah	1839	York Boro	-
,	Sophia	1844	"	-
,	Susannah	1781	York	w/o Henry
,	Susannah	1809	"	single
Speck,	Martin	1849	Washington	-
Speer,	James	1823	Chanceford	-
,	James	1826	Hellam	-
Spence,	George	1797	Newberry	-
,	Isaac	1819	Fairview	filed Henry

File Name		Date	Twp.	Misc. Info.
Spence,	Isaac	1825	Fairview	Esq.
,	Jane	1788	Cumberland*	single
		1798		vendue
,	John	1833	Fairview	-
Spencer,	William	1779	Manallen*	-
Spessert,	Michael	1815	Shrewsbury	-
Spices,	Christopher	1821	Paradise	-
,	Ludwig	1780	Dover	Montg. Co. Md.
Spickert,	Henry	1769	Hellam	-
Spiese,	Peter	1785	Dover	-
Spiess,	George W.	1820	Hanover Boro	-
Spitzer,	Conrad	1812	Fairview	-
Sponseller,	Abraham	1797	Cumberland*	-
,	George Sr.	1778	?	-
Spotz,	Frederick	1828	York	-
,	Jacob	1799	Chanceford	-
Sprenkle,	Ann Maria	1825	York	-
		1825		vendue
,	Frederick	1817	York	-
,	George	1828	Codorus	-
,	George Sr.	1805	W. Manchester	-
,	Hannah	1824	"	-
,	Peter	1789	Manchester	-
,	Peter	1813	York	-
,	Peter	1831	Codorus	-
,	W. Daniel	1849	W. Manchester	-
		1849		2nd inv.
,	William	1826	Windsor	-
		1826		vendue
,	William	1772	York	-
Spring,	Justina	1774	?	-
Springer,	Ann	1789	York Boro	-
,	George	1762	Windsor	-
,	Jacob	1830	Fairview	-
Sprogle,	Joanna C.	1791	York Boro	-
,	Michael	1755	?	-
Sprout,	Samuel	1791	Chanceford	-
Spyker,	James	1850	Hellam	-
Squibb,	Eli	1828	Washington	-
,	Joanna	1828	"	-
,	Robert	1823	Warrington	-
,	William	1826	Washington	Esq.
,	William	1832	Newberry	-
Staab,	Adam	1773	Mt. Pleasant*	-
,	Catharina	1785	Heidelberg	-
,	Mathias	1770	?	-
Stabler,	Christian	1784	Shrewsbury	-
,	Jacob	1837	Hopewell	-
		1837		vendue
,	Jane	1850	Shrewsbury	-
Stabley,	Adam	1792	"	German
,	John	1829	Fairview	-

137

File Name		Date	Twp.	Misc. Info.
Stacy,	William	1802	York Boro	–
Staeble,	George	1809	Shrewsbury	–
Stagner,	Jacob	1803	Fairview	–
,	Nicholas	1764	Windsor	–
Stahl,	Henry	1777	Manheim	–
,	Henry	1808	"	–
Staiger,	Conrad	1760	?	–
Stair,	Jacob	1850	York Boro	–
,	Philip	1854	"	–
Stake,	Catharina	1812	"	–
,	George	1789	Yorktowne	Esq.
,	Jacob	1801	Hellam	–
Staley,	Andrew	1794	Chanceford	–
,	Jacob	1772	"	–
,	Jacob	1775	Germany*	–
,	Jacob	1796	"	–
,	Melchoir	1786	Newberry	–
,	Peter	1777	Chanceford	–
Stambaugh,	Henry	1833	Codorus	–
,	Henry	1841	Paradise	–
,	Jacob	1842	"	–
,	Jacob Sr.	1848	Codorus	–
,	Jacob	1826	Paradise	–
,	Jacob	1814	Manheim	German
,	John	1824	Paradise	–
,	Michael	1835	Codorus	–
		1835		vendue
,	Michael	1826	Paradise	–
,	Michael	1803	Codorus	German
,	Nicholas	1759	?	–
,	Philip	1811	Codorus	–
,	Philip	1800	"	–
Stammers,	John Sr.	1791	Hamilton Ban*	army Pvt.
,	John	1795	"	–
Stark,	John	1825	Hanover Boro	–
Starr,	Ezya	1823	Dover	–
,	John	1803	Fairview	–
,	Samuel	1843	"	–
Staub,	Adam	1826	York Boro	–
,	John	1834	"	–
Stauch,	John	1844	Dover	–
Stauffer,	Abraham	1785	Monaghan	–
,	Christian	1812	Manheim	–
,	Christian	1835	Spr. Garden	–
		1835		vendue
,	Daniel	1818	Hellam	–
,	George	1813	Heidelberg	–
,	Henry	1827	Hellam	–
,	John	1803	Chanceford	–
,	John	1840	Franklin	–
,	John	1821	"	–
,	John	1807	Paradise	–

File Name	Date	Twp.	Misc. Info.
Stauffer, Peter	1795	Newberry	-
Staugh, George	1844	Dover	-
Stauler, John	1823	Hanover Boro	-
Steahr, Jacob	1840	Conewago	-
Stedham, Christopher	1756	?	-
Steel, James	1805	Hopewell	-
, John	1781	Hamilton Ban*	-
, Thomas	1816	Peach Bottom	-
Steffe, George	1824	Manheim	-
Steffee, Catharine	1841	"	-
Steffie, Peter	1832	Codorus	-
	1836		vendue
Steiner, Jacob	1823	W. Manchester	-
Steinfeld, Henry	1840	York	-
Steinfort, John	1847	Shrewsbury	-
Steng, Frederick	1754	?	-
Stentz, Henerich	1758	Hellam	German
, Jacob	1784	"	-
Steohr, Henry	1821	Conewago	-
Stephen, Anna Maria	1824	Windsor	filed w/Henry
, Henry	1812	"	h/o Anna
, Peter	1776	Manheim	-
	1800	"	?
Stermer, Eve	1839	Shrewsbury	-
, George	1810	"	-
, John George	1777	Strasbg. twn.	-
, Michael	1844	Chanceford	-
Sterner, Barnet Sr.	1808	Manheim	-
Stetler, Jacob	1804	Hellam	(Stadtler)
, Samuel	1823	Fairview	-
Stevenson, Robert	1779	Warrington	-
Steward, Asahel	1826	Peach Bottom	-
, George	1798	Hopewell	-
Stewart, Elizabeth	1812	York Boro	-
, Jacob	1850	Fairview	-
, James H.	1850	Lw. Chanceford	-
, James	1787	Hamilton Ban*	-
, James	1791	"	-
, James	1829	Lw. Chanceford	-
, John	1778	Hamilton Ban*	-
, John	1770	Cumberland*	-
, John	1780	York	-
, John	1826	Chanceford	-
, John	1820	Lw. Chanceford	-
, John	1809	York Boro	-
, Patrick	1825	Hopewell	-
, Robert	1793	Chanceford	-
, Robert	1784	Manallen*	-
, William	1771	Cumberland*	-
, William	1849	Lw. Chanceford	-
, William	1787	Mt. Joy*	-
Stick, Casper	1817	Manheim	-

File Name		Date	Twp.	Misc. Info.
Stickel,	Christopher	1797	Warrington	-
,	Peter	1848	Fairview	-
Stickler,	Jacob	1796	Warrington	-
Stiegel,	Jacob	1779	"	-
Stiegelman,	Peter	1845	Fairview	-
Stiffler,	Elizabeth	1821	Heidelberg	-
Stillinger,	Charles	1832	York Boro	-
,	Richard	1783	Yorktowne	-
Stillwell,	Jeremiah	1751	?	-
Stine,	Abraham	1800	Newberry	-
,	Frederick	1815	"	-
,	Frederick	1816	York Boro	-
,	Frederick	1827	Shrewsbury	-
,	Jacob	1803	"	(Stein)
Stockton,	Joseph	1784	Straban*	-
Stoeher,	John Sr.	1815	?	-
Stoehr,	Christopher	1833	York Boro	-
Stom,	Henry	1760	?	-
Stoner,	Abraham	1799	Hellam	German
,	Christian	1786	"	-
,	Christian	1833	"	-
,	Christian	1831	"	-
,	George Jr.	1845	Newberry	-
,	Isaac	1791	Manchester	-
,	John	1825	Hellam	-
Stouffer,	Christian	1839	Chanceford	-
,	Christina	1809	Franklin	-
,	Jacob	1824	Dover	-
,	Jacob	1840	Paradise	-
,	Mary	1835	Franklin	-
		1835		vendue
,	Susannah	1847	Heidelberg	-
Stough,	Anna Barbara	1824	Dover	filed w/Geo.
,	David	1839	"	-
,	Frederick	1835	"	-
,	George	1803	Dover	h/o Anna B.
,	George	1841	York Boro	-
,	Godfrey	1793	Dover	-
,	Godfrey	1810	"	-
,	Jacob	1831	"	-
,	John	1805	"	-
Stover,	Christian	1843	Heidelberg	-
,	Frederick	1796	Paradise	German
,	George	1806	"	"
,	Henry	1850	Conewago	-
,	Isaac	1846	Paradise	-
,	Michael	1781	"	-
,	Michael Sr.	1847	"	-
,	Michael Jr.	1846	"	-
,	Nicholas	1810	Dover	-
Strain,	John	1774	Fawn	Rev.
Strale,	Jacob	1830	Dover	-

File Name		Date	Twp.	Misc. Info.
Straley,	Andrew	1767	Reading*	-
Strang,	Adam	1834	Hellam	-
Strasbaugh,	Catharina	1835	Paradise	-
		1835		vendue
,	Conrad	1797	York Boro	-
,	Elizabeth	1841	Paradise	-
,	John	1846	N. Codorus	-
,	Michael	1794	Paradise	h/o Cath/Ger
,	Nicholas	1753	?	-
		1753		vendue
Strausbach,	Peter	1822	Heidelberg	-
Strawbridge,	James	1839	Fawn	-
Strayer,	Adam	1775	?	-
,	Adam	1849	Hopewell	-
,	Jacobina	1823	Dover	-
,	John	1832	"	-
,	Mathias	1767	?	-
,	Nicholas	1836	Hopewell	-
		1836		vendue
,	Peter	1817	Hopewell	-
,	Peter	1794	Dover	-
Strealy,	Stephen	1824	"	-
Streber,	Peter	1814	York	-
Strebig,	Catharine	1809	"	German
,	Michael	1842	Hellam	-
Streibig,	George	1822	York	-
Stretch,	Richard	1845	Washington	-
Strickhouser,	Barbara	1844	Codorus	-
,	Catharine	1844	"	-
,	Elizabeth	1839	N. Codorus	-
,	Henry	1837	Codorus	-
		1837		vendue
,	Jacob	1830	Codorus	-
,	John	1777	"	-
,	John	1822	"	-
,	Peter	1827	"	-
Strickland,	Amos	1828	Manchester	-
,	Joseph	1832	Newberry	-
,	Samuel	1825	Manchester	-
Stricklen,	Christian	1841	Spr. Garden	-
Strickler,	Anna	1848	Hellam	-
,	Christina	1798	"	w/o Conrad/Ger
,	Conrad	1793	"	-
,	Henry	1835	Spr. Garden	-
,	Henry Sr.	1793	Hellam	-
		1824	"	?
,	Jacob	1774	York	-
,	Jacob Sr.	1837	Hellam	-
,	Jacob	1802	"	German
,	John	1810	"	"
,	John	1817	York	-
		1821	"	2nd inv.

File Name	Date	Twp.	Misc. Info.
Strickler, John	1777	Windsor	-
, John	1850	Spr. Garden	-
, John	1836	Hellam	-
	1837		vendue
, John	1777	Hellam	-
, Ulrich	1749	"	-
Strine, George	1796	Newberry	-
, Johan Adam	1787	Manallen*	-
, Peter	1834	Conewago	-
	1836		vendue
Strohmenger, Jacob	1786	Windsor	-
Stroman, Eve	1850	York Boro	-
, John	1843	"	-
, John Jr.	1817	"	Esq.
Stromans, John	1764	Yorktowne	(Stowman)
Strome, Emanuel	1842	Lw. Chanceford	-
Strominger, Jacob	1849	Newberry	-
, Michael	1837	Fairview	-
	1837		vendue
, Rachael	1849	Fairview	-
Strong, James	1804	Windsor	-
Stuart, Charles	1828	Fairview	-
Stuck, Conrad	1770	Codorus	-
, Jacob	1829	York Boro	-
, Martin	1783	York	-
, Peter	1807	Codorus	German
, Peter	1817	"	"
Stuckslager, Albertus	1777	Cumberland*	-
Studebaker, Clement	1762	?	-
Studebecker, Clemon	1840	Paradise	-
, Rebecca	1838	"	-
Stump, Adam	1835	York	-
	1835		vendue
, Matthias	1784	Paradise	-
, Peter	1791	Manheim	German
Styer, Henry	1834	"	-
, Tobias	1772	"	-
Suchrist, Veronica	1841	Shrewsbury	-
Sullivan, Timothy	1785	?	-
Sultzbach, Magdalena	1797	Hellam	child
, Margaret	1833	"	w/o Philip
, Philip	1784	"	-
Sultzberger, Anna B.	1789	York Boro	-
, Jacob	1784	Yorktowne	-
Sumberland, John	1775	Berwick*	-
Summe, John	1775	?	-
Summer, Eve	1792	?	w/o John
, John	1773	Manheim	-
Sunday, Christina	1798	Paradise	filed w/Jac.
, Jacob	1825	Paradise	-
, Jacob	1788	"	h/o Christ.
, Joseph	1844	"	-

File Name		Date	Twp.	Misc. Info.
Sutor,	George	1794	Fawn	-
,	William	1771	"	-
Swaab,	Adam	1809	Hellam	German
,	Margaret	1809	Windsor	-
Swan,	Robert	1798	"	-
,	Robert	1800	Chanceford	-
Swartz,	Abraham	1806	Shrewsbury	German
,	Andrew	1789	"	-
,	Andrew	1804	"	-
,	Andrew	1777	Yorktowne	-
,	Anna Mary	1821	Shrewsbury	-
,	Charles	1804	Hanover	-
,	Christian	1795	Paradise	-
,	Conrad	1831	Shrewsbury	-
,	Daniel	1846	"	-
,	Elizabeth	1833	"	-
,	George	1789	"	-
,	George	1817	York	(Shwartz)
,	Henry Sr.	1844	Springfield	-
,	Henry	1819	Manheim	-
,	Henry	1799	Shrewsbury	-
,	Jacob	1804	"	-
,	John Sr.	1845	York Boro	-
,	Ludwig	1843	Paradise	-
,	Mary	1847	York Boro	-
,	Michael	1786	Newberry	-
Swartzbaugh,	Adam	1792	Codorus	-
Swartzfelter,	Elizabeth	1845	York Boro	-
Sweeny,	James	1820	Lw. Chanceford	-
,	John	1820	"	-
,	Mary	1813	Hopewell	-
Sweigart,	George	1808	Chanceford	-
,	Hanna	1839	Washington	-
,	Jacob	1820	Chanceford	-
Sweney,	Isaac	1780	Cumberland*	-
,	James	1809	Shrewsbury	-
Swinehard,	George	1846	Fairview	-
Swing,	Michael	1782	Yorktowne	-
Swope,	Anna	1767	Paradise	-
,	Conrad	1799	Hanover Boro	-
,	George	1755	?	-
,	John	1844	Hanover Boro	-
Sykes,	Henry H.	1849	York Boro	-

−T−

Talbot,	Moore	1796	Cumberland*	(Torbet)
Tarbert,	Andrew	1837	Fawn	-
,	Robert	1832	"	-
,	William	1839	Hopewell	-

File Name	Date	Twp.	Misc. Info.
Tarney, Andrew	1819	Chanceford	-
Tate, Archibald	1794	Cumberland*	-
, Isaac	1799	Straban*	-
, Jermiah	1799	Newberry	-
, Jacob	1798	"	-
, John	1834	Chanceford	-
, Solomon	1815	Fairview	-
, Susanna	1830	Monaghan	-
Tawney, John	1795	Straban*	(Taney)
Taylor, Benjamin	1752	York	-
, Catherine	1834	York Boro	-
, George	1763	?	-
	1769	Fawn	?
, John	1752	?	-
	1750	?	?
, John	1834	Newberry	-
, John	1823	Fairview	-
, Joseph	1813	Warrington	-
, Joseph	1816	Newberry	-
, Phebe	1844	"	-
, Philip	1815	Hopewell	-
, Robert	1762	Fawn	-
, Samuel	1762	?	-
, Susanna	1825	York	-
, Thomas	1779	?	-
, Thomas	1840	York Boro	-
Teaffe, Michael	1772	?	-
Teatery, William	1770	Mt. Joy*	-
Teitsch, Philip	1789	York Boro	(Deitch)
	1792	?	?
Templeton, James	1829	Fawn	-
Test, George	1795	York Boro	-
Theaker, John	1810	Fawn	-
, Samuel	1823	?	-
Thoman, Benedict	1771	Codorus	(Thomin)
, Jacob	1805	Manheim	(Thomen)
, John	1829	Codorus	names Jacob
Thomas, Abraham	1832	Heidelberg	-
, James	1813	Warrington	-
, James	1830	"	-
, John	1771	"	-
, John	1808	Hanover Boro	-
, Nathan	1822	Newberry	Blacksmith
, William	1839	Carroll	-
	1839		2nd inv.
Thompson, Alexander	1766	Cumberland*	-
, Andrew	1759	Mt. Pleasant*	-
, Andrew	1768	?	-
, Archibald	1764	?	-
, Archibald	1850	Chanceford	-
, James	1784	Hopewell	-
, James	1847	W. Manchester	-

144

File Name		Date	Twp.	Misc. Info.
Thompson,	John	1774	?	-
,	John	1793	Hamilton Ban*	-
,	John	1794	Huntington*	Teacher
,	John	1842	Fairview	-
,	Jonathan	1762	?	-
,	Joseph	1816	Chanceford	-
,	Mary	1822	York Boro	-
,	William	1790	Cumberland*	-
,	William	1797	Straban*	-
,	William	1794	Windsor	Teacher
,	William	1750	?	-
Thorley,	Abraham	1823	Fairview	(Tholey)
,	Florenda	1846	"	-
,	George	1787	Newberry	(Thorly)
,	George	1803	Fairview	-
,	George	1798	Newberry	-
,	Joseph	1808	?	-
,	Thomas	1828	Fairview	-
,	William	1795	Newberry	-
Thornburgh,	Robert	1817	Fairview	-
		1817	Newberry	?
Thron,	Abraham	1820	Heidelberg	(Throne)
,	Abraham	1801	Manheim	-
Throne,	Catharine	1837	Heidelberg	-
		1838		vendue
,	George	1836	Heidelberg	-
		1836		vendue
,	George	1778	?	(Trone)
,	John	1789	Manheim	(Thron)
,	John	1847	Hanover Boro	Cordwainer
,	John	1847	"	-
,	Magdalen	1811	Manheim	filed as John
,	Samuel	1816	Heidelberg	-
Tilden,	Susanna	1842	Manchester	-
,	Ulysses	1835	"	-
Todd,	James	1767	Newberry	(Tod)
,	James	1827	"	Esq.
,	Joseph	1793	"	-
,	Robert	1767	Huntington*	-
,	William	1810	York Boro	Doctor
Tome,	Benedict	1806	York	-
,	Christian	1826	Chanceford	-
		1837	York	vendue?
,	John	1823	Chanceford	(Tomb)
Tomlinson,	Charles	1838	York Boro	-
Tompkins,	Benjamin	1799	Fawn	-
,	John Jr.	1824	"	-
,	John	1813	"	-
Tompson,	Alexander	1843	Hopewell	(Thompson)
Toner,	Neal	1755	Chanceford	-
Toomey,	Thomas	1815	Dover	-
Torbet,	Allen	1806	Monaghan	-

145

File Name	Date	Twp.	Misc. Info.
Torrence, Aaron	1769	?	-
, David	1750	?	poor cond.
, William	1751	Shrewsbury	-
Towele, Ambers	1754	?	-
Townshend, George	1799	?	-
Townsley, John	1791	Mt. Joy*	-
Traup, Paul	1787	Reading*	-
, Peter	1806	Washington	-
Treiber, Ludwick	1772	Manchester	-
, Michael	1808	"	German
Treichler, Barbara	1839	Hellam	(Treighler)
, John	1756	?	-
Treighler, Dorthea	1810	York	-
, John	1799	"	-
, Martin	1801	Paradise	German
Trimmer, Andrew Sr.	1795	Reading*	-
, Anna	1826	Dover	-
, Barnet	1848	Paradise	-
, John	1832	"	-
, Peter	1790	Reading*	-
, William	1844	Paradise	-
	1841	"	?
Trine, George	1847	Dover	-
, Peter	1821	"	German
Tristler, George David	1796	?	-
Trone, Jacob	1837	Manheim	-
	1837		vendue
Trostle, Abraham	1819	York Boro	-
, Susanna	1826	"	-
Trout, Elizabeth	1825	Hopewell	(Traut)
, George	1848	Shrewsbury	-
, Wendell	1820	Hopewell	-
Troutwine, Christian	1831	Manheim	-
, Nicholas	1799	Chanceford	-
Trump, John	1796	Paradise	-
, Peter	1804	"	-
Tschopp, Henry	1847	Windsor	-
Tschudy, Nicholas	1821	Hanover Boro	-
Tucker, John	1750	?	-
Tull, Conrad	1766	?	(Dull)
Turk, Ephraim	1839	Lw. Chanceford	-
Turner, David	1751	?	-
, John	1839	Chanceford	-
, William	1766	Straban*	-
Twigs, John	1804	Hopewell	-
Tyson, Elizabeth	1850	Windsor	-
, Hannah	1839	"	-
	1839		vendue
, Isaac	1817	Hellam	-
, Jacob	1822	Windsor	-
, John	1846	Springfield	-
, Sarah	1820	Windsor	-

-U-

Uhland, Michael	1812	Codorus	-
Uhler, Adam	1770	Manchester	-
, Deter	1765	"	-
Ulrich, Michael	1774	?	-
, Nicholas	1819	Windsor	-
Underwood, Alexander	1768	Warrington	-
, Ann	1815	Washington	-
, Benjamin	1803	Warrington	-
, Elihu	1801	"	-
, Elihu	1803	"	-
, Jacob	1784	"	-
, John	1776	"	-
, John	1809	Washington	-
, Joseph	1842	Dillsbg. Boro	-
, Nehemiah	1810	Fawn	-
, William	1785	Warrington	-
Ungefehr, George	1764	Heidelberg	(Unkafare)
Unger, Baltzer	1783	Manheim	-
Unky, John	1759	?	-
Updegraff, Abraham	1781	Dover	-
, Benjamin	1847	York Boro	-
, Harmon	1758	?	-
, Herman	1806	Monaghan	-
, Jacob	1787	Yorktowne	-
, Jacob	1845	Newberry	-
, Joseph	1819	York Boro	-
, Joseph	1802	"	-
, Mary	1803	"	-
, Samuel	1790	"	-
Upp, Catharine	1828	W. Manchester	-
, Jacob	1835	York Boro	-
Urey, Anthony	1779	Warrington	-
, Barbara	1844	Lw. Chanceford	-
, George	1826	"	-
	1844	"	?
, William	1842	Chanceford	-
Urich, John	1842	Warrington	-
, John	1848	Dover	-
, Margaret	1833	"	-
, Michael	1814	Washington	-
, Michael	1826	York Boro	(Eurish)
, William	1841	Dover	-
Usher, Dorothy	1837	(New York) Saratogo Co.
Utz, Adam	1844	Manheim	-
, Daniel	1818	Heidelberg	-
, George	1849	Manheim	-
, Jesse J.	1849	Codorus	Doctor

File Name	Date	Twp.	Misc. Info.

—V—

File Name	Date	Twp.	Misc. Info.
Vale, John	1821	Warrington	–
, Joshua	1831	Washington	–
, Peter	1834	"	–
, Robert	1799	Warrington	–
, Robert	1817	"	–
, Robert	1823	"	–
, William	1838	"	–
	1838		vendue
Valentine, Michael	1761	?	–
Vanarnsdale, Simon	1788	Straban*	–
Vanasdak, Cornelius	1787	"	–
Vanasdale, David	1815	Warrington	–
, David	1835	Franklin	–
	1836		vendue
, Garret	1784	?	–
, Isaac	1772	Berwick*	–
, John	1772	"	–
, Simon	1783	?	illegible
Vance, Adam	1777	Cumberland*	–
, Ezakiel	1768	Manallen*	–
, John	1773	?	–
Vanderbilt, Ida	1799	Straban*	–
, William	1769	?	–
Vandersloot, Frederick	1831	Paradise	Rev.
Vandyne, David	1795	?	–
Vangundy, Peter	1820	?	Bonds only
Vansant, William W.	1850	Fawn	–
Vanscyoc, Aaron	1772	Huntington*	–
, Rebecca	1773	?	–
Vaught, Susanna	1833	Windsor	–
Venus, Elizabeth	1823	Hopewell	(Venis)
, Frederick	1820	"	–
, Henry	1829	"	(Venis)
, John	1827	Shrewsbury	–
, Philip	1777	?	–
Vernon, Aaron	1799	Newberry	–
Vernum, Johannes	1780	Codorus	–
Versh, Christopher	1814	Hellam	–
Vickers, Daniel	1824	Newberry	–
Voght, Daniel	1830	Hellam	(Focht)
Voglesong, Daniel	1848	York Boro	–
Von Beoman, Charles A.	1847	Lw. Windsor	–

—W—

File Name	Date	Twp.	Misc. Info.
Wadsworth, Frederick M.	1830	York Boro	Esq.

File Name		Date	Twp.	Misc. Info.
Wagner,	Anna Maria	1837	York Boro	(Wagoner)
,	Barbara	1800	"	"
,	Casper	1830	Paradise	-
,	Conrad	1793	?	-
		1793		vendue
,	Daniel	1811	(Fred. Co.)	Md./Rev.
,	Daniel	1837	York Boro	-
		1838		vendue
,	George	1772	Reading*	-
,	George	1830	Dover	-
,	Jacob	1791	Manchester	(Waggoner)
,	Jacob	1813	Monaghan	-
,	John	1836	Spr. Garden	-
,	Jost	1786	Manheim	-
,	Philip	1778	Windsor	German
,	Philip	1835	York Boro	(Wagoner)
Wagoner,	Daniel	1847	Paradise	-
Wahly,	Adam	1802	Warrington	(Wahle)
,	Catherine	1802	Newberry	"
Walck,	Mary	1823	Chanceford	-
Waldenberger,	Daniel	1799	Manchester	German
Walgamuth,	Rebecca	1842	Warrington	-
Walker,	Abel	1817	"	-
,	Ann	1823	"	filed in 1832?
,	Benjamin	1822	"	-
,	John	1814	Hopewell	-
,	Joseph	1788	Tyrone*	-
,	William	1825	Peach Bottom	-
Wall,	Mary	1845	Carroll	-
,	William	1839	"	-
Wallace,	Aaron	1765	Chanceford	-
,	Agnes	1772	Hopewell	-
,	Alexander	1767	Shrewsbury	-
,	Alexander	1842	Hopewell	-
		1843		
,	Ann	1842	Hopewell	-
,	Daniel	1752	?	-
,	David	1831	Hopewell	-
,	James	1778	"	-
,	James	1777	?	-
,	John	1783	?	-
,	Mary	1832	Hopewell	-
		1782	?	?
,	Mathew	1831	Lw. Chanceford	-
,	William	1756	Chanceford	-
Wallick,	John	1835	Windsor	-
Waltemeyer,	Charles	1834	Hopewell	-
,	Christian	1843	"	-
,	David	1790	Huntington*	-
,	Ludwig	1782	Yorktowne	-
,	Philip	1829	York Boro	-
Walter,	Andreas	1779	Dover	-

File Name	Date	Twp.	Misc. Info.
Walter, Elizabeth	1794	York Boro	German
, George	1829	Codorus	-
, Henry	1781	"	-
, Henry	1792	York Boro	large inv.
, Jacob	1784	Codorus	-
, Joseph	1775	Yorktowne	-
, Paul	1754	"	(Walther)
Waltimeyer, David	1844	Hopewell	-
, Magdalena	1850	"	-
Waltman, John	1785	Hanover Boro	-
, Lewis	1822	Chanceford	-
Wambaugh, George	1809	Windsor	-
, George	1804	"	-
, Mary	1810	"	-
, Michael	1845	"	-
, Michael	1802	Newberry	-
, Peter	1806	Windsor	-
, Peter	1828	Fawn	-
, Susanna	1849	Fairview	-
Wampler, Henry C.	1836	Hanover Boro	-
, Henry C.	1837	"	Doctor
.	1836		2 vendues
, Jacob	1819	York Boro	-
, John	1822	Manheim	-
, Lewis	1820	York Boro	-
, Ludwig	1772	Yorktowne	-
Wanbaugh, Jacob	1822	Fairview	-
Wantz, Jacob	1821	Heidelberg	-
Warner, Adam	1775	Germany*	-
, Charles	1812	Manheim	-
, Christly	1842	Chanceford	-
, Jacob	1846	Codorus	-
, Samuel	1839	Chanceford	-
	1840		vendue
, William	1821	Manheim	-
, William	1846	Codorus	-
Warren, David	1842	Newberry	-
Warrick, Andrew	1818	Hopewell	-
Watson, Hugh	1768	Straban*	(Wattson)
, James	1836	Fawn	-
	1837		vendue
, John	1754	?	-
, William	1803	Chanceford	-
Watts, Andrew	1831	Newberry	-
, Thomas	1795	Chanceford	-
, William	1848	Newberry	-
Waugh, John	1777	Hamilton Ban*	-
Waughtel, George	1798	Windsor	-
Waughtle, Jacob	1819	"	-
Weal, Peter	1845	Newberry	-
Weatherill, Thomas	1832	Spr. Garden	-
Weaver, Daniel	1845	York Boro	-

File Name		Date	Twp.	Misc. Info.
Weaver,	David	1820	Washington	-
,	Henry	1835	"	vendue
,	Jacob	1821	York Boro	-
,	Melcher	1783	Reading*	-
Webb,	Eleanor	1790	Fawn	-
,	Elizabeth	1796	"	-
,	James	1788	"	-
,	Joseph	1821	Newberry	-
,	Joseph	1845	Peach Bottom	-
,	Joseph	1832	York Boro	-
Weber,	Philip	1807	Yorktowne	-
,	Sebastian	1789	Germany*	-
Wecker,	Baltzer	1773	Yorktowne	h/o Marg.
Weems,	Thomas	1796	Mt. Joy*	-
Wehler,	Frederick	1847	Washington	-
,	Henry	1799	Paradise	(Wheallar)
,	Henry	1827	Washington	-
,	John	1839	Paradise	-
		1839		vendue
Wehr,	George	1800	York Boro	(Where)
Weibling,	George	1831	Codorus	-
Weidler,	Jacob	1814	Shrewsbury	-
Weigel,	George	1842	Conewago	-
,	Henry	1841	Manchester	-
,	Henry	1843	E. Manchester	-
,	Martin	1822	W. Manchester	German
,	Sebastian	1807	"	-
Weigle,	Anna Mary	1847	Manchester	(Weigel)
,	Henry	1812	W. Manchester	-
,	Jacob	1804	Dover	(Weigel)
,	Leonard	1825	W. Manchester	German
,	Magdalena	1836	Manchester	-
		1836		vendue
,	Margaretta	1845	Hanover Boro	-
,	Maria Margaret	1838	Manchester	-
,	Martin	1759	?	(Weikel)
,	Peter	1828	W. Manchester	-
Weikert,	John	1797	Mt. Pleasant*	-
Weimer,	George	1762	Dover?	-
		1762		vendue
,	Jacob	1773	Dover	(Wymer)
,	Jacob	1823	Franklin	-
,	John	1784	Germany*	(Wymer)
Weimert,	Andrew	1819	W. Manchester	-
Wein,	Jacob	1789	Heidelberg	(Wine)
Weirich,	Elizabeth	1843	Hanover Boro	-
,	Michael	1825	"	-
,	Nicholas	1810	"	-
Weiser,	Daniel P.	1849	York Boro	-
,	John Sr.	1847	York	-
,	Martin J.	1829	York Boro	-
,	Martin	1822	"	-

File Name	Date	Twp.	Misc. Info.
Weiser, Samuel	1838	York Boro	-
Weitter, Michael	1781	Yorktowne	-
Weitzel, John	1844	Fairview	-
Welch, William	1767	Windsor	-
, William	1794	Newberry	-
, William	1816	York Boro	-
Welker, George	1827	?	-
, Stronica	1823	Newberry	-
Weller, George	1780	York	-
, Jacob	1845	Spr. Garden	-
, Martin	1788	York	-
Wells, John	1756	?	-
, William	1826	Lw. Chanceford	-
Welsh, Andrew	1759	?	-
, Anna M.	1822	Washington	-
, Barbara	1832	York Boro	-
, Charles	1822	Washington	(Walsh)
, Elizabeth	1832	York Boro	-
, Elizabeth	1796	"	filed w/Jacob
, George	1791	Manchester	-
, Henry	1827	Hanover Boro	-
, Jacob	1773	Yorktowne	h/o Eliz.
, Jacob	1813	Washington	-
, Jacob	1815	Hanover Boro	-
, James	1807	Newberry	-
, James	1770	"	-
, John	1818	York Boro	-
, Julianna Cath.	1838	"	-
, Michael	1805	"	-
, Michael	1832	"	-
, Michael	1789	"	-
, Nicholas	1795	Tyrone*	German
, Susan	1844	York Boro	-
, Valentine	1825	Fairview	-
Welshans, Aaron	1838	Wrgvlle. Boro	-
	1838		vendue
, Joseph	1836	Hellam	-
	1836		vendue
Welshantz, Eve Eliz.	1795	York Boro	-
, Jacob	1763	York	-
, Jacob	1819	York Boro	-
, Joseph	1790	Yorktowne	-
Welty, George	1819	Manchester	-
, Henry	1822	"	-
, Jacob	1826	"	-
, John	1794	Manheim	German
, Peter	1755	"	-
, Philip	1813	Dover	-
, Philip	1835	E. Manchester	-
	1835		vendue
Wentz, Anna Maria	1816	Dover	German
, John	1842	E. Manchester	-

152

File Name		Date	Twp.	Misc. Info.
Wentz,	John	1816	Dover	-
		1837	"	widow
		1837		vendue
,	Margaret	1815	Dover	German
,	Mary	1818	"	filed w/Phil
,	Michael	1825	Manchester	-
,	Peter	1835	"	-
		1835		vendue
,	Philip	1795	Dover	h/o Mary
,	Valentine	1788	Manheim	-
,	Valentine	1846	"	-
Werking,	Jacob	1763	"	(Wirking)
,	Mary	1835	"	"
		1835		vendue
,	Nicholas	1782	?	-
,	Philip	1829	Manheim	-
Werner,	Anna Mary	1837	Shrewsbury	vendue
,	Daniel	1821	Manheim	-
,	George	1827	"	-
,	George Jacob	1812	Shrewsbury	-
,	Henry	1833	Chanceford	-
,	John	1805	Codorus	-
,	John	1837	"	-
		1837		vendue
,	John	1847	Shrewsbury	-
,	Melchior	1802	Manheim	-
,	Udith	1829	Codorus	-
Wert,	Thomas	1805	Chanceford	-
Wertz,	Daniel	1832	Codorus	shoemaker tools
,	Jacob	1778	"	-
,	Jacob	1844	N. Codorus	-
,	John	1782	Codorus	(Wartz)
,	John	1824	"	-
,	John	1823	"	-
,	John	1843	N. Codorus	-
,	Peter	1783	Reading*	-
,	Willhelmus	1784	"	-
West,	Charles	1789	Newberry	-
,	Pricilla	1804	?	-
,	Samuel	1786	Fawn	-
Westhafer,	Abraham	1815	Newberry	-
,	Levi	1848	Conewago	-
Westhoffer,	Catharine	1839	Manchester	-
		1839		vendue
,	Jacob	1839	Conewago	-
Wetzel,	Jacob	1779	Mt. Joy*	-
Weverling,	John	1771	?	-
Weyand,	John	1824	Warrington	(Wyant)
Weyer,	Andrew	1804	W. Manchester	-
,	Barbara	1836	York Boro	(Ingles)
		1836		vendue
,	Daniel	1829	Conewago	-

File Name		Date	Twp.	Misc. Info.
Weyer,	John	1834	Spr. Garden	vendue
,	Ludwig	1823	Newberry	-
Wherley,	George Sr.	1841	Shrewsbury	-
Whiery,	Robert	1792	Newberry	-
Whinright,	Edmond	1791	Dover	-
White,	Archibald Jr.	1763	Fawn	-
,	Elizabeth	1778	Windsor	-
,	George	1789	Paradise	-
,	Hannah	1804	"	-
,	James Sr.	1782	Reading*	-
,	John	1752	Hamilton Ban*	-
,	John	1783	Cumberland*	-
Whittakery,	Thomas	1813	York Boro	-
Whittelsey,	Eleazer	1752	?	Rev.
Wickersham,	Anna	1815	Newberry	-
,	James Sr.	1815	"	-
,	Jesse	1803	"	-
,	Richard	1779	Warrington	-
Wierly,	Fetrick	1750	?	(Verly)
Wierman,	William	1830	Franklin	-
Wiest,	Catharine	1833	Paradise	-
,	Jacob	1814	"	-
,	John	1837	W. Manchester	-
		1837		vendue
Wiestling,	Jacob H.	1826	Hanover Boro	Rev.
Wildanger,	Mathias	1832	"	-
Wildasin,	Jacob Sr.	1814	Manchester	-
,	Margaret	1820	Heidelberg	-
,	Peter	1819	Manheim	-
,	Samuel	1804	"	-
,	Samuel	1805	"	-
Wilderness,	Abraham	1778	Tyrone*	-
Wiley,	Andrew	1822	Peach Bottom	-
,	David	1817	Hopewell	-
,	James Sr.	1837	Fawn	-
,	John	1801	Chanceford	-
,	Nathaniel	1812	Fawn	-
,	Robert	1755	?	-
,	William	1813	Hellam	-
Wilhelm,	Frederick	1790	Codorus	-
,	John S.	1847	Shrewsbury	-
,	Michael	1824	Dover	Jr.
		1825	"	Sr.
,	Peter	1783	Codorus	-
,	Peter	1778	York	-
Wilkinson,	Charles	1766	?	-
,	Jesse	1840	Lw. Windsor	-
,	John	1769	Newberry	-
,	Joseph	1817	Manchester	-
Will,	Martin	1817	Hanover Boro	-
,	Michael	1773	?	-
Willet,	Anthony	1828	Manheim	-

File Name		Date	Twp.	Misc. Info.
Williams,	Benjamin	1785	Warrington	-
,	Catharine	1849	Springfield	-
,	Frederick	1847	"	-
,	George	1819	Windsor	-
,	Henry	1845	Hellam	-
,	Hezekiah	1805	Fairview	-
,	Isaac	1838	Chanceford	-
		1838		vendue
,	Mordecai	1811	Warrington	-
,	Roger	1758	?	-
,	Thomas	1832	Wrgvlle. Boro	-
,	Thomas	1799	Windsor	vendue
Willis,	Henry	1761	Newberry	-
,	Henry	1764	"	-
,	Joel	1814	"	-
,	Samuel	1848	Manchester	-
Willoughby,	James	1761	?	-
Willson,	David	1848	Windsor	(Wilson)
Wilson,	Abraham	1813	Monaghan	-
,	Andrew	1778	Newberry	-
,	Andrew	1752	?	-
,	Andrew	1804	Monaghan	-
,	Andrew	1793	"	-
,	Andrew	1790	"	Captain
		1803		2nd inv.
,	Catharine	1846	Spr. Garden	-
,	Charles	1780	Mt. Joy*	-
,	David	1793	Mt. Pleasant*	-
,	David	1827	Hopewell	-
,	Francis	1820	Monaghan	-
,	George	1830	Chanceford	-
,	George	1785	Manallen*	-
,	Henry	1779	Monaghan	-
,	Henry	1840	Wrgvlle. Boro	-
,	Henry	1757	?	-
,	James	1797	Monaghan	-
,	James	1837	Lw. Chanceford	-
		1837		vendue
,	James	1779	Hamilton Ban*	-
,	James	1809	Hopewell	-
,	Jasper	1770	Tyrone*	-
,	John	1792	Huntington*	-
,	John	1802	Newberry	mill
		1802		vendue
,	John	1849	Wrgvlle. Boro	-
,	Joseph	1789	Franklin*	-
,	Josias	1812	?	Rev.
,	Margaret	1847	Spr. Garden	-
,	Margaret	1811	Chanceford	-
,	Mary	1792	Tyrone*	-
,	Mary	1804	Chanceford	-
,	Patrick	1760	?	-

155

File Name		Date	Twp.	Misc. Info.
Wilson,	Rachel	1827	Hopewell	-
,	Robert	1834	Spr. Garden	-
,	Ruth	1824	Lw. Chanceford	-
,	Thomas	1777	?	-
,	Thomas	1768	?	-
		1770		2nd inv.
,	Thomas	1779	Cumberland*	-
,	Thomas	1825	Chanceford	-
,	Thomas	1826	Conewago	-
,	Thomas	1828	Monaghan	-
,	William	1765	Reading*	-
,	William	1766	Hamilton Ban*	-
,	William	1773	?	-
,	William	1781	Chanceford	-
,	William	1792	Paradise	-
,	William	1807	Chanceford	-
,	William	1815	Lw. Chanceford	-
,	William	1812	Hopewell	-
Wilt,	Daniel	1826	Conewago	-
,	Jacob	1839	York Boro	-
		1840		vendue
,	John	1847	York Boro	-
,	John	1823	Conewago	German
,	Nicholas	1786	Manchester	-
,	Paul	1803	Dover	German
,	Peter	1849	York Boro	-
,	Sarah	1844	"	-
,	Solomon	1834	"	-
		1836		vendue
,	Valentine	1755	?	-
Winand,	John	1821	Hopewell	-
Winebrenner,	Catharine	1791	Hanover Boro	German
,	Christina	1755	Dover	poor cond.
,	George	1840	Heidelberg	-
		1840		vendue
,	George	1780	Hanover Boro	-
,	Peter	1789	"	German
,	Peter	1839	"	vendue
Wineholt,	George	1826	Windsor	(Winehold)
Winemiller,	Catharine	1847	Shrewsbury	-
,	Francis	1813	Hopewell	-
,	Francis	1812	"	-
Winkelfus,	Mary A.	1838	?	-
Winn,	Thomas	1748	Hellam	oldest inv.
		1749		2nd inv.
Winnagle,	Mathias	1846	Newberry	-
Winter,	Anna Maria	1820	Conewago	-
,	George	1814	Codorus	-
,	George	1814	Shrewsbury	-
,	Jacob	1850	"	-
,	John	1816	Hopewell	-
,	Margaretta	1834	Codorus	w/o Geo.

File Name		Date	Twp.	Misc. Info.
Winter,	Peter	1818	Windsor	-
Wintermeyer,	Catharine	1818	Dover	German
,	Philip	1807	Manchester	(Windermyre)
Wintermyer,	Anthony	1798	Dover	-
,	Valentine	1844	Conewago	-
Winteroth,	Jacob	1797	Germany*	-
Winters,	Daniel	1821	Codorus	-
,	Jacob	1800	"	German
,	Philip	1780	Chanceford	(Winter)
Wirt,	Christian	1842	Hanover Boro	-
,	Jacob	1834	"	-
Wirth,	Henry	1764	Manheim	(Wirt)
Wise,	Casper	1782	Berwick*	-
,	Christina	1815	Chanceford	poor cond.
,	George	1804	"	-
,	George	1789	Manheim	German
,	George	1834	Chanceford	-
		1834		vendue
,	John	1813	Dover	(Weiss)
,	Sebastian	1802	Paradise	"
Wisehart,	Henry	1750	Hellam	-
		1750		vendue/Ger.
Witerecht,	Peter	1825	Manchester	-
Witherow,	Michael	1793	"	German
,	William	1781	?	-
Witherspoon,	Thomas	1759	Cumberland*	-
Witman,	Jacob	1816	Chanceford	-
,	Leonard	1813	Paradise	-
,	Michael	1813	Chanceford	-
Witmer,	David	1843	Spr. Garden	-
,	Fraeneca	1820	Monaghan	-
,	Henry	1814	Dover	-
Witmeyer,	Simon	1834	Windsor	-
		1834		vendue
,	Simon	1806	Manchester	-
Witrecht,	John	1849	York Boro	-
Wittig,	Frederick	1815	Windsor	(Whittig)
Wogan,	Ann	1799	Manchester	-
,	Jacob	1841	"	-
,	Jacob	1850	"	-
,	John	1835	E. Manchester	-
		1835		vendue
Wolaver,	Henry	1850	Windsor	-
Wolf,	Adam Sr.	1835	York Boro	-
		1835		vendue
,	Agnes D.	1797	York Boro	-
,	George	1781	Manchester	-
,	George	1788	York Boro	-
,	Henry	1793	Windsor	-
,	Henry	1817	Hellam	-
,	Henry	1767	?	-
,	Henry	1809	York Boro	-

File Name		Date	Twp.	Misc. Info.
Wolf,	Henry	1828	Manchester	-
,	Henry	1835	W. Manchester	-
		1835		vendue
,	Jacob	1750	?	-
,	Jacob	1775	Yorktowne	-
,	Jacob	1850	Manchester	-
,	John	1773	"	-
,	Jonas	1787	Berwick*	-
,	Magdalena	1823	W. Manchester	-
,	Michael	1822	Fairview	-
,	Michael	1847	Chanceford	-
,	Peter	1771	Yorktowne	(Woolf)
,	Peter	1844	Codorus	-
,	Peter Sr.	1850	W. Manchester	-
,	Peter	1796	Manchester	Esq.
,	Peter	1774	(Shepherds twn)	Va.
Wolfahrt,	Peter	1830	Manheim	(Wolford)
Wolfart,	Christopher	1821	"	-
Wolff,	John	1803	York Boro	-
Wolffram,	August B.	1822	Codorus	-
Wolford,	Maria	1838	Manheim	-
Wolgamuth,	Henry	1798	Warrington	-
,	Maley	1835	Dover	(Wilkamuth)
		1835		vendue
,	Peter	1821	Washington	-
Wolgemuth,	Abraham	1835	Warrington	(Wolkemuth)
		1837		vendue
,	David	1814	Dover	-
Wolhaft,	Jacob	1843	Spr. Garden	Freystwn.
Wolleber,	Francis	1803	Windsor	-
Wollet,	Elizabeth	1797	Paradise	-
,	Frederick	1842	Spr. Garden	-
,	George Adam	1789	Paradise	-
,	Lewis	1840	Warrington	-
		1840		vendue
Woltzhover,	Jacob	1758	?	-
Wonder,	Henry	1759	?	poor cond.
,	Stephen	1795	Huntington*	-
Woods,	Rachel	1845	Fairview	-
Worley,	Abigail	1830	Newberry	-
,	Daniel	1805	York Boro	-
,	David	1795	Huntington*	h/o Anna
,	Francis	1768	Manchester	-
,	Francis	1798	"	-
,	George	1850	York Boro	-
,	Jacob	1812	Manchester	-
,	John	1823	Dover	-
,	Nathan	1823	"	-
Worrell,	Benjamin	1843	Lw. Windsor	-
Worst,	Mary	1830	Hanover Boro	-
Wren,	Joseph	1827	York Boro	(Renn)
Wright,	Eleanor	1778	Hellam	-

File Name		Date	Twp.	Misc. Info.
Wright,	John	1760	Hellam	–
,	John	1784	"	–
,	Samuel	1789	Manallen*	–
Wyant,	Frederick	1759	?	–
,	Jacob	1755	?	–
,	Johan William	1791	Paradise	(Weyand)
Wysong,	Conrad	1789	"	–
,	Ludwick	1784	Heidelberg	(Weisong)

-Y-

Yager,	Henry	1807	Manheim	–
Yeager,	John	1790	Manallen*	–
Yessler,	Henry	1813	Paradise	–
Yinger,	Anthony	1829	Newberry	–
,	George	1790	?	–
,	George	1840	Fairview	–
,	Jacob	1813	Newberry	–
,	Magdalena	1846	"	–
,	Samuel	1816	"	–
Yocum,	Isaiah	1820	"	–
,	William	1847	Shrewsbury	–
Yoder,	John	1788	Reading*	–
Yoe,	John	1835	Paradise	–
		1835		vendue
Yoest,	Sophia	1846	Hanover Boro	–
Yohe,	Abraham	1823	York	–
,	Michael	1785	Dover	(Yow)
Yoner,	Elizabeth	1793	"	–
,	Nicholas	1788	"	–
Yost,	Catharine	1793	York Boro	–
,	Conrad	1760	Manheim	–
,	Gerhard	1842	Hanover Boro	–
,	John	1825	Dover	–
,	Nicholas	1785	Shrewsbury	–
,	Nicholas Sr.	1787	Yorktowne	–
Youce,	Frederick	1818	York Boro	(Youse)
Young,	Andrew	1823	Spr. Garden	–
,	Andrew	1774	Chanceford	–
,	Christian	1815	?	German
,	Daniel	1831	York Boro	Rev.
,	Devalt	1773	Mt. Pleasant*	–
,	Elizabeth	1850	Hanover Boro	–
,	Frederick	1793	Mt. Pleasant*	German
,	Frederick	1827	Shrewsbury	–
,	George	1827	Windsor	–
,	Hannah	1808	Dover	–
,	Henry	1809	Hanover Boro	large inv.
,	Henry	1827	Shrewsbury	–
,	Henry	1833	"	–

File Name		Date	Twp.	Misc. Info.
Young,	Jacob	1838	Windsor	-
,	James	1798	Hamilton Ban*	-
,	James	1842	Chanceford	-
,	John	1813	York Boro	-
,	Margaret	1767	Cumberland*	-
,	Rebecca	1837	Springfield	-
,	Sarah	1797	York	-
,	Susanna	1830	Fairview	-
,	Tobias	1808	Codorus	(Yung)
,	William	1850	Hanover Boro	-
,	William	1795	Manallen*	-
,	William	1779	Chanceford	-
Youse,	John	1823	York Boro	-
,	Mary	1838	"	-
		1838		vendue
,	Rife Jacob	1847	Washington	-
Yunt,	Samuel	1847	Hopewell	-

-Z-

File Name		Date	Twp.	Misc. Info.
Zacharias,	George	1806	Manheim	-
Zanckel,	John	1815	York	-
Zarbach,	Charles	1827	Codorus	-
Zech,	Dorothea	1834	Shrewsbury	-
,	Michael	1817	"	-
,	William	1823	"	-
Zeigler,	Adam	1822	Codorus	-
,	Barnet	1797	"	-
,	Frederick	1779	York	illegible
,	George	1819	Hanover Boro	-
,	George	1764	?	(Zigler)
,	George	1840	York Boro	-
		1840		vendue
,	George Philip	1804	W. Manchester	-
,	Gotlieb	1779	Yorktowne	-
,	Jacob	1785	Huntington*	(Zeagler)
,	Jacob	1810	Codorus	-
,	John	1799	Huntington*	-
,	John	1814	W. Manchester	-
,	John	1836	Spr. Garden	-
		1836		vendue
,	Killian	1808	Paradise	-
,	Magdalena	1840	York Boro	-
		1840		vendue
,	Margaret	1841	Spr. Garden	-
		1841		vendue
,	Martin	1824	York Boro	-
,	Mary	1837	Hopewell	-
,	Michael	1814	Codorus	-
,	Michael	1819	"	-

160

File Name		Date	Twp.	Misc. Info.
Zeigler,	Michael	1793	Windsor	-
,	Michael	1850	Shrewsbury	-
,	Nicholas	1791	Codorus	German
,	Peter	1819	Spr. Garden	-
,	Philip	1756	?	-
,	Philip	1828	Dover	-
,	Rosina	1819	Codorus	-
Zeller,	Bartholomew	1779	Windsor	-
		1791	"	widow
,	Bartholomew	1826	Hopewell	-
,	Catherine	1824	York	-
,	Jacob	1824	Shrewsbury	-
		1815	York	filed wrong
,	Jacob	1845	Spr. Garden	-
Zenker,	Anthony	1794	Manheim	-
Zercher,	Baltzer	1781	Dover	-
,	Conrad	1786	Manheim	German
,	Philip	1815	Newberry	-
Ziebler,	Christian	1850	Windsor	-
Ziegel,	Thomas	1817	York Boro	-
Ziegler,	Adam	1849	Paradise	-
,	George D.	1847	Shrewsbury	-
,	Jacob	1848	Dover	-
,	John	1846	W. Manchester	-
Zigle,	Gotlieb	1816	?	-
Zimmerman,	Conrad	1823	Newberry	-
,	Jacob	1817	"	-
Zinlaub,	George	1791	Germany*	German
Zinn,	Anna Cunta	1813	Dover	-
,	Jacob	1841	Paradise	-
,	Jacob	1845	Dover	-
,	Jacob	1809	"	-
,	John	1804	York Boro	-
,	Margaret	1806	"	-
,	Mary (Molly)	1808	Dover	-
,	Mary	1815	"	-
Zollinger,	Peter	1791	Paradise	-
Zorger,	Elizabeth	1844	Conewago	-
,	Jacob	1833	"	-
,	Maria Eliza.	1830	"	-
,	Michael	1843	Fairview	-
,	Peter	1845	Conewago	-
Zoug,	Henry	1775	Germany*	-
,	John	1823	Newberry	(Zuck)
Zutelgte,	Henry	1841	Hellam	-

-The End-

.

www.ingramcontent.com/pod-product-compliance
Lightning Source LLC
Chambersburg PA
CBHW071441090426
42737CB00011B/1744